Shooting the
Shaman

Lynda Rose

Copyright © 2001 John Hunt Publishing Ltd
Text © 2001 Lynda Rose

ISBN 1 903019 77 X

Design: Nautilus Design (UK) Ltd

Write to:
John Hunt Publishing Ltd
46A West Street
Alresford
Hampshire SO24 9AU
UK

Printed in Guernsey, Channel Islands

Visit us on the Web at: www.johnhunt-publishing.com

Contents

1

In the Reverend Dr Dougal Sampratt's eyes, he was a pillar of ecclesiastical rectitude. He did not lust after small boys or pubescent girls. He did not drink excessively and had never taken drugs (apart from the socially acceptable dosage of caffeine and occasional aspirin) and he was kind to animals and to the old ladies who seemed to litter the congregations with which he was familiar. Also, and perhaps most important of all, he held no belief to excess. Apart, that is, from an almost rabid commitment to 'Restore', the group opposed to women in holy orders, of which, for the last two years, he had been a member.

On this particular issue, of course, it was different, and he prided himself that he stood at the rock face of opposition to the heretical changes introduced by a Synod overly swayed by the influences and opinions of the world. Despite his high churchmanship, however, this was not because he subscribed to the opinion that any fundamental change affecting Church order required the sanction of Rome - in fact he rather disapproved of the suggestion that a foreigner should have that much control of the Anglican Church. But he was ruled by an unshakeable inner conviction, grounded on his long study of theology and objective personal observation, that women were temperamentally and spiritually unfitted to hold any kind of clerical office. God, he was fond of telling people, had placed authority with men.

If the uninitiated were foolish enough to show any interest, he would explain. It all had to do with the pre-lapsarian condition, he would say. Christ certainly had redeemed mankind from the disastrous effects of the fall and, more specifically, the curses pronounced upon Adam and Eve. But, given that woman was first created merely as the helpmeet of man, which was clearly on the grounds of congenitally diminished responsibility, the hierarchical structures remained intact. What women needed, therefore, was to cease their unhealthy pursuit of power – which of course was grounded in their predisposition to rebellion first manifested in Eden – and simply accept, with meekness and due reverence, their position of service and inferiority to men. The universe thus secured, Dougal firmly believed that men would then look after women in the way God had clearly first intended. And all would be right with the world.

Dougal was not a bad man, neither was he unduly stupid. But he liked very much to have his own way and, perhaps unfortunately for the continuance of his own wellbeing, he had for most of his life been accustomed to getting it. Amanda was then, to all intents and purposes, the perfect companion for his life's journey. In so far as he knew, she harboured no great ambitions of her own. Although she had once shared with him that she would like a kitchen with a fully functional Aga, which she intended to be used mainly by the nanny they would employ as soon as the first of their many offspring came along. When Dougal had raised an enquiring eyebrow at this (the nanny, it should be said, not the children), she had explained that she intended, once they were married, to devote herself to the performance of charitable acts, thus becoming in time a model for the perfect vicar's wife. Dougal had been entranced and his opinion of her had been confirmed. She may be a little up-market for a vicar's wife, it was true, and the cost of the lifestyle she appeared to be envisaging would undoubtedly be prohibitive but, with her father a retired bishop and wealthy in his own right, he felt she could perhaps be indulged in this.

Needless to say, he had chosen her with great care, mindful of the advice his father – an archdeacon – had given him when he had first learned that Dougal intended to follow in the family footsteps. 'Get yourself a wife, my boy,' he had said sententiously. 'Your average parish likes a married man with a stable home. A wife who is available. And at least two children.'

From that moment, even though at the time only seventeen, Dougal had been on the lookout. In the event it had proved to be quite a long search because, try as he might, he had discovered that a large number of girls did not want to be married to a clergyman. In fact many of them seemed not to want to be married at all. But as soon as he had seen Amanda and learnt of her pedigree, he had known instinctively that she was right.

He had told her he loved her, though at that particular juncture without actually giving the matter much thought, about six weeks after they had first met. They had been at a party at Walsingham, the theological college where Dougal was reading theology and undergoing ministerial training, after completing his first degree in Greats at the University of Carbery just down the road. That particular weekend, Amanda had been visiting a rather lonely old schoolfriend who was in her first year at the university, but Dougal had met her in the afternoon walking down the High Street, and she had agreed excitedly to come along to the party they were having that night, provided she could bring her friend.

Amanda herself had an 'absolutely super job' at an art gallery in London. She was terribly enthusiastic about this, telling everyone about the famous artists she regularly met, but from what Dougal could make out in conversation with her, she didn't actually spend very much time there, and seemed to know very little about art. It was, he felt, immaterial.

For Amanda's part, as Dougal had gazed meltingly into her eyes and told her, in his rather serious way that he loved her, she had dimly caught a glimpse of the fulfilment of a childhood dream. This was to marry a vicar who would one day follow in her father's footsteps - thus making her, at the very least, a bishop's wife. From their first meeting, those few short weeks ago, she had thought Dougal rather sweet. But she had also heard that he was tipped to go far. And so she had responded to his overtures in kind.

Dougal had hardly been able to believe his luck, and within days they had decided to marry. Once, that is, Dougal had been priested and achieved a secure position in life.

It had been Amanda who had actually suggested this, but Dougal fully agreed. He thought such measures prudent, though it had sometimes occurred to him recently that their engagement (now entering its sixth year) had perhaps been rather long. When he had mentioned this to the light of his life, however, Amanda had been adamant. There was plenty of time, she had assured him blithely. They must not rush into things. Dimly it occurred to Dougal that a little bit of rush might be nice, but Amanda was not to be moved. Once he had a suitable position, she assured him, *then* they would marry.

When Dougal finished his doctorate at Cambridge, where he had gone on completing his ministerial training at Walsingham, he had then returned to his theological alma mater to teach patristics. He had rather assumed that after that he would remain in academia for life. Others might say that the ivory tower existence of theological training was too far removed from any kind of real spiritual engagement, but Dougal rather liked it. And besides, as he had argued forcibly to Amanda when she had complained that such a life was too insular for the realisation of their plans, there were many bishops today coming from an exclusively academic background.

He had, however, reckoned without the policy of retrenchment that hit university establishments, and theological colleges in particular, at around the same time his contract came up for review. He had thought himself secure for life but, to his very great astonishment, as the time for the expiration of his current five-year contract drew near, he found himself summoned by the college principal, Father Goody, and, instead of being asked whether a further five-year term would be acceptable (or even tenure, which was what he had been anticipating), it was put to him that perhaps this would be a good point in his career to venture out into the wider and less rarified world of parish life.

'You must understand,' Father Goody said to him silkily, 'our resources are limited, and the very standing of theological colleges is under review at this time. We must be seen to be fulfilling a real need within the wider communion of the Church, and it has been pointed out to me recently by the Bishop himself that Walsingham is unfortunately made distinctive by its total lack of female staff. If we wish to survive into the next decade we must demonstrate that we are neither at odds with, nor in any way opposing, current trends. We must, at the very least, present a facade of catering equally for the needs of female students, alongside our men.'

Dougal felt himself grow pale. He had done so much around the college that he had thought his position inviolable. 'Are you trying to tell me,' he brought out at last, in strangled tones, 'that you are intending to give my appointment to a woman?'

The idea was so horrendous that he felt his mouth go unnaturally dry, but it was no good. Father Goody was beaming benignly. 'So glad you understand, dear boy,' he murmured. 'If there were any other option, of course, I'd take it. But with funds being so limited ...'

He trailed off and smiled again. Dumbly Dougal nodded. 'Am I to be allowed any extension of time,' he asked at last, 'in order to find another position?'

The principal frowned as if Dougal had suggested something improper, and looked down at his hands. He was silent. In the absolute quiet that followed, Dougal felt that the painful thudding of his heart must be audible but, if it was, Father Goody gave no sign. 'You must understand, dear boy,' he said finally, 'my hands are tied. If it were up to me, of course I would give you all the time in the world. But it's not.' He shrugged. 'There is, after all, your successor to be thought of. We've already inserted advertisements in the *Church Times* and the *Higher Ed*. Indeed, I believe we've already had some preliminary enquiries, and I know of at least one person who has made an application.' He did not add that the person in question was a woman, who had done so only at his instigation, but he did not need to. Dougal was fully aware of the machinery underlying the appointment system at Walsingham.

'I see,' the young priest said stiffly. He rose painfully to his feet. In the space of twenty minutes he felt as if his entire world had been upended, and he felt lost. He had no idea even how to go about the process of finding an appointment in a parish. He had never been interested. He supposed he ought to go and see the Bishop. And then the most ghastly thought occurred to him. He had been priested, of course, and helped out at weekends in a local church, but he had never yet served a curacy. What if they now said that he had to? The thought was so appalling that he staggered in mid step and almost fell. Whatever would Amanda say?

'Are you alright, dear boy?' enquired Father Goody, all false concern as he too now rose to his feet.

'Ye ... yes,' faltered Dougal. Then, more firmly as he saw the steely glint of the principal's piggy eyes reflected through the lenses of his half moon glasses, 'Yes, of course I am. I just caught my foot.'

'Of course,' murmured Father Goody. He glided forward and held open the door. 'Then just let me wish you luck in your search, and say that I shall of course be happy to render whatever assistance I may.'

Dougal was dismissed. He found himself outside in the gloomy corridor, standing on the beige carpet that he had always hated, with the door closed firmly on his back.

Amanda, when he told her, was jubilant. 'Thank God!' she burst out, before she could help herself. 'Now at last you can leave this hole and get a proper job. Something that's going somewhere!'

Dougal was offended. 'I've been happy here,' he said huffily. 'I like it.'

'Oh don't be so silly,' snapped Amanda. 'It's been alright for a while,

I suppose, but it's such a backwater. It's about time you stopped all this self-indulgence and thought a bit about our future. A nice city parish, that's what we need! Somewhere smart. Big congregation ... I'll phone Daddy.'

Dougal was appalled. 'Good heavens, Amanda,' he expostulated, 'you can't do that!'

But Amanda was genuinely puzzled. 'Why ever not?' she asked. 'It's the way things are done.'

'No,' said Dougal firmly. His chin lifted. 'I'm perfectly capable of finding a parish for myself, thank you. I shall go through the normal channels.'

'Which are?'

Dougal's chin lifted even higher. He did not like to admit that he had not the slightest idea. 'I shall go and see the Bishop,' he said stiffly.

Bishop Hubert had been in post only about a month, and was still struggling valiantly to deal with the chaos left behind by his predecessor, who had caused acute shock to the country at large by running off with another woman and, at a stroke, abandoning both the diocese and his wife. The tabloids had had a field day, and the diocese had still not recovered. In the general confusion that had been left, Bishop Hubert had been seen as a good appointment – by which it was meant that he had never in his life said anything to offend anyone, and that, in so far as anyone could be sure, there had as yet been no hint of scandal attaching to his rather boring life.

In fact, the appointments board had had a horrendous job finding anyone at all, because in the wake of the scandal it had been felt that they had to find someone absolutely safe. First of all they had tried to find someone unmarried, but then it had been pointed out to them that such a candidate might well be a closet homosexual, and so they had hastily abandoned that strategy and looked instead for a family man. Those they had approached, however, had declined the honour, and for a while it had looked as if they were not going to be able the fill the vacancy at all. And then, at last, someone had come up with the name of Hubert Higgins.

It was rumoured by the unkind that his name had been drawn out of a hat, but this was untrue. What had actually happened, was that a junior chaplain, serving one of the bishops on the appointments board, had come across a pamphlet Hubert had written on medieval graces. It had struck him at the time as totally inane and he had giggled about it with his wife, but not long afterwards his Bishop had given him the task of compiling yet another list of possible candidates for Carbery and, in a fit of extreme pique because he was sick of the whole business, the chaplain had included the Reverend Higgins' name.

Three weeks later, no one had been more surprised than the Reverend Higgins himself, when a letter had landed on his doormat asking him – nay, begging him – to accept the appointment of Bishop of Carbery.

Boring he most certainly was, but the Reverend Higgins was also a man of very sincere faith and profound (if rather naive) integrity, and so he had prayed a bit about the letter, and then gone off by himself on a long walk and had a think, and then he had come back and said to his wife Myra, 'You know, my dear, I really think this may be of God. The poor people of Carbery are in such a state. I think I shall accept.' Which he did. And a month later (before, as the Archbishop said, he could change his mind) amidst general relief and public rejoicing, he was enthroned; the forty-third Bishop of the ancient see of Carbery.

The first thing he did on taking up his new appointment was to introduce extremely long prayer meetings, not only at the start of every working day, but also before any decision was made that would affect the running of the diocese. 'We are simply servants of the Lord,' he was fond of saying. 'Therefore, on all matters of importance, we must consult the Almighty so as to discover His will!'

The diocesan staff, who were accustomed to rather different methods, were appalled and it looked for a while as if there might be a strike. Then, however, the Archbishop's press officer pointed out to his diocesan counterpart that coverage of this kind of activity was exactly what was needed to restore public confidence, and so the practice had been leaked to the press. Overnight Hubert was hailed as a new broom who was going to sweep the diocese clean.

It was this selfsame bishop that Dougal now found himself trying to see. Under this new regime, however, he found that making an appointment was no easy task. 'He could possibly fit you in in about six weeks time,' said the Bishop's chaplain gloomily. 'It's this new system, you see. He simply doesn't have time for individual appointments any more.'

'But I've got to see him before that,' said Dougal. 'My contract at Walsingham runs out before then.'

'I can't help that,' replied the Bishop's chaplain testily.

At that moment, however, fate intervened in the person of the Bishop himself. That worthy had just been passing through the outer office on the way to his inner sanctum, when he had overheard the buzz of Dougal's distraught tones on the phone. 'Who is that, Nicholas?' he asked, poking his head round the door.

The chaplain blanched guiltily, and then attempted to look nonchalant. 'It's Dougal Sampratt from Walsingham, Bishop. Asking for an appointment to see you.'

'Sampratt?' repeated the Bishop. 'Sampratt? I know that name, don't I?'

The chaplain put his hand firmly over the mouthpiece of the receiver. 'He's the tutor you were talking about with Father Goody when you were discussing the future of the college,' he hissed. 'You know, the one Father Goody said they'd be happy to replace with a woman.'

The Bishop frowned. 'Ah,' he said measuringly. A look of deep concentration settled on his face, and then he said, 'Tell him to come and see me tomorrow.'

'But, Bishop,' began the chaplain plaintively, 'you've got your council tomorrow morning, followed by the Portfolio training review assessment at three, and a delegation of factory workers from Luton at five ...'

It was too late. The Bishop had gone. 'Fit him in at one,' floated back over his shoulder. 'Pastoral care of my priests is very important.'

The chaplain scowled and turned back to the phone. 'Dougal,' he said, forcing himself to smile into the handset, but through clenched teeth. 'I find we do have a window after all. At one tomorrow. But you'll have to be prompt.'

'Thank you,' said Dougal fervently. 'I shall be.'

Dougal arrived ten minutes early, and found himself installed in a small waiting room, with a cup of coffee and the promise that the Bishop would not be long. Eight minutes later, bang on time, the chaplain appeared and bore him upstairs.

Dougal discovered that he felt slightly nervous. He had not actually met the new Bishop before, but he had, of course, heard all the stories that were flying around the diocese, and hitherto had shared the general view at Walsingham that Hubert was, in all probability, a very bad appointment. 'A bloody disaster!' as Father Goody had put it one morning, rolling his eyes dramatically. Dougal found, however, in the general turmoil of his spirits, that he was no longer quite so disposed to trust his principal's assessment. The Bishop, he felt, might well be his only line of hope. It was with mixed feelings, therefore, that he followed in the chaplain's wake.

'Dougal!' exclaimed the Bishop, rising immediately to his feet and surging forward as the chaplain, still sulking, opened the door and prepared to usher him in. 'Dear boy!' With a sense of acute shock, Dougal found his hand firmly grasped and then pumped up and down energetically. 'Come along in and sit down. I'm so glad you've come to see me.'

An arm was placed in fatherly fashion round Dougal's shoulders, and he found himself being propelled forward. Then he was inserted into an armchair, and the Bishop dismissed the chaplain with a brief nod of his head. 'Let's pray,' he said, settling himself opposite.

Dougal blinked. He was not used to the evangelical practice of praying aloud at the drop of a hat, and disliked it intensely. He squirmed as the Bishop launched forth and then, resigning himself to the inevitable, shut his eyes.

'Father Almighty,' began the Bishop loudly, 'please be with us now and guide us by your Spirit as we meet to discuss this young man's future. We know that you have a plan, Lord, and so we ask that you will show us exactly what that is, and how best he may be used.'

There was a silence. Dougal opened his eyes warily, and found the Bishop staring at him. There was a huge beam on his face. 'I've read your file,' he said warmly. 'And I think we may have just the thing!'

Half an hour later Dougal left. Reeling. The 'thing' that the Bishop was so enthusiastic about had turned out to be a parish on the outskirts of Carbery, which had the mixed blessings of a run-down council estate on the one side (notorious throughout the city for its vice and crime), and a pig farm on the other. This last gave off the most appalling smell and presented, to the eye of any passing pedestrian, a broad tract of unrelieved mud. Dougal had blanched, and stammered that he was not quite sure he had the appropriate gifts for such an appointment. But the Bishop had waved aside such protestations as merely evidence of a becoming humility.

'Nonsense,' he said kindly. 'You must have more confidence in yourself and your abilities. I am absolutely convinced you are just what the parish of St Prosdocimus the Inferior needs.' Which, for some extraordinary reason, was absolutely true.

The file for St Prosdocimus had, on his arrival, been placed on the Bishop's desk as a longstanding problem. Not, as he had thought on first reading, because they could persuade no sane priest to look at it, but because the parishioners (who though small in number were resolutely charismatic in attitude) had turned down everyone they sent along. Quite why, therefore, he should have thought Dougal, a conservative Anglo-Catholic down to his black polyester/nylon socks, could possible be the right man for the job was something of a mystery, and there was no little sniggering by the staff of Church House when the chaplain first appraised them of the Bishop's scheme. But it was undeniable that, after praying about the problem at staff prayers in the morning, the Bishop was sure that Dougal *was* the right man, and the staff were now all agog to see the outcome.

Dougal, of course, knew none of this. He had heard only that St Prosdocimus was an area where one did not venture alone after dark. In vain he attempted again to protest, at which point the Bishop's eyes narrowed and he said, though still not unkindly, 'I think I should explain. It's either St Prosdocimus the Inferior or nothing. There are no other vacancies within the diocese that would be at all appropriate. And St Prosdocimus will be a challenge for you.'

With this last Dougal entirely agreed. But there were some challenges he felt were better avoided. The church, built of concrete in the sixties, had latterly achieved acclaim as having had to be surrounded by a fence of barbed wire, after a group of rowdies had blocked off the entrance with a stolen car and then torched it, so that the whole building had seemed in imminent danger of going up in flames. It was rather a pity Dougal thought, sitting there opposite the Bishop, that they had not succeeded.

The chaplain smiled maliciously as Dougal came out. 'Any joy?' he enquired innocently.

Dougal gurgled inarticulately and the chaplain's beam grew. 'Here's the file,' he said sweetly. 'The Bishop thought it would be a good idea for you to go away and study it. Then you can get back to him when you've had a think. He told me to tell you, by the way, that the diocese will be quite happy to pay for the upgrading of the current security system on the vicarage. In the circumstances.'

'Thank you,' said Dougal. Hardly even conscious of what he was doing, he took the file held out to him in a nerveless hand, and left.

2

Ten days later Dougal and an unwilling Amanda dutifully went to view the parish of St Prosdocimus the Inferior. It was a grey, miserable day and as they set out, the streets were wet with rain. When they arrived forty minutes later, having been held up by an accident at the roundabout leading on to the estate (six teenagers who had been racing stolen cars had managed to drive into each other) they discovered the churchwardens, looking wet and bedraggled under a battered golfing umbrella, waiting for them just outside the porch.

'Oh God,' said Amanda, taking in the barbed wire around the outside of the building and their glum faces, 'they've got guards!'

She slid down lower in the seat of Dougal's ancient Fiesta with a sulky expression on her face, and Dougal frowned. 'Don't be ridiculous, Amanda,' he said reprovingly. 'We must at least view the parish.'

'Huh!' said Amanda.

They clambered out and squelched their way up the muddied concrete path. Squashed Coke cans, empty bottles and bits of paper littered the edges, and across the balding grass that ran off on either side and trailed dispiritedly round the building, Dougal saw little piles of dog mess and the disintegrating remains of faded confetti. It had a depressed feel about it. Then, as he raised his eyes, he saw, away off to the left, the blackened remains of the famous car. He was slightly puzzled that no one had removed it but, whatever the reason, it still stood there, isolated in all its destroyed glory, like some kind of monument asserting the victory of chaos.

Just then a voice said reprovingly, 'You here at last! We dun almost give you up, you so late.'

Dougal blinked, tearing his eyes with difficulty away from the car, and found himself staring straight into the eyes of the woman, who now came forward and planted herself firmly in front of him. She was only about five foot three, but easily fifteen stone, and almost as broad as she was tall, so that the buttons of her grey coat strained indignantly across the heaving expanse of her bosom. Around her head, and framing her shiny black face, was tied a rusty looking scarf.

'My name's Regina,' she announced. 'And this here's Eliston.' She indicated the timid little man standing behind her with a belligerent jerk of her head and the man cowered, as if fearful she was going to round on him. Then, as if he had just seen something of the most tremendous importance, he turned and began to stare fixedly at the notice board just inside the porch. Puzzled, Dougal followed the direction of the man's gaze, and discovered three rusty drawing pins and a tattered leaflet warning people against theft.

'How do you do,' said Amanda, at her most superior. 'How nice.'

It was a tone that had quelled whole classrooms of uppity juniors when she was a house captain at school. The latter part of her remark did not seem to be addressed to anything in particular, rather it was simply part of an all-embracing disdain, and Regina bristled. The front part of her wiry hair, just visible under the edge of the headscarf, literally seemed to stand on end, and Dougal was reminded of a porcupine. But she looked like a porcupine about to go on the attack. 'How do you do,' he said hastily, stepping forward and interposing himself physically between the two women. 'My name's Dougal Sampratt, and this is my fiancee, Amanda.'

'I know who you are, Reverend.' Regina sniffed, but the hair subsided. 'De bishop, he tell us you comin'. He tell me an' Eliston to come an' meet with you.'

Amanda, who had been scrutinizing the outside of the church as if she still could not quite believe it, remarked casually, 'How considerate of him. I expect he wanted us to get the full flavour.'

'Yes, well!' Dougal gave an uneasy laugh as Regina again swelled up. He hated it when Amanda went into patronising mode. She became so obtuse and difficult. But, looking at Regina, he dimly realised that war had been declared between the two women. His heart sank.

With immense dignity Regina unlocked the three padlocks on the double doors and led the way into the church. With surprise Dougal discovered that the interior was circular, with the altar placed in a cleared space in the centre. Directly above, a cross of thorns, twisted and strangely beautiful, hung suspended from the wooden roof, and from the stained glass windows set high in the walls, a soft blue light shone. The effect was one of peace, and of a kind of ordered indestructible calm that refused to be overcome by all the surrounding chaos. On the grey cement walls were hung huge brightly coloured banners, with flames of the Holy Spirit licking their way upwards and the words 'Jesus is King' emblazoned across them. Surprised, he drew up short and Regina stared at him approvingly, the first faint glimmerings of a smile just touching her lips.

'You like it?' she demanded.

Dougal swallowed. 'Yes,' he said. 'Yes, I do. It's not at all what I expected.'

He walked forwards into the stillness, taking in the neat pine seats and brightly coloured kneelers placed on the floor in front of each one. 'It's beautiful,' he said, in tones of surprise, his voice catching.

Regina looked at him closely and then sniffed with satisfaction. 'Yes,' she agreed. 'It am de home of de Lord.'

Amanda, who had followed Dougal in and was now examining a particularly large banner, said sulkily, 'I prefer a more traditional setting myself. This kind of place always reminds me of a bunker.' She shivered ostentatiously. 'It's so cold in here and damp.'

'That's because the heatin's broken,' announced Eliston mournfully. It was the first time he had spoken and they all three turned and stared at him in surprise. He was hovering just inside the door and, as they all gazed at him, he shook his grizzled grey head sadly, 'We can't afford to mend it. Not since the boys broke in and smashed the thermostat on the boiler. The gasmen, they say it cost a lot of money to put right.

'Really?' Amanda looked unimpressed. 'Makes you wonder why they don't just close the place really, doesn't it?'

The church inspected, they trooped off through the rain to look at the rectory. As they drew near, Dougal noted that the windows had all been boarded up, but even so someone had still managed to smash the security lights set high up on the walls. 'It's bin standin' empty for goin' on a year now,' said Regina apologetically. 'We had de squatters in, but de police, dey moved dem. Now de diocese says we must keep it like dis.'

'I can't live in there!' exploded Amanda, taking in the full glory. 'It's horrible.'

Dougal found himself laughing uneasily, 'It's the weather,' he said. 'I'm sure it will look better in the sun.'

'No,' said Amanda. 'I am not going to live here and that's flat. If you do insist on coming to this hell hole, the diocese has got to find us another house. I can't be expected to live somewhere like this.'

Regina was looking at her narrowly. 'Der ain't no more big houses round here,' she announced. 'It's eider here o' one of de tower blocks, but dat would mean a lot o' climbin for you because de lifts don't generally work.'

'Oh God,' said Amanda.

Matters did not improve when they went inside, especially when a small brown mouse ran across Amanda's foot in the kitchen. She screamed and leapt backwards, and Regina said tranquilly, 'We get a lot o' dem round here. Lucky really it wasn't a rat.'

Amanda looked at her with loathing.

Next the two churchwardens insisted on taking them on a walking tour of the parish. The rain had eased slightly now, but it was getting dark, and the street lamps glimmered palely off the sodden streets. Between them Regina and Eliston seemed to know most of the people they passed, and they called out greetings, and when Regina stopped in front of an arthritic old woman, walking with difficulty along the pavement, she introduced Dougal as, 'De new vicar.'

'Oh bless you,' said the woman. 'We knew as how you'd come.'

Dougal felt himself freeze with horror. 'No,' he began, 'really ... I need to find out more about the church. There's nothing settled yet.'

'It will be,' said Regina firmly. She appeared to have come to a decision. 'You'll do us just fine.'

All the way back to Walsingham, Amanda maintained a frigid wall of icy silence. 'It's no good,' she exploded, as soon as Dougal stopped the car, 'I simply cannot live in that place.'

'But, Amanda,' he said patiently, turning to her, 'there really doesn't seem to be any other option at the moment.'

She glared at him mulishly, 'I could still phone Daddy.'

Dougal felt torn. His heart also quailed at the prospect of St Prosdocimus. It was so alien to everything he knew. Such a wasteland. But quite paradoxically, with Amanda's words, a little spirit of independent rebelliousness reared itself in his heart. 'I think that would be most unwise,' he said stiffly. 'It would be totally immoral to rely on your father for preferment. Neither you nor I would ultimately be satisfied with that.'

Amanda privately thought that she would be quite satisfied with that and opened her mouth to protest, but Dougal gave her no chance.

'I must find my own way in the world. Besides which the good people of St Prosdocimus are obviously in need. Perhaps it really is God's will that I go there.'

Amanda emitted a sound midway between a steam train and a ruptured balloon. 'Oh Dougal!' she screamed, 'You can be so obtuse sometimes.' And to his intense surprise, she flung open the door and stormed out into the torrential rain, leaving her umbrella reclining soggily on the floor.

The fact that, in the short run to the closed doors of the college, she got drenched, did nothing to improve her mood, but Dougal remained obstinately unrepentant. Warning bells screamed in his head that St Prosdocimus would be an absolute disaster, but still ... but still that little appealing voice he had first heard inside the church kept whispering, 'Come.'

He phoned up the Bishop's office and accepted.

Amanda phoned up her mother. 'It's absolutely awful,' she wailed. 'All the roads have bumps to stop the joy riders.'

Her mother was momentarily nonplussed. 'Does that mean it's one of those charismatic parishes, dear?' she enquired.

There was a moment's silence as Amanda attempted to digest this, but she proved unequal to the task. 'What the hell are you talking about?' she demanded. 'What's the parish's churchmanship got to do with anything?'

At the other end of the line her mother blinked. Dear Amanda was obviously upset. 'Well, dear,' she said vaguely, 'I simply thought you meant there were divisions within the congregation.'

Amanda ground her teeth. Mummy was obviously going to be not the slightest use at all on this one. 'Put Daddy on please,' she said ominously.

But her father too proved unexpectedly obdurate. 'I really think, darling,' he said mildly, 'that we must respect Dougal in this. He has suffered a setback in career terms, but he obviously feels he has to redeem the situation himself.'

'But, Daddy,' shrieked Amanda, unable to help herself, 'it's a dreadful place. It's in the middle of a council estate, and the people are absolutely ghastly. And the church looks as if a bomb's hit it. They had a riot last year.'

Her father swallowed. He could imagine St Prosdocimus all too well. Not for the first time he began to wonder about the wisdom of Amanda's engagement to Dougal. He had always felt slightly uneasy about that young man. There was something about him not quite pukka. He had always thought it was because he was academic, but now he was beginning seriously to wonder. Still, at this particular point in time there seemed very little he could do.

'Daddy,' said Amanda quietly, wheedling. 'I want you to get him a decent parish. Somewhere nice. He's shell-shocked at the moment, poor lamb. He can't think straight. I really am beginning to worry for his sanity. But if there was some sort of alternative in front of him, and it was presented in the right way, I'm sure he'd see sense. Please, Daddy.'

Her father was lost. Whenever his little girl spoke in those tones he always found himself giving way. He adored her. 'All right,' he promised. 'I'll see what I can do.'

Having accepted so precipitously in face of Amanda's displeasure, Dougal found himself suddenly overwhelmed with doubt. It swept over him like a great and torrential flood, smashing all his carefully maintained constructs and the ordered landscape of his mind. With terror, it suddenly hit him how stupid he was being. The area of St Prosdocimus was alien to him. And it was evangelical! Regina had informed him very sniffily that they would not countenance lace cottas while, as for incense, the parishioners would think he was introducing drugs. 'Dem's heathenish practices,' she had announced dismissively. 'We don't hold no truck with dat kind of thing.'

Yet this was Dougal's world. For him pageant was an integral part of faith. Strip away the trappings and what was left? Thinking of St Prosdocimus he had the uncomfortable feeling he was about to find out.

Over the following days, the rest of the staff at Walsingham appeared to view his imminent move with cautious commiseration. The announcement that Dougal's contract was not to be renewed had left them all feeling decidedly uneasy. 'Only think, darling,' said Brian the ethics tutor, to his friend and colleague, William Seminopolus. 'What's this going to mean for the rest of us? That's what I'd like to know. Are they going to replace us all with women?'

They were sitting in Brian's rather untidy study, toasting crumpets on the little gas fire set in the wall, and William now leant forwards, inspecting his bun carefully. 'No, B,' he said judiciously. 'I think the trouble is poor old Dougal is just so rabid on this women thing, and someone had to go. He's always banging on about how they ought to be excluded. I mean I agree entirely, you know that, but it's just not politic these days to be quite so vocal. Now they're in, we'd have had to take women some time. Dougal's mistake was that he just wouldn't shut up.' He decided the crumpet was done to his satisfaction and transferred it to a waiting plate. 'I think that provided we keep our heads down we'll be okay. Timbo's got his woman now I hear, and that ought to keep the Bishop happy.'

'I hope you're right,' said Brian gloomily. 'I don't think I could bear to go out into one of those nasty parishes.'

William laid a reassuring hand on his knee. 'Believe me, dear,' he said. 'It won't come to that, I'm sure.'

All this, of course, was of absolutely no comfort at all to Dougal and whenever his colleagues bumped into him, which was as infrequently as they could contrive, they gave every impression of tip-toeing round him as if he was somehow infected. It hurt Dougal sorely. Almost overnight he felt he had become some sort of pariah and, though St Prosdocimus still filled him with feelings of deepest apprehension, he began to have a strange kind of longing to go. Then forms and papers relating to St Prosdocimus began to arrive daily on his desk. The Diocesan Parsonages Board contacted him to let him know they had arranged for new security windows with reinforced glass and steel bonded doors to be fitted at the rectory. 'Yes,' said the unknown male voice cheerfully from the other end of the phone, 'a tank wouldn't get through this lot. And we're thinking of fitting retractable steel shutters on the insides too. In addition to the usual vicarage security system, of course – you know the kind of thing; alarms, outside security lights. The Bishop says he wants to make you really secure. He doesn't want a repeat of anything like what happened to the last incumbent.'

'What did happen to the last incumbent?' asked Dougal, swallowing.

There was a silence. 'Ah,' said the voice. 'You didn't know. Sorry, I hadn't realised.' He stopped, as if hoping to avoid having to say anything more but then, as Dougal said nothing, he added reluctantly, 'Some kids broke in, that's all.'

'Yes?' said Dougal ominously.

The man laughed nervously. 'Honestly, he was alright. Once they'd managed to remove the tar and feathers. It was just a prank really. And he was fully compensated for the loss of possessions.'

Dougal hung up, feeling numb, but the next day colour charts arrived, along with samples of fabric for the curtains, and he found himself staring at a long letter informing him, among other things, that in the circumstances the diocese was not just going to redecorate, but would also recarpet the entire house, and could Dougal let them know as soon as possible his preferences, because the decorators wanted to make a start the following week. Dougal, who had no idea about this kind of thing, handed the entire communication over to Amanda, and asked her to choose what she thought would go best. She, however, rather frostily handed it back and informed him that, as he was going to living there, it ought to be his decision. Dougal felt this did not augur well, and he began to think that he had after all perhaps been a trifle hasty. The doubt grew, and then suddenly exploded into a massive rock of terror after Brian casually mentioned to him in passing that he believed St Prosdocimus went in for a totally free liturgy, and, for preference, favoured the Toronto style and no bells. He had just made up his mind to refuse after all, when he had a visitor.

Puffing and blowing like a small, rather disreputable galleon under full sail, and clutching the now furled golfing umbrella before her like a battering ram, Regina waddled her way up to his study on the second floor of Walsingham. 'I come to see you,' she announced, flinging back the door in answer to his quiet, 'Come in'.

Dougal blinked, stunned by this wholly unexpected invasion into his world, but Regina was unabashed. 'De diocese, dey tell us you coming. So I come to say how very pleased me and Eliston are. We both knew you was right, de moment we saw you. And we dun had signs too.'

She paused, staring at him expectantly, and Dougal attempted a feeble smile. 'What signs?' he asked.

He had evidently asked the right question, because Regina beamed. 'Dere was a prophecy,' she announced, 'at our prayer meetin'. Delbert, he say de Lord sendin' a warrior.'

'A warrior?' repeated Dougal faintly.

Regina nodded her head enthusiastically. 'A warrior,' she reiterated firmly. 'Delbert, he say de sword of de Lord is hoverin' over us because He has seen the plight of His people, and He goin' make a mighty deliverance. Delbert say de Lord is startin' a new thing, but dat de warrior is unexpected. Delbert say de Lord promises great things for de warrior. A shatterin' of de old and much pain, but new beginnin's ... much glory for de man of faith. Delbert, he say you dat man. He say he see you in de street, and he see de Lord's hand upon you. He knowed you de right man, so I come to tell you we right behind you, Reverend.'

'Please, call me Dougal,' said Dougal absently.

When Regina burst in, he had been in the act of beginning his letter to the Bishop retracting his acceptance, and now he covered it guiltily with his hand. He would have liked to have avoided this meeting, but it occurred to him that, since she had made the effort to come and see him, he should at least try to be honest with her and let her down gently. She would be bound to understand, he thought, once he had explained. 'My dear Regina,' he began gently, 'I'm deeply touched by your coming to see me like this.' Regina beamed. 'And I understand of course how very much you are all wanting a new vicar but ...'

'It not just a new vicar we want,' interrupted Regina firmly. 'We want de right man. Dat what we bin waitin' on de Lord for.'

'Quite,' said Dougal.

'We tell de Lord, we not have no one dat not His choice!'

'Of course,' said Dougal, 'and that's very commendable.'

'We turned down three people already.'

In spite of himself, Dougal's attention was caught. He had not known this. 'Have you?' he asked, interested. 'But I understood there had been difficulties filling the vacancy.'

Regina nodded her head vigorously, 'Yes, but only because we refuse to have de men dey send. We urban priority,' she added proudly. 'We good parish for man with right calling.'

Vainly Dougal clutched at the straw being proffered. 'Yes, but that's just it,' he said, 'you've put your finger on the very problem. St Prosdocimus is a wonderful parish for a man with a calling to that specialised form of ministry – but that's not me. I'm not an urban priority kind of a priest.'

To his intense surprise and not a little chagrin, Regina laughed. 'Rev ...,' she began, 'I mean, Dougal – you ain't got no choice what kind of priest you are. De Lord, He chooses, not you, and He chosen you for dis parish.'

Dougal had the strangest sensation of the ground beneath his feet slipping, as if he were standing on sand. 'But my fiancée,' he said plaintively, 'she doesn't like St Prosdocimus.'

Regina looked at him speculatively, 'Maybe,' she said, considering, 'dat because she *not* called.'

Amanda was at that very moment paying a visit of her own. She went to see the Bishop. 'Ah,' he said, his face breaking into a smile when he realised who she was, 'Dougal's fiancée. How nice!'

Amanda found herself thrust into the selfsame leather armchair in which Dougal had sat only days before, and a glass of sherry was placed in her hand (the Bishop, who was learning fast, had remembered who her father was). This, Amanda felt, augured well. 'It's about Dougal,' she said firmly, as soon as she had answered all the inquiries about her parents' health. 'I'm extremely concerned about him.'

The Bishop raised an enquiring eyebrow. Undeterred, she went on, 'Ever since he learned his contract was not going to be renewed at Walsingham, he has been behaving most strangely. And now this awful business at St Prosdocimus!'

The Bishop frowned. 'I was not aware that anything untoward had happened.'

'No.' Amanda struggled for words. 'I mean accepting the place.'

The Bishop examined his knees. 'Are you suggesting,' he enquired finally, 'that you believe Dougal is having some sort of breakdown?'

Amanda pulled up short. The last thing she wished to imply was that Dougal was somehow unstable. She knew perfectly well the effect that such information on his file would have on his career. He would never become a bishop with that hanging over him. 'No,' she temporised. 'Of course not.' She thought for a moment. 'It's just that in career terms he's somehow adrift. He doesn't know what he ought to be doing, and so that makes him open to every lunatic suggestion that comes along. But he's just not the sort of priest for a place like St Prosdocimus. He doesn't know the first thing about inner city ministry. His gifts are much more ...' Words failed her and she looked at the Bishop appealingly, fluttering her lashes. She had not the slightest doubt he would know exactly what she meant.

She was wrong. Bishop Hubert was of a rather different make from her father, and for all he was learning to assimilate some of the social niceties of higher Anglicanism, he had not the slightest intention of jettisoning what he felt to be his spiritual duty. 'Perhaps, my dear,' he said reprovingly, 'God wishes Dougal to move in a new direction. He seems to me ideally suited to St Prosdocimus, and I know for a fact that the churchwardens and parishioners are most excited by news of his acceptance.'

This was too much. 'They'd be excited by news of a one-eyed sloth,' exploded Amanda, 'if it meant they were going to get a new vicar. They can't get anyone!'

The Bishop stared at her. 'In that, my dear,' he said levelly, 'you are entirely wrong. They have had three candidates already offered and have turned them all down. The problem has not so much been finding someone, as finding someone they would be happy to have minister to them. And in this particular case, given the sensitivity of the area, we have taken the views of the parishioners very seriously indeed.' Then his eyes narrowed. 'Tell me,' he said enquiringly, 'does Dougal know you are here today?'

Amanda had the grace to blush. 'No,' she said, through gritted teeth, 'and I would very much appreciate it if you didn't tell him. My object in coming here today was simply to ask you to help him see sense.' She placed the barely touched sherry glass down on the table between them, and then said with dignity, 'I can see now how wrong I've been. You are clearly unable to see how wasted his talents would be in that awful place.'

There seemed nothing to say after that. With studied politeness, the Bishop held the door of his study open for her, and shut it quickly on her retreating back. Once outside, Amanda stamped her foot with rage, and then pulled up short as there was a slight cough behind her.

'Difficult time?' asked the Bishop's chaplain sympathetically as she spun round. Amanda nodded. 'Wouldn't listen to a word you said?' Amanda nodded again. The chaplain sighed. 'He's always like that,' he confided. 'He's driving us all mad. Won't listen to anything any of us say.' And then he looked at her more closely. He discovered she was rather attractive. 'Tell you what,' he said brightly, 'why don't you come and have lunch at the pub over the road and tell me all about it.'

3

Dougal was lost. Faced by Regina's certainty, he found he entirely lacked the spirit to resist. She was, he felt, like a tidal wave – uprooting trees, flattening houses ... smashing to a pulp all that stood in her way, not from any consciously focussed effort or malice, but from the sheer force of her gargantuan personality.

The service of induction was fixed for the evening of Wednesday, August 8th. Secure in the knowledge that this meant Dougal was definitely going to go, Walsingham now decided to throw behind him the full weight of what, up to then, had been its ambivalent support. A month beforehand Father Goody sent round a memorandum to all members of staff, urging them to cancel whatever prior commitments they might have had and attend en masse. Cassock albs and cottas were washed and pressed and, as a leaving present, Dougal's brother priests determined on presenting him with an ornately embroidered cope, specially designed by Brian, along with a set of matching stoles in the full range of liturgical colours. Brian was especially pleased with the Advent one. 'Such a wonderful shade of violet,' he confided to William. 'They've captured the real essence of my design. Honestly, darling, I think the pomegranates were an inspiration.'

The Friday before, mindful that Dougal was to spend the three days prior to his induction in retreat, the college arranged a small leaving party for him and Amanda, inviting along members of staff and their families and friends, and others whom it was felt might have some kind of interest in the move. In an attempt to curry favour and at the last moment, Father Goody also arranged for invitations to be sent to the Bishop and his wife, along with the Archdeacon and Registrar of the diocese.

Dougal felt wretched when he was informed of the arrangements, and Amanda looked mulish, but there seemed nothing they could do and so, barely speaking to each other, they suppressed the hostility still bubbling away between them over the move, and went along to the upper common room where the party was to be held.

Walsingham was not a large college. It numbered only some twelve permanent members of staff, and four part-timers. Of these, three were married, four had girlfriends (including Dougal), two had professed celibacy, one felt he was facing a crisis of gender, and the remaining four indulged in frequent and heartsearching discussions on the expression of love – and how that expression of itself was good, while repression of desire was contrary to the will of God, who had himself first implanted it. Occasionally they brought along others from outside the college to these discussions, all men and most of them in orders, but sometimes they just met together, and offered each other support through the trials and tribulations of life, and especially in those areas surrounding their many and varied relationships. Despite the occasional temporary lapse it was, however, now generally recognised that Brian and William were an established couple, almost of the same status as the more conventional male/female partnerships. As a result, the other two now came along to them for advice and recently, as an affirmation of his sexuality, Brian had taken to wearing heavy black eyeliner and mascara.

He was wearing this tonight, combined with eye shadow in a rather startling shade of electric blue, and he surged forward as Dougal and Amanda entered the room, a bottle in one hand, and a plate of vol au vents in the other. 'Darlings!' he enthused, 'What an age you've been. We were beginning to think you weren't coming.'

Dougal and Amanda stared at each other, and then Amanda attempted a hard smile, the merest brittle curve of her lips, but which left her eyes cold. 'Brian,' she said distinctly, 'how nice to see you.' Then she took in the full glory of his eyes and a curious kind of sheen seemed to settle on her face.

'Come and say hello to Tim,' said Dougal hastily, intercepting and rightly interpreting the look. He took her elbow in an attempt to steer her away before she could give voice to the comment he felt she was about to make, but he was too late.

'Isn't that shade a little heavy for you, Brian?' Amanda said distinctly. 'You remind me of an Egyptian rent boy, the way your eyes go up at the corner like that.'

Brian's face went purple and, on the far side of the room, William's head reared up and round like an affronted meercat. Dougal wasted no further time. His grip on Amanda's elbow tightened and, giving her a sharp shove, he propelled her none too gently away. 'Ooh, the cow!' floated after them. 'At least I don't walk around with my knockers flopping out.'

Halfway across the room Amanda, with a violent shove, struggled free of Dougal's restraining hand and whirled back round. 'That, my dear Brian,' she said nastily, 'is because you don't have any. Men, in case you haven't noticed, have testicles. Though on reflection you probably don't know about that.'

A shocked silence fell on the room, and then one of the wives laughed uneasily. Father Goody, obviously feeling matters were about to get out of hand, surged forwards and planted himself firmly in Amanda's way, at the same time signalling furiously with his hand for Brian, who looked as if he was about to explode, to be temporarily removed. 'Amanda! Dougal!' he exclaimed, sweat breaking out across his forehead, 'Wonderful! Come along in.'

At that moment there was a little flurry from over by the door, and they all turned in time to find the Bishop standing there, an expression of the deepest shock on his face. At his side was his wife, Myra, and behind them and peering over the Bishop's shoulder, Dougal made out the grinning face of Nicholas, the chaplain. Only Brian, now struggling with his captors who were trying vainly to march him from the room, was oblivious. 'I'm not going to let her get away with that!' he shrieked. 'She's never liked me. She's a bitch.'

The Bishop's clear tones fell like ice. 'Is there a problem here?' he asked ominously.

The Bishop had actually come with the intention of trying to mend a few fences. For the past few weeks, in fact ever since he had first met Dougal, he had had the uneasy feeling that he might have been a shade too hasty in his actions towards Walsingham. On first arriving in the diocese, he had been shocked by the reputation attaching to the college and he had determined either to make it clean itself up, or close it down. But he had liked Dougal, and though he genuinely believed the Lord was calling the young man to St Prosdocimus, it had occurred to him that an establishment that ranked him among its staff could not be all bad. He had even begun to wonder if he had been misinformed. Now, however, taking in the noisy scene being played out before him, in one fell swoop he felt his worst fears confirmed.

Father Goody, becoming aware of the august presence glaring at him from the door, was engulfed by a wave of horror. 'Ah no, Bishop. No,' he burbled, half stumbling as he hurried forward, 'there's not a problem. Dear me, no.' And then he had a brainwave. 'It's amateur dramatics.'

'Amateur dramatics?' repeated the Bishop, staring at him as if he was mad.

But Father Goody was in full flight. 'Of course,' he said, resolutely thrusting Amanda aside, 'we pride ourselves on our theatrical tradition here at Walsingham. Amanda and Brian were simply rehearsing a little impromptu entertainment for us all. They didn't mean it. Good heavens no! They weren't arguing. They're the best of friends – we're all the best of friends here.'

He waved his arms expansively and from behind Amanda looked as if she might hit him. But a tiny grain of common sense was beginning to reassert itself, and so instead she breathed deeply, her bosom rising and falling as she strove to control the indignation that was threatening to choke her. She was helped by the thought that a blazing row in public with Brian now would do little to further her intended's career.

The Bishop came further into the room and his wife, who hated any form of conflict, said brightly, 'Oh I see, you mean you're playing charades or something. Do we have to guess? What is it? Is it a film?'

There was a moment's silence, and then Father Goody said glassily, 'Yes, that's right ... a film.'

'What fun. What was it? Had you guessed?'

Father Goody strove to take command of the mire into which his own words had plunged them. And failed. 'Er, no,' he said feebly. 'I'm really not sure what it was.' He turned to Amanda and, safe in the knowledge that his back was to the Bishop, glared at her, 'Do tell us, Amanda, what was it?' The expression on his face seemed to imply that she had got them into this mess, so it was up to her to get them out.

Amanda stared back at him stonily, and then smiled. Straight into his eyes. '*Prick Up Your Ears*,' she said distinctly. 'I was doing *Prick Up Your Ears*. You know the Joe Orton biography. He was homosexual. But I'm not really sure what Brian was doing.'

Facing her, Father Goody went purple, but then he forced himself to laugh. 'Oh dear, Amanda! Such a sense of fun. Where are we all going to be without her?'

The Bishop opened his mouth as if to tell them, but perhaps

fortunately was prevented by his chaplain suddenly stepping forward and saying loudly, 'We used to play charades at school. I was quite good at it. Shall we try another one? Amanda, would you like to partner me?'

He seemed almost to prance forward, interposing himself between the Bishop and the rest of the room. At Amanda's side, Dougal frowned. He had met Nicholas for the first time when he had gone to see the Bishop in his quest for a parish. He had not realised that Amanda and Nicholas knew each other. He blinked as the chaplain now stepped forward, gave a huge flourish and then gallantly held out his hand. In response, Amanda gave an odd little mewing simper and said, 'How sweet.'

'Do you two know each other?' asked Dougal, even more astonished.

'Oh yes,' said Nicholas casually, his eyes never leaving Amanda's face. 'I feel like I've known Amanda for ever.'

Dougal was not entirely satisfied. He was not exactly jealous, but still something, from their manner, felt to him a little strange. He had no chance to pursue the matter, however, because the Bishop at that moment descended on him, while Amanda disappeared off to the drinks table with Nicholas. Dougal stared after them for a second, torn, but the Bishop was asking him how things were going and so, with difficulty, he dragged his attention back and tried to form some kind of reply.

It was a difficult evening. Everyone seemed on edge, and Father Goody kept trotting round distractedly, trying desperately to avoid any further conversation with the Bishop. In other circumstances, since the Bishop seemed equally determined to try and catch him, this might have afforded Dougal no little amusement. Now, however, he discovered he felt depressed.

Brian returned to the room some twenty minutes later, subdued and with his face washed, and with a stern-looking William in tow. For the rest of the evening the ethics tutor avoided Amanda ostentatiously and, when the Bishop's wife cornered him and asked him which film he had been doing, he stared at her blankly and then, with a baleful glance in Amanda's direction, said, 'I know which one I'd like to do.'

The party was not an unqualified success. At about half past nine, Father Goody called them all to order and said that, on behalf of the college, he wished to make a small speech and presentation. Dougal found himself pushed forwards, and the eyes of everyone in the room turned and fixed on him. There followed a fulsome eulogy from Father Goody on Dougal's many talents, coupled with ardent assertions of how much they were all going to miss him, and how deeply sorry they all were to see him go, and then he found an extremely large box with a pink satin ribbon attached to the top thrust into his hands, and there were cries of, 'Open it! Go on, open it now!'

He looked round for Amanda, but she was standing over by the wall in conversation with Nicholas, and she looked away. Dougal sighed. He felt she was punishing him but, with the eyes of everyone still fixed on him, there was nothing for it. Forcing a smile to his face, he rather glumly took the scissors held out to him and snipped the ribbon. Hands reached forward to help him, excitedly tugging away the lid, and then Dougal found himself staring down into layers of tissue paper. Brian, who had recovered some of his customary ebullience, could restrain himself no longer. 'Come along, Dougal,' he said, surging forward, 'Don't be so slow.'

His pudgy hands reached into the box and then, with one deft movement, he seized and shook out the heavy folds of the embroidered cope. The light winked off the gold thread that ran through the fabulous design, and there were little 'Oohs' and 'Aahs' of admiration. Standing there, huddled together and clutching their half empty glasses, the debris of nibbled sandwiches and squashed fairy cakes littering the small tables and chairs that stood dotted around the dingy room, it seemed almost too rich. Dougal stared at it, appalled.

'Do you like it??' asked Brian excitedly.

'Yes. Y ... yes, of course I do,' stammered Dougal. 'It's beautiful.'

Something in his tone percolated through to them all and, over by the wall, Amanda looked up. 'So what's wrong then?' asked William.

Dougal shook himself. 'Nothing,' he said resolutely. 'It's a wonderful present.' And then, as they all still continued to look at him, 'It's just that St Prosdocimus is evangelical.' He bit his lip. 'They don't use vestments, or even stoles. I won't be able to wear any of this.'

Brian's face fell. 'Do you mean you won't be able to dress up at all?' A look of horror came over his face as Dougal nodded. 'How ghastly,' he exclaimed. Then he brightened. 'But you can at least wear it for your induction. The parishioners can't possibly object to that.'

They did. Five minutes before the service was due to start, Dougal found himself being severely reprimanded by Regina. 'Dis de wrong season of de year for dressin' up,' she informed him stoutly. 'You look like de fairy on top of de Christmas tree.'

Dougal drew himself up awkwardly. The cope was truly magnificent, but he found he rather agreed with Regina. It felt like something the Archbishop of Canterbury might wear for a state occasion and, rather to his surprise, Dougal realised he didn't like it. He was beginning to feel slightly uneasy with all the emphasis on show. He was not even sure why, but it was somehow as if, after what felt to be his rejection by Walsingham, he was seeing everything in a new light. And that light was very bright and, rather uncomfortably, seemed to expose harshly all the deficiencies and faults that he had been blind to before. But when he tried to look beyond, he was not sure what was there, and he found that that disturbed him, as if he had discovered a void in his life.

Regina snorted crossly, and he realised she was still staring at him accusingly, expecting an answer. Embarrassed, he attempted a feeble smile. 'It's just that it was a leaving present from the college,' he explained. He thought of Brian. 'They'll be upset if I don't wear it.'

Regina sniffed disdainfully. 'Seems to me,' she announced, 'you ought to think more of what de Lord wants.'

Dougal wore the cope, but throughout the service he was uncomfortably aware of Regina's eyes fixed on him sourly. That his finery far outshone that of the Bishop did little to help, and he began to wish heartily that he could take the thing off.

All of the staff of Walsingham, mindful of Father Goody's instruction, had rallied to his support, and throughout the service they clustered behind him like so many lace clad, gently bobbing birds. Behind them were gathered the rest of the priests from the deanery, who had all come along to welcome Dougal and say hello. But, even though robed, they were all far more restrained in dress than the Walsingham contingent and, taken en masse – in the rather stark surroundings of St Prosdocimus – they could almost have been rival factions from alien planets. Dougal discovered St Prosdocimus did not boast a large congregation, but they were all extremely committed and, as Regina had informed him, they had all turned out to welcome him that evening and offer their support. He felt rather touched.

The Walsingham brigade had insisted on candles and incense. Brian had said they wanted to give Dougal a good send-off and spiritually set the atmosphere for his new ministry. St Prosdocimus had never seen anything like it before. Through the writhing clouds of smoke that curled around the altar and licked up towards the iron cross, Dougal could only dimly make out the rather perplexed faces of his new parishioners. Black, brown and white, they all looked mystified. At the same time, as he knelt before the Bishop, and then rose to his feet to read out the declaration of assent, Dougal was acutely aware of Amanda's eyes glued on him disapprovingly. She was wearing a long, floaty chiffon dress that, Dougal knew, she had bought specially for the occasion from an extremely expensive little shop she frequented in Bond Street, and on her head was a chic little straw hat, with a pale drooping rose attached to the crown. Her expression was hard and then, as he stared at her apprehensively, he saw her glance swiftly aside and give a small smile. Surprised, Dougal turned to follow the direction of her gaze, and found himself staring straight into the eyes of the Bishop's chaplain, now standing just behind his lord and master and carrying the mitre and crook.

Swallowing, Dougal looked away. He had a sudden horrible feeling of a shadow resting over them all. He cleared his throat and began to read the words that now swam before his eyes on the page. But he had hardly managed two sentences when there was a loud bang on the outer wall, as if something extremely heavy was being dragged along the side. All over the church peoples' heads jerked round, and Dougal faltered and then stopped. There was another bang, not so loud this time, and then the doors were pulled roughly back. In the rush of cool air that blew in the candles flickered and one went out, and then into the doorway came a group of boys. As far as Dougal could make out they were all of them dressed in black, rough and untidy looking, and one of them had a dog. He counted five, and then very arrogantly the group sauntered down the aisle and flung themselves into the nearest seats.

'Get on with it then!' shouted one, waving his hand imperiously. 'We just come to sus out the opposition.' He laughed unpleasantly.

It was too much. Before anyone could stop her Regina rose to her feet and set off in full sail down the aisle. 'You get out!' she shouted, waving her arms. 'We don't want yo kind in here. We know you. You de boys what torched de car. You get out now!' And then she seized the ringleader by the scruff of his leather jacket and began to try and manhandle him out of his seat. There were jeers and catcalls from the youth's mates. He looked stunned for a second and, before the violence of her attack, fell from his chair. It was a mistake. He swore viciously and the next second had twisted up and grabbed her arms. 'You just watch it, darlin'!' he shouted viciously.

Regina gave two affrighted steps back and there were gasps of horror from the congregation. But it was as if they were all mesmerised, and not one of them did anything to help.

Behind their leader, the intruders began to chant and the boy pushed Regina steadily before him up the aisle, prodding the older woman roughly in the chest as he went. As he drew abreast of Amanda he paused, and stared at her insolently, 'Caw,' he shouted, 'What we got 'ere then?'

For Dougal it was as if the words released him. Even afterwards he was not sure exactly what happened, but he suddenly found he had lain down the charge the Bishop had handed to him, and was striding down the aisle. He saw Regina's petrified eyes fixed on him pleadingly, and the next instant he had reached out and grabbed the young man by the scruff of his neck. Dougal was quite large and, until he had decided at the end of his college days that it was no longer seemly, he used to play fly half for the college rugger team. He had actually been rather good and had achieved a half blue, but the consequence of all that sporting activity was that he had built up a not inconsiderable amount of muscle. Now, thrusting aside the heavy folds of the cope which were getting in the way, he lifted the young man bodily into the air, and then began to frogmarch him back down the way he had just come. The youth struggled indignantly, his jaw dropping open, but he was no match for Dougal, who was now thoroughly roused. With one almighty heave, the priest flung him out of the church door, and the boy fell heavily on the path. 'And stop out!' roared Dougal. 'You can come back in when you want Christ, and not before.'

Then he swung back round, the cope flying out from his shoulders and making him, had he but known, look like some huge and terrifying avenging angel. That at least was what the remaining yobs appeared to think. As he turned and stared, gathering himself up to expel them, they took one look and then, almost falling over each other in their haste to get out, hurtled past him through the door. There was another moment's silence, and then the congregation cheered. 'Dat de way!' shouted Eliston, who now sprang to his feet and ran forwards. He threw both arms round Dougal and gave him a great hug. 'Welcome, reverend!' he shouted. 'Yo home.'

Over his shoulder Dougal saw Regina. After all the upset she was trembling violently and her face looked grey but, catching his look, she nodded and gave a weak, approving smile.

The Bishop waited another minute and then stepped forward, his hand upraised. 'Alright. Thank you, everyone!' he called. 'It's over now. Let's get on with the service.' He motioned to Dougal. 'If you'll please come back, Dougal, and proceed with the declaration of assent.'

Dougal came to a decision. Shrugging off the heavy folds of the cope, he laid it into Regina's outstretched hands as he walked past. Then, coming to a stop just in front of the Bishop, he turned and, in a rather firmer voice, pledged himself to bring the grace and truth of Christ to those now committed to his care.

'Well, I don't know,' said Brian afterwards, 'whoever would have thought Dougal could be so macho? My heart was all of a flutter when those dreadful boys came in. But Dougal was magnificent.' He laughed guiltily, catching William's surprised blink, and said, 'Oh don't worry, dear, I'm not about to run off with him. He's a bit *too* macho for me, but you've got to admit, he was impressive.'

Amanda evidently thought so too. As soon as she could, she sidled up to him and slipped a hand through his arm. 'You were absolutely wonderful, darling,' she breathed. 'I never knew you had it in you. You certainly put them in their place. I shouldn't think they'll dare try that again.'

Regina, who had overheard, looked concerned. Dougal noticed her shake her head and then mutter something aside to Eliston, but she stepped forward and said firmly, 'You was wonderful, Dougal. But I not sure dat de end of dem. Dey very bad boys. Dey de ones dat broke in before and burned de car.'

Amanda laughed. 'Yes, but you didn't have a vicar then, did you? Now you have, and now they know him. I really don't think there'll be any more trouble.'

Nicholas came up. 'Well done,' he said drily. 'St Dougal to the rescue – we will have all the young girls' hearts a-flutter.'

He looked at Amanda and smiled, and Dougal had the satisfaction of seeing her turn away from the chaplain and back towards himself. She squeezed his arm. 'Well they'll have to get behind me then,' she murmured. 'He's taken.'

Out on the street, to restore their pride, Danny and his mates had pinched some beer and fags from the shopping parade opposite. 'I vote we get him,' said one. 'He didn't ought to be allowed to get away with that.'

'No,' said another. 'Shoving Danny round like that!'

Danny looked sulky. 'He caught me off guard,' he muttered belligerently. 'But I'll get him for that. I will.' He took another swig of beer and the others gathered closer, admiringly.

'How?' demanded one. 'What you going to do?'

Farther along the street a car pulled up, and there were negotiations with the girl standing nearby on the corner. It was a big car and the boys watched with interest, momentarily diverted. The girl, wearing a skirt so short it was almost a belt, opened the door and got in. 'Drive over there,' they heard her say. 'Into the car park. You don't need a ticket at this time of night.'

'What d'you reckon, Biff?' said one, staring at his watch. 'Seven minutes?'

'Pepper? No way,' said the other jeeringly. 'Five minutes max. She won't hang about.'

'I'll give you a quid for six, Darren,' said another.

They exchanged bets and Danny's scowl grew. He liked Pepper, though she was at least five years older than him and he had the uncomfortable feeling she was out of his league. Still, he harboured fantasies about her and he had even, once or twice, toyed with the idea of trying to buy her favours for himself – he did not delude himself that she would look at him any other way. But the trouble was, at forty quid a go he could not really afford it. And besides which, he was worried that if his mates ever found out that he had paid for sex (even with Pepper) they would call him sad, and maybe even boot him out of the gang. And Danny did not want that; he wanted to belong.

As the throbbing of the engine died and the tail lights of the car went out, his friends began to count the minutes.

'I wouldn't mind a piece of that action,' remarked Darren inconsequentially.

After precisely four minutes and thirty-two seconds Pepper re-emerged, walking launguidly out from the dark car park and back towards the street. Behind her the car slid slowly out and away. She did not look round.

'I win,' crowed Biff. 'I was closest.'

From her position under the street light Pepper turned and stared at them. 'Don't you saddos have anything better to do?' she remarked. 'Shove off. You'll put the punters off.'

Biff was feeling pleased with himself. 'Come on, Pepper,' he shouted, 'it's only a laugh. Why don't you take a break? Come over here and have a beer.'

He held up a can and she stared at him consideringly. 'Come on,' he repeated.

'Okay.'

She glanced quickly round to make sure there was no one about, and then walked slowly across towards them. She had on platforms that gave a good three inches to her height, and as she walked she gave the slightest alluring roll with her hips. Danny could hardly believe how sexy she was. He watched her approach with unconsciously bated breath, taking in her long, naturally curly red gold hair and huge velvety eyes. But what really attracted him were the pert little breasts thrusting upwards through her thin cotton top, the nipples forming prominent little inviting peaks. He could see that she was wearing nothing underneath, and he felt a sudden spurt of desire.

His mates were oblivious. 'How's trade?' remarked Darren, as Biff undid the can and handed it to her.

She shrugged. 'Alright. Bit slow.'

'Where's Carl?'

Carl was her pimp, and not overly nice. She shrugged. 'Dunno. Around ... Don't care.' She took a long swig of the beer, tilting back her head and exposing the long line of her throat, so that Danny felt a cold sweat break out on his forehead. Feeling his eyes upon her, she lowered the can and looked at him lazily. 'What you been up to then?' she asked.

Embarrassed, Danny's scowl grew even darker. 'Don't take any notice of him,' jeered Biff, giving a hoot, 'he just got chucked outta the church.'

'So did you,' retorted Danny.

'No ... o!' Biff started to his feet. 'I left voluntarily, I did.'

The others snorted, and Darren said, 'Only because you was scared that if you didn't, you'd get thrown out too.'

They dissolved into noisy laughter and Pepper asked, 'So what happened then?'

'Oh, you know.' Danny shrugged.

'We thought we'd go and welcome the new rev,' volunteered Darren. 'There's a big service tonight over at the church. We went along.'

'And?' Pepper looked bored.

'The new vicar, he asked us to leave.'

As if this was enormously funny, Biff fell around laughing. 'You mean he threw us out. At least, he did Danny. The rest of us left before he could get to us.'

'Really?' For the first time Pepper looked genuinely interested. 'I thought vicars was supposed to love everyone. I didn't know they could throw people out.'

'This one did.'

'What's he like then?'

Danny glowered. 'He's big,' he said quickly, before any of the others could interrupt. 'He's built like a brick shithouse. I reckon he works out.' His scowl grew. He discovered just at that moment that he had an almost unassuagable physical longing for the girl standing opposite him. 'I'll get him,' he asserted. 'He'll be sorry for what he done.'

But Pepper was already rising to her feet. 'Yeah, yeah,' she said nonchalantly, discarding the can. 'And I'm going to go to Hollywood. Never mind, back to work. Thanks for the drink, lads.' And she was gone.

Danny stared after her retreating back gloomily. She never took him seriously, he thought. In that moment his resolve hardened. She might think he was a joke, but he'd show her. He'd do exactly what he'd said. He'd get that poncey vicar, if it was the last thing he did.

4

Bishop Hubert looked annoyed.'Nicholas,' he said with some acerbity, 'exactly why is it that none of my instructions seem to have been carried out?'

The chaplain smiled blandly.'But they have been, Bishop,' he said reassuringly. 'It's just that these things take time.' His tone seemed to imply that the Bishop, a mere newcomer to the higher echelons of power, did not fully appreciate the workings of diocesan machinery.

'But I asked you to sort this out over a month ago,' the Bishop said plaintively. 'Surely a simple thing like the analysis of clergy deployment within the diocese shouldn't take this long!'

The chaplain tutted and allowed himself the merest of patronising smiles. 'Oh, Bishop,' he began sententiously, 'you've no idea. For a start we have had to differentiate between non-stipendiaries and part-timers, then non-stipendiaries in secular employment, and non-stipendiaries in full ministry but without reimbursement. Then we have had to divide up clergy in parochial and non-parochial forms of ministry – and of course the different types of non-stipendiaries within those two categories are enormous. And for these purposes, where should we place chaplains?' He paused and appeared to ponder the question. 'For example, should we differentiate between hospital, college and industrial chaplaincies? Or should we lump them all together, in which case some of the fringe ministries, like the football club or theatre chaplains, might well feel slighted. The reverberations could be enormous.'

He beamed, and the Bishop breathed heavily. Lying in bed one night a couple of months ago, unable to sleep, he had hit upon what had seemed to him the absolutely brilliant scheme of implementing what, in the stillness of the night, he had called 'triplet evangelism'. It had seemed to him so blindingly obvious that he was at a loss to understand why no one had ever done it before. The idea was that diocesan clergy should link up with two others in related areas of expertise or strength. These three should then meet together on a regular basis for prayer and mutual support but, even more importantly, they should then make themselves available as a practical resource to other parishes where there was need but not the necessary know-how. For example, the Bishop had said excitedly to Nicholas the following morning, if a parish had a large number of Asian shopkeepers, or well-to-do but unchurched commuter types, then the local vicar could call upon the appropriate evangelistic team to come along and help set up a mission that would really hit to the heart of the problem. 'That way,' he had finished excitedly, 'we could evangelise – even convert – the whole diocese!'

Nicholas had gone pale with horror. It all sounded to him like the most enormous amount of work and, therefore, a very bad idea. Besides which, he was not sure he actually liked the idea of a sudden influx of Asian or hard-nosed business-type converts. 'Wonderful, Bishop,' he had said, swallowing, and thinking fast, 'But we mustn't rush into this. It's obviously going to need a lot of groundwork.'

'Like what?' the Bishop asked, surprised but willing to be instructed.

'Oh, you know,' Nicholas said vaguely. And then inspiration had struck, 'Well for a start, we're going to have to have a survey of exactly what talents we have available, but before we can even begin to think about that, we'll need to ascertain the exact nature of self-perceived ministries. But of course before *that* – we're going to need a list of exactly who is employed.'

The Bishop had frowned at this juncture. He had thought the last point would be obvious and that they would simply include everyone, but Nicholas had assured him they could not possibly do that, and had then gone on to instruct him at length on the full diversity of ministry at diocesan disposal.

Afterwards he had said to Bob Myers, the Communications Officer, 'Ghastly idea, isn't it? The old boy hasn't got a clue.'

'So what are you going to do?' Bob had asked mildly, and Nicholas had smiled – a rather evil little smile.

'Well for a start,' he said, 'I reckon if we can take long enough sorting out the clergy deployment lists, he might forget about the whole thing. Either that, or get so bogged down in everything else he'll run out of steam. But of one thing I am sure, we are *not* going to do this.'

So far he had been very successful, but of late Bishop Hubert had begun to start pressing him to try and move the process on. Dougal's induction at St Prosdocimus had acted as a spur. It had been forcibly borne in upon the Bishop by the noisy intrusion of the yobs, that his new priest's strongarm tactics might be effective in clearing the church, but that, in order to fill it, Dougal might perhaps need to learn how better to communicate with his flock. And the Bishop had been acutely aware that public school, followed by college at Carbery and then Walsingham, was not perhaps, for these purposes, the best preparation. 'Poor Dougal,' he muttered now, 'I fear he's going to need help.'

Dougal was also thinking something along these lines. He had discovered his refurbished rectory was quite comfortable, although each time he came through the front door and disarmed the burgular alarm, it put him in mind of the security measures around Fort Knox. The alarm had at first floored him and he had managed to set it off three times, but then the community policeman had very patiently and slowly taken him through the mechanism, step by step, and now at least he felt he could arm and disarm it without mishap.

In the week following his induction he had resolved personally to visit every member on the electoral roll. It had been an eye-opener. He had discovered the first lady on his list, Anna Ardetti, lived on the twelfth floor of one of the two tower blocks that dominated the estate. As warned by Regina, he discovered that the lifts did not work, and so he had had to labour up all twelve flights of urine-smelling stairs. Once arrived at the appropriate floor, he had found himself confronted by a long balcony. Anna lived two doors along – behind a door that was bound across with steel bars. 'Who is it?' shouted an Italian voice in answer to his ring.

'Er ... hello,' shouted Dougal. 'My name's Dougal Sampratt. I'm the new vicar at St Prosdocimus.'

There was a long pause. 'How I know you who you say you are?' demanded the voice, nearer now.

Dougal had the impression she was standing right behind the door, listening intently. 'Well I am,' he said helplessly. 'Open the door and you'll see.'

Another pause, so long that Dougal thought that maybe she had got bored and gone away and sat down. 'Hello!' he called desperately.

There was the grating sound of a chain being put on, and then the door was drawn slowly back. A dark, bird-like eye peered at him suspiciously. 'Hello,' said Dougal, trying to pin a reassuring smile on his face. 'I wondered if I might come in and say hello?'

'You said that already,' said the voice ungraciously.

Dougal breathed heavily. 'Yes, I know,' he began, 'but I meant I would like to get to meet you properly.'

The eye regarded him for perhaps another thirty seconds, and then the door was shut. Again the chain rattled, and the next second Dougal found the door had been opened all of ten inches. 'Quick,' hissed the voice, from out of the darkness beyond, 'come in!'

Dougal stepped through into the tiny hall, and the door was instantly slammed behind him. Through the gloom he found himself staring at a tiny little old lady, with beady black, apprehensive eyes, and hair scraped back into a bun. 'You really the vicar?' she asked.

Dougal discovered Anna had not been out of her flat at all for the last four months. She was too scared, she explained. A neighbour did the shopping and, since the council had fitted the door after her last one had been kicked in for the third week running, she had not dared to venture outside. A sad look had flitted across her face when Dougal spoke about the church. 'I no come now,' she said. 'I worried that if I leave here something terrible happen. To me maybe, or to my home when I am gone.'

Dougal was appalled. 'Do come,' he said, 'it can't be that bad. Why not try it next Sunday and see?'

But she shook her head dismally. 'No,' she said. 'You new. You don't know what it like.'

Everywhere he went he found it was the same story. People were scared. Scared to go out. Scared to stay in. The kids, they all said, had run wild. It wasn't safe any more. Dougal began to understand why his congregation was so small. He determined to visit the local community centre and try and find out what, if anything, was being done to improve matters. When, however, he discovered the grafitti-covered building to which he was directed by Eliston, he found it was shut, and there was a heavily defaced notice on the door, 'Shut till further notice'; only a wag had crossed out the first 'u' and substituted 'i' instead. It felt, he thought, somehow appropriate.

Depressed, he went back alone to the rectory that night and made himself cheese on toast. Dismally reviewing the day, he worked out that of the eight visits he had made, three had refused point blank to let him in; one family, so far as he could make out, had been out; and one of the addresses on his list belonged to a house that was clearly derelict, the frames surrounding the smashed windows blackened by fire. On top of that he had discovered that the old swimming pool that served the area as its only recreational facility was also boarded up, and half the shops on the estate were shut. There was, therefore, nowhere that local people could go in safety and meet. Consequently, as far as Dougal could make out, the elderly cowered in their homes, and the young hung about aimlessly on the streets, getting into trouble. Dougal had already noted the spots frequented by the prostitutes and drug dealers. They were almost on his front door, and impossible to ignore.

Wearily, he flung himself down into a chair and absently flicked on the radio to hear the news. This was not a parish, he thought bitterly, it was hell. No wonder Amanda was so cross and had threatened to break off the engagement if he remained. Of course she could never live here, and neither could he. He came to a sudden decision. He would phone up the Bishop the next day and resign. He didn't care how it seemed. He was going to look for a new parish.

At that moment, as if in response, the radio crackled and a voice announced, 'We're going over to Naples in Italy now, to meet a local priest who's been causing quite a stir.'

In spite of himself, Dougal's ears pricked up and he began to listen. The reporter said how a young priest, Father Luigi, had caused chaos to the local establishment by ministering to the prostitutes, transvestites and drug dealers who filled the city. By day, said the voice, he was a normal parish priest but every night he toured the streets and red light districts, looking for lost souls to save. And then a rolling Italian voice took over, 'Every nighta, I go around de streets, and I ask, 'Do you lova Jesus?' They say 'Yes, Father. I lova Jesus'. *Siempre*. So then I aska them, 'Why you do this? You want me pray?' Dougal felt a wave of incredulity sweep over him, but the voice went on, 'And alaways they say yes, and so we pray on the streets. This my mission. To sava their souls!'

There followed soundbites of various Italian speaking voices, with an interpreter translating over the top. 'I was a student,' began one. 'I could not afford my studies. It seemed so easy and I fell into this life – but then I could not get out. Father Luigi, he helped me.' Then another voice, male this time, carried on, 'I got involved with drugs when I was twelve. I was a bad boy. I got into trouble with the police. Father Luigi brought me back to Jesus. He saved me. Now I live for the Lord.'

Dougal was riveted. He had never heard anything like it, and at the same moment it struck him with the most appalling clarity that this was a mirror image of the situation in which he now found himself. He wasn't anywhere as exotic as Naples, it was true, but he too was surrounded by the dregs and flotsam of society. Unlike his Italian counterpart, however, who apparently so bravely sallied forth each night into the murky wastelands where his flock resided, and entered into what sounded like both physical and spiritual combat in order to rescue them and bring them back, he, Dougal, was all set to abandon them. But what would happen to them all he wondered? If he left St Prosdocimus now, like everyone else appeared to have done, who would be left to try and seek out the lost and help them?

The rest of the report swept over him in a blur of sound as Dougal was suddenly filled with shame. He realised he could not do it. He couldn't run away just because it was tough. That way would be to let chaos and darkness win. Dazedly, as if he had been almost physically assaulted, he staggered to his feet and stumbled across to the window. The steel security shutters, that he had not bothered to draw back when he came in, made a diamond pattern against the gathering gloom of the night. Beyond he could see the dark outline of the tower blocks, illuminated all the way up by little squares of pale light. It struck him again how isolated they all seemed, and then his eyes travelled down to the barren, bottle-littered square that stood in front of the rectory, and on to the dreary houses beyond. On the corner stood a pub, The Wigspittle and Pole. Dougal had barely registered it before, but now over its doorway, to his horror, he saw a huge cross. He stared at it transfixed, and it seemed to him that that moment the air about his head seemed to crackle, as if there was a sudden discharge of electricity. Surely that had never been there before?

It was so totally unexpected that, in the quiet that seemed suddenly to fall, Dougal felt as if it was a sign straight from God. You may go, God seemed to be saying to him, but I won't. I'll never go, because my lost children are here, and they need me.

Dougal could not help himself. 'Oh, God!' he muttered. He half collapsed onto his knees and, unable to hold it back, let out a sob. 'I'm so sorry,' he said aloud, as if the Almighty himself really was standing there listening, 'I never thought. But you're right. If I go now ... if I abandon them ... there won't be anyone here, will there? But what can I do?'

Almost like an answer, he had a sudden compelling image of Father

Luigi sallying forth onto the streets, cassock flapping around his sandalled feet, a huge crucifix clutched in his hand. It was so bizarre that Dougal laughed, but at the same time he felt absolutely certain he was being given an answer. He too had to go out onto the streets, and not cower inside the concrete of St Prosdocimus waiting for the world to come to him. He had to seek out the lost.

Some time later – he was not sure how long had passed – he rose shakily to his feet and, in a gesture of defiance, flung back the steel shutters. Immediately the inky blackness of the night seemed to surge towards him, but Dougal no longer felt afraid. He peered out, raising a hand and rubbing a patch on the glass in order to see more clearly. At the same moment there was a sudden gust of wind and, with an audible squeak, the cross on the pub opposite suddenly lifted and the middle bit swung out. His attention caught by the movement, Dougal laughed. Of course, that was what it was, the 'cross' was no more than the pub sign seen from the side. He had never noticed it before. Not a cross after all. But in a sudden explosion of mind-illumining clarity, he realised that that was irrelevant. The sign may not have been intended as a cross but, from his perspective, that was what it most certainly was – a whispered intimation of God's hidden presence. Dougal felt he knew what he had to do.

*

Back in her flat in London, Amanda was having revelations of a different kind. Lying full length on the maroon check sofa that graced her living room, and wiggling her toes, Amanda giggled into the phone. 'Oh, Nicholas,' she said, 'it sounds wonderful, but I can't.'

At the other end Nicholas made a little mewing sound of dissent. 'But you'd be helping me out,' he protested. 'I've got these two tickets for that new musical, *Fire Eaters* that you were talking about, and if I can't find someone to come along with me they'll be wasted.'

He did not add that he had moved heaven and earth in order to get the tickets, after Amanda had happened to mention at Dougal's induction that she had heard it was very good. Neither did he tell her that, as a last resort, and all normal channels having proved useless, he had paid the most exorbitant sum to a tout. In fact the carefully edited version he had put to her had been that an old college friend involved in the production had given him the tickets out of the blue. It was so exciting he had said, and so kind, but he had no one to accompany him. There was no way he wanted to go by himself, and she was the only person living in London he felt he *could* ask at such short notice.

'Please,' he added pleadingly. 'After all, there can't be any harm. And I'm sure Dougal would want you to come if he knew.'

'Nicholas, there must be dozens of people you could ask,' cooed Amanda, flattered by his insistence.

'No,' he said again. 'Honestly. I know hardly anyone up in London these days, and it's always a bit difficult asking a female along. You know, they're all either attached or think you want a permanent relationship or something. They're not as understanding as you.'

It crossed Amanda's mind that she was herself attached, but she let that pass. 'Isn't there anyone special you could invite?' she asked.

'No,' said Nicholas fervently, 'No one at all.'

Amanda was tempted. She had of course read all the reviews about *Fire Eaters* and had been wanting to go ever since it had first opened a couple of months ago, but, as she had mournfully informed Nicholas, each time she suggested it to Dougal, he put her off. 'Not just at the moment, old thing,' he kept saying. 'Let me get the move sorted first. I can't even begin to think about anything else at the moment.'

Amanda had felt cross. The fact that Dougal had still been intent on going to St Prosdocimus was bad enough, but to have her pleasures interrupted by that fact had made her see red. Besides which, she suspected that a major part of his lack of enthusiasm derived not so much from overwork, as he maintained, but from the fact he did not really like musicals ... or ballet, or opera, or any of the other things, come to that, so dear to Amanda's heart. In fact the more Amanda thought about it, the more she decided the light of her life was something of a cultural pygmy, and that made her even more annoyed.

Listening to Nicholas now, it occurred to her that an evening spent in the company of the attractive young chaplain, given that Dougal had refused to take her, might be very pleasant. And after all no one could blame her, she reasoned. It was all perfectly innocent. She would simply be, as Nicholas was insisting, helping him out. And then a little spark of malice, that even she had not realised was there, reared itself in her breast and looked her firmly in the eye. Even if it wasn't innocent, it said severely, it would serve Dougal right!

'Alright,' she said, making up her mind, and before conscience could intervene. 'I'd love to come.'

Nicholas was overjoyed. 'Splendid,' he said. 'Terrific. I'll pick you up at seven, and then we'll eat after.'

Promptly at seven the following night, as promised, he arrived on her doorstep. Amanda was rather taken aback, because it had occurred to her later in the evening that he did not know her address. She had immediately wanted to phone him back, but had then realised that she was in exactly the same position herself. She had not the slightest idea where he lived. Nothing daunted, she had attempted the following morning to phone his office at Church House. There, however, she had drawn a blank. 'Sorry,' said the secretary she was eventually put through to, 'he's away at a conference in Wales at the moment. We're not expecting him back till Monday. Would you like to leave a message?'

'No,' said Amanda, puzzled, 'I wouldn't.'

Bemused, she had hung up and had then spent the rest of the day wondering whether or not she was supposed to be seeing him that night after all, or whether she had in fact made a mistake about the date. Perhaps he had meant next week. She had passed the day hoping he would phone, but he hadn't and so, at around six, she took out from the wardrobe the little black dress she had been intending to wear, and looked at it speculatively. But there seemed not a lot of point in changing and so, after a second, she put it back.

Consequently, when his ring sounded at the door, she was still in jeans and an old sloppy Joe sweatshirt. 'Hello,' she said surprised, opening the door and finding him standing there, grinning inanely, a single red rose clutched in his hand.

Nicholas, in his turn, was taken aback. 'Ah,' he said. 'Sorry. Am I early?'

'No ... o,' said Amanda. 'Not at all.' And then, realising he was staring at her, she explained, 'I thought I must have made a mistake that's all. I realised after we spoke last night you didn't know my address. And then when I phoned your office this morning, the secretary said you were away in Wales.'

Amanda was not sure whether she imagined it or not, but she thought he went slightly pale, 'You'd didn't tell them why you were phoning, did you?' he asked.

'No,' she said. 'There didn't seem much point leaving a message if you weren't going to be back before Monday.'

'Thank God for that.' Nicholas relaxed visibly, and then gave a slightly embarrassed laugh. 'I did go to a conference in Wales this morning,' he explained, 'and it does go on till Monday. But it was deadly boring, just as I'd anticipated, and I left at lunchtime. It's alright,' he added, seeing her look, 'no one'll miss me, and I can always go back tomorrow.'

Amanda was dazzled. She was so used to Dougal's pedestrian insistence on always keeping to the rules that, at that moment, Nicholas' rather cavalier flouting of them seemed to her incredibly alluring. 'Gosh,' she said. 'How naughty.' And then she glanced down at her jeans. 'Come in and give me five minutes. I'll change.'

Fire Eaters was tremendous. They both agreed. It was fun and, in parts, extremely risqué. 'Dougal would hate it,' Amanda confided during the interval. 'He disapproves so terribly of all this kind of thing. He says it leads people astray.'

Nicholas took a leisurely sip of his wine. 'Yes,' he agreed, 'Dougal does seem a shade straightlaced.'

Amanda looked at him for a second. 'You're very different,' she observed.

They were sitting opposite each other on tall stools in the theatre bar. Nicholas had on a velvet jacket of impeccable cut and a pale apricot silk shirt underneath, open at the neck. 'In fact you don't look like a clergyman at all,' she added after a moment.

He laughed. 'May I take that as a compliment?'

'I'm not sure.' She looked at him quizzically. 'How far does the difference extend?'

'From Dougal?' He looked surprised, and then appeared to consider the question more carefully. 'Well,' he said at last, 'I think you could say we have a different style that's all. Dougal always strikes me as doing everything by the book. A bit unimaginative perhaps – and maybe he puts people off because of that. But I'm much more of a social animal, and I like to keep in touch with what's going on. It's all very well making the Church into some sort of Puritan ghetto, but at the end of the day that's very unattractive. So I try to stay involved.'

An odd kind of look flitted across Amanda's eyes. 'Dougal says St Prosdocimus is 'involved',' she said levelly.

Nicholas pulled a face. 'I'm sure it is,' he agreed. 'Very socially relevant and all that. I just feel my calling's a little bit more – how shall we say – directional. You need men on the ground, the foot soldiers, I couldn't agree more. But then you need the generals and strategists too. And the diplomats. The people who are going to build the bridges for everyone else to cross. I'm good with people, so I suppose I feel my calling is more that end. And after all,' he added with a laugh, 'God does love the wealthy too.'

Amanda knew exactly what he meant. 'That's the sort of thing Daddy might say,' she said wistfully. 'I always thought Dougal was like that too, but just recently ... I don't know. He's been so strange.'

The bell rang for the end of the interval. 'Dear me, we seem to be getting a bit gloomy,' Nicholas remarked. 'Come on, drink up.' He drained his glass and stood up, smiling at her. Behind them the crowds surged towards the doors and a buzz of excited sound suddenly, and unexpectedly, seemed to explode into the air. Nicholas continued to stare at her for the briefest of seconds, the smile still hovering about his lips, and then he leant forwards and took her hand.

Startled, she looked at him for a moment, and he raised a questioning brow. Abruptly she smiled back. 'I like being with you,' she said. 'You make it all seem fun again.' Hand in hand they walked back into the auditorium.

5

'You goin' do what?' demanded Regina.

Dougal took a deep breath. 'I'm going to try and befriend the prostitutes and drug addicts,' he repeated clearly.

Regina looked at him as if he was mad. 'What for?' she asked.

They were in Dougal's study. Following his experience of the other night, Dougal had felt that his proposed plan of action was so momentous, not just for him personally, but for St Prosdocimus as a whole, that before doing anything he had to tell the churchwardens and ask for their prayers and support. Accordingly he had asked Regina and Eliston to come round to the rectory at five that afternoon, and they had arrived bearing tins of buns and a cake baked by Regina, huge beams pinned on their faces. Their general demeanour had seemed to suggest that they were extremely pleased with their new vicar, but that on the whole they still felt that, at this stage, he needed looking after. They had been solicitous, and Eliston had insisted on making the tea, which he had then carried in ceremony into the study.

'How you doin' then?' Regina had enquired, as soon as they were all seated. Dougal's response had wiped the smile from her face. Now she said vehemently, 'You won't get nowhere doin' that. You saw what dey like de other night, when those boys came into church. Dey not speak de same language we do.'

'They are still God's children,' said Dougal, in a tone that sounded pompous even to his own ears. 'I believe their current mode of behaviour is simply an example of their deep-rooted alienation.' They both stared at him blankly, as if it was he who was speaking another language and, seeing their bewilderment, he took a deep breath and tried again. 'They act like that because they feel rejected.'

'Pah!' Eliston gave a small explosion of disgust. 'They act like that because they're bad. All they want to do is mock the Lord. They not want God. They want to destroy everything.'

'Yes,' said Dougal patiently, 'but that's only because they don't know any better, and they're lost. They may not know it, but they are. And unless we try and help them, then they haven't a hope. They'll stay out in that wilderness.'

'Best place for dem,' grumbled Regina. Then she looked at Dougal's face. 'I'm tellin' you, it won't be no good!'

'We can't know that,' said Dougal reasonably, 'unless we try.'

They both stared at him, but then it seemed to dawn on them that he was perfectly serious and that there was nothing they could say that would change his mind. 'Well, jus how you propose to do it?' Regina asked finally.

Inwardly Dougal breathed a sigh of relief. 'I've been thinking about that,' he said slowly. 'I thought I'd begin just by going out onto the streets at night where they hang out, and getting to know them. Tell them about Jesus – you know the kind of thing.'

'You mean distributin' scriptures and things?' asked Eliston. His tone was slightly grudging, but Dougal could tell his interest was aroused.

'Yes, that's the sort of thing,' he agreed. 'But the main thing would be I'd be there to talk, and help if I could.'

Eliston nodded his head. 'My granddaddy used to do that, back in Jamaica,' he said slowly. 'He said it the only way to reach people, out on the street.'

'Exactly,' said Dougal excitedly. 'They're not going to come to church, so we need to take it out to them. And then in time, who knows? Maybe we could set up some sort of drop-in centre in the church hall? I mean, I know it's a bit much to expect them all to start coming along to church and changing overnight, but a drop-in centre might be a kind of halfway house. We could offer them practical help and, at the same time, demonstrate Christ's love.'

Eliston nodded his head slowly as Dougal's vision began to communicate itself to him, but Regina was still staring at him with what looked like extreme apprehension. 'Exactly who you goin' get to man this centre?' she enquired.

Dougal looked at her. This, he knew, was the weak spot in his plan.

'Oh, no,' she said. 'Not me. You way out of de line there.'

'Please,' said Dougal pleadingly. 'Can't you see? It's what we have to do. They're the people of this parish, and they're lost sheep. If we're going to be faithful to God, then we've got to go out there and round them up. I really believe this is what God wants us to do.'

He managed to persuade them at least to give it a try, but they were still, he knew, not entirely happy. Especially Regina, who kept shaking her head and muttering darkly about 'biting off more dan we can chew'. Dougal discovered he was becoming quite fond of her, but her patent unease did nothing to build up his confidence. He prayed about it all the next day and then, at eleven o'clock in the evening, screwed up his courage and went out onto the street.

It was dark as he emerged, with a thin sliver of moon showing intermittently through the clouds scudding cross the sky. His footsteps took him in the direction of the church – to be precise, the small square in front of the church, where, Regina had informed him, the working girls most liked to ply their trade. 'Dey use de car park jus round de corner,' she said. 'On a good night some of dem get as many as thirty customers.' Then her face screwed up in disgust, 'Filthy goin's on. I think de men are more to blame dan de girls.'

To his surprise, Dougal found he agreed. Temperamentally he had always felt rather bemused by prostitution and, in the past, had tended simply to condemn the women involved for their laziness and greed. Yet now, with his expanded vision, he began to feel that maybe he had been wrong and that, just possibly, it was the girls who were the victims. He felt rather virtuous.

Walking quickly down the dark streets, his footsteps echoing on the empty pavement, his thoughts took flight, and he began to ponder the desperation that could compel a woman to sell her body. Society must have gone badly wrong, he reflected sadly, when any individual could be forced to such measures merely in order to survive. But the further he went, despite all his good and rather patronising intentions, the more he began to feel that he was advancing into a kind of no man's land, and he began to feel rather scared. Then, confronted with the cheerless reality of the night, his do-gooding zeal faltered, and collapsed. Unable to think what to do, but determined not just to turn tail and flee, he began to pray. 'God,' he muttered, 'I feel a complete idiot, but if this is your idea and not just mine, then please let me find the people you want me to help without looking. Bring them to me, Lord.' He laid particular emphasis on the 'me'. 'Let them cross my path.'

He became so engrossed in his inarticulate burblings to the divine, that he hardly even noticed when his footsteps brought him to the pathway leading up to the church, and consequently almost jumped out of his skin when a form suddenly detached itself from the shadows and a grating female voice demanded, 'Got the time?'

'What?' Dougal blinked. 'Oh yes, sorry.' He lifted his wrist, straining to see its face in the poor light. 'Just gone eleven ... Ten past, I think.'

The woman regarded him with disgust. 'I didn't mean that,' she said. 'I meant *have you got the time?*' Stupefied, he stared at her, wondering if there was something in the conversation he had missed, and she suddenly flared angrily, 'What's up then, don't you fancy me?'

He stared at her, appalled, and for the first time fully registered her appearance. She looked to be in her late forties and was easily seventeen stone. Her greasy hair was scraped back into a ragged bun, and she had on a grey coat that was too small. Under the coat she wore a grubby mini skirt, and beneath that sprouted her pudgy, stockingless legs. It was her feet, however, that most drew Dougal's attention. Instead of shoes, she had on men's carpet slippers, the backs trodden down and frayed around the toes. Dougal gulped. It occurred to him that God had answered his prayers rather more promptly than he had anticipated, but he had no time to give thanks for this because the apparition before him was evidently expecting some sort of response.

As he failed to reply she glared at him angrily, breathing heavily, and Dougal had the unpleasant realisation that if she were physically to assualt him, given her superior weight and girth, she might very well win. Then he remembered his mission, and the words of Father Luigi floated into his brain. 'Do you know Jesus?' he asked, in strangled tones.

'What?' said the woman, surprised.

A cold sweat broke out across Dougal's brow. 'I said, do you know Jesus?' he repeated.

A look of menace crossed the woman's face and she took a step forward. Dougal stepped back, but it was too late. Her fist reached out and grabbed the collar of his jacket, simultaneously twisting viciously and yanking him towards her. So extreme was the movement that the air was forced out of his lungs and he thought for a second he was going to choke. Then she brought her face up close up to his, so that her tobacco-filled breath hit him squarely between the eyes, and hissed, 'You some sort of pervert? Or are you just trying to be funny?'

Half choking, Dougal scrabbled to regain his balance. He had never in his life hit a woman before but, through the swirling tide of red that suddenly rose before his eyes, he dimly realised it was either that or be suffocated. Giving one almighty shove, he planted his hands on her shoulders and heaved her aside and then stood panting on the pavement, fighting to regain his breath. Surprised, the woman shook herself like an affronted and extremely large hen, and then again stepped forwards as if to resume the attack.

Dougal raised a hand to ward her off. 'No,' he panted, still breathing heavily and tugging at his collar in an effort to take more air into his lungs. 'No, I'm serious. I'm the new priest at St Prosdocimus. That's my church behind you.'

The woman turned and glared suspiciously in the direction of Dougal's feebly waving hand.

'I really wanted to know, do you know Jesus?'

She turned her gaze back onto him, little piggy eyes becoming slits in the fleshy folds of her face as she obviously tried to work out whether or not this was a trick question. She stared at his collar, now dimly visible in the light, and a look of bovine puzzlement spread over her face. But the effort was clearly too much. 'You are a pervert,' she snapped. 'Go on, shove off! You ain't got no call botherin' people like that.' She made a violent gesture with her arm. 'Push off and let me get on with me business.'

Shaken, Dougal stumbled back. But he was breathing more easily now and the unpleasant singing in his ears had stopped. He opened his mouth to protest but the woman, as if sensing some sort of opposition, squared up to him belligerently and then, mumbling imprecations, turned and shuffled off back into the shadows from whence she had come.

Dougal stared after her retreating back, half wondering whether he ought perhaps to go after her, but something told him that this might be a bad idea and so, after a moment's indecision, he turned and walked on. But he went more slowly this time – and he kept away from the bushes, looking around nervously in case anyone else should be lurking there.

From the chippie on the other side of the square, Danny and his mates watched the exchange with interest. 'I don't think he fancied her,' remarked Darren.

There were ribald comments and sniggers, and then Danny heaved himself up and went and stood in the door. 'What's 'e up to then?' he asked. 'Where's 'e going?'

'We could follow 'im and see,' suggested Darren.

Clutching their greasy bags of half-eaten chips, the rest heaved themselves up, and then they sauntered slowly out onto the street.

Dougal decided to try again. Over on the far corner he saw a group of young girls. They were scattered along about twenty yards of pavement, five of them, but every so often they would break away from what was evidently their patch, and go and have a chat with one of their mates. Then they would amble back and position themselves again on the edge of the kerb, leg thrust provocatively forward, hair tossed back, an expression of intense boredom on their faces. Dougal watched, fascinated, as a car pulled up. The driver leant across and chatted briefly to the adjacent girl, then she got in and the car slowly inched its way towards the car park Regina had told him about. Now that he had actually seen this for himself, he felt rather shocked. He stood and watched this happen perhaps four more times, then the first girl came back, pulled down her short skirt, lit a cigarette and resumed her position. It all seemed to happen with incredible speed and Dougal felt stunned, astounded both by the number of cars, and by the speed with which the transactions were apparently accomplished.

After about ten minutes he made up his mind. These girls looked a lot younger than the woman who had just accosted him. He could imagine Father Luigi talking to them, brandishing his crucifix before their eyes and then praying over them, before they fell down with noisy sobs of repentance at his feet. Yes, he decided, these were definitely the type of girls he was called to save. They might not listen, but he was sure at least that they would not attack him, and perhaps he might be able to offer help. Taking a deep breath and screwing up all his courage, he walked determinedly across the road.

'Blimey,' said Darren behind, ''e is. 'E's after a girl! Bleedin' pervert.'

'Only way 'e'll get it, I expect,' said another. They huddled into the shadow of a nearby alley, from where they could observe what happened next.

Oblivious, Dougal carried on across the road. 'Hello,' he called cheerily, coming up to the first girl. 'How are you tonight then?'

The girl turned and stared at him. She was about eighteen or nineteen, Dougal thought, with long blonde hair and huge black-ringed eyes. 'Twenty-five quid basic,' she said unenthusiastically. 'Blow job, a tenner more, and if you want to go all the way, it's forty and a condom.'

'No,' said Dougal, feeling embarrassed, 'I don't want any of that, I just wanted to talk.' He raised his chin slightly, hoping that his collar was visible and the girl continued to stare at him.

'What about?' she demanded at last. She dropped the cigarette she was holding onto the pavement, grounding the butt with the heel of her stiletto, then blew out a long, casual stream of smoke.

'Cor,' breathed Danny, from the darkened alley across the street where the boys had clustered, ''e's gone for Shelley.' His mates sniggered.

'I ...' Dougal had been about to say, 'I was wondering if you knew Jesus', but remembering his last success with this gambit, he changed his mind. 'I was wondering if you had any kind of faith,' he said nervously.

The girl regarded him. 'Yeah,' she said after a minute. 'I do as it 'appens. I'm a Buddhist.'

Dougal blinked. This possibility had not previously occurred to him and he was unsure how to respond. 'Ah,' he said carefully, 'are you?'

'Yeah. I think I was Egyptian in a past life. That's why I do me eyes like this.'

There seemed no answer to this, and Dougal stared at her, nonplussed. 'Maisie, over there,' the girl continued, 'she's pagan, she is. She'll tell your fortune if you ask her. And she's good. She told me when my gran was going to die.'

'Did she?' Dougal was floored. He felt his training in pastoral evangelism had not quite prepared him for this. He wondered how Father Luigi would respond. He flapped his mouth uselessly, and the girl suddenly looked at her watch. 'Look, darlin',' she said, 'I don't mean to be rude, an' it is really lovely talking to you. We heard you'd come to the church ... but I really got to get on now, otherwise I won't 'ave too much of a future to talk about. Know what I mean?'

Dougal felt the conversation was not going at all the way he had envisaged. 'But I wanted to talk to you about what faith really is,' he said desperately. 'And about Jesus.'

A shade of annoyance crossed the girl's face. 'That's really nice, and I'd love to some other time. But just at the moment I'm busy.' A car pulled up and she pushed past him. 'Twenty-five quid basic,' Dougal heard her say, 'Blow job a tenner more ...'

Defeated, he turned away and looked up the street. 'Shelley's given 'im the flick,' remarked Darren. 'Wonder what 'e'll do next.'

'Try the rest, by the look of it,' remarked another.

It was true. Dougal was bearing down on the little knot of girls now standing chatting together in the doorway of the launderette. 'Hello,' he boomed with forced jocularity, 'I'm the new vicar over at St

Prosdocimus. I just thought I'd come and say hello.'

Silence fell as they all turned, and four pairs of eyes looked him up and down suspiciously. 'Hello,' replied one at last. Her tone did not seem encouraging.

'Beautiful night,' said Dougal, forcing an inane grin onto his face.

It was beginning to rain and they did not respond. 'Bit chilly though,' he tried again.

'What d'ye want?' said one of them finally.

Dougal chose to take this as encouragement.

'Well,' he said, stepping forward and swallowing, 'I suppose you could say I wanted to talk to you about Jesus really. I wanted to tell you He loves you.'

They looked at him as if he was mad, and then one of them, in a broad Liverpudlian accent, said sarcastically, 'Yeah, 'im and the rest of Carbery.'

Disconcerted, Dougal blinked. 'Pardon?' he said. 'I'm sorry. Have I said something wrong?'

The girl who had spoken flicked an imaginary speck from the sleeve of her jacket. 'Look,' she said, 'we've 'eard it all before, but at the end of the day, you don't really want to know about us. You don't care about what 'appens. All you lot want to do is clean up the streets.' She stared at him insolently, 'We're a problem that needs to be sorted, right?'

Dougal frowned. 'No, it's not like that.' And then it struck him that maybe it was, and he dried up.

'Oh, you mean we're not a problem then?'

At that moment Shelley joined them, having just returned from her last stint. 'Don't be 'ard on 'im, Maisie,' she enjoined. ''E wants 'is fortune told.'

Dougal blinked. He was unprepared for this turn in the conversation. 'Er, no,' he began.

But the girl addressed as Maisie was ignoring him. 'Does 'e?' she asked. ''Ow'd 'e 'ear about me then?'

'I told 'im, didn't I.'

'Wow.' Maisie was obviously impressed by this information. 'Well, why didn't 'e just say then, if that's what 'e wants?'

'Dunno, shy probably.'

They all turned again and regarded him now with interest, and Maisie smiled. 'Course I'll tell your fortune, luv,' she announced, 'but not now. Come and see me tomorra.'

At that moment an invisible cat let out an eerie yawl of distress, and there was the sound of a can skittering up the street. They all turned and looked. 'Blimey,' said one of the others fearfully, 'It's Carl.' She turned to Dougal, 'You'd better clear off,' she advised, ''E won't like you wasting our time.'

'But I ...,' began Dougal. As if at a signal, the girls evaporated, gliding with affected unconcern back to their posts, leaving Dougal alone.

A large black man suddenly materialised in front of him. He looked Dougal up and down coldly, eyes finally coming to rest on his priest's collar. 'Yes, reverend,' he said silkily, 'what can I do for you?'

Dougal felt himself at a disadvantage. So once again he said, 'I'm the new priest over at St Prosdocimus. I just wanted to tell the girls – and you too of course,' he added hastily, 'that we're going to be setting up a drop-in centre over at the church hall and that you'll all be very welcome.'

The man regarded him through narrowed eyes. He was tall and had on a black leather jacket, and there was the glint of silver around his neck. Staring, Dougal made out a small skull on a leather thong. 'Tea?' enquired the man sarcastically. 'Biscuits? Somewhere warm to wait in between punters? How nice – but I don't think so.'

Dougal flushed. He felt angry at this unexpected interruption. But he suddenly discovered that, confronted by another man, he felt he was on firmer ground. He knew how to respond. 'I simply wish them to know God's house is open to them,' he said, chin lifting.

They were about the same height, and a curious transformation suddenly came over the man's eyes staring levelly into his. They grew hard and dark, and a strange, menacing 'something' Dougal could not quite define seemed to uncoil in their depths. 'Let's get this straight, reverend,' he snarled softly, bringing his face up close, 'they're my girls. You don't mess with them. Not you. Not anybody. And I don't want you filling their heads with ideas.'

Dougal was unused to this kind of behaviour, but he was no coward. 'Redemption is not an idea,' he said, drawing himself up in turn and taking a step forward, so that now the other was forced to retreat. 'And those girls are *not* yours. No human being belongs to another. They're free under God, and they can choose for themselves.'

For perhaps a minute the two men glared at each other, and Dougal wondered fleetingly whether he was going to be attacked, but then Carl laughed softly. It was not a pleasant sound. 'I'm giving you warning,' he said. 'Just stay away.' Then he spun on his heel and walked away, towards the nervously watching girls.

Over in the alley, Darren let out a low whistle. ''E certainly knows 'ow to pick em,' he remarked. 'Seems a bit unwise to me, to get on the wrong side of Carl.'

'Yeah,' agreed one of the others. 'I don't reckon our vicar friend is going to last too long.'

''Ere, Danny,' said another, 'you'd better get in quick if you want to do 'im. Ain't goin' to be much left for you. Not if Carl has a go.'

When Dougal told her what had happened, Regina was round eyed. 'That's Carl,' she breathed. 'Yes. I know him. We all know him. He very bad man.'

'I take it he's their pimp,' said Dougal dryly.

Regina pulled a face. 'Among other tings,' she agreed. 'De word on de street is that he Mr Big. He supplies all de drugs. Most of de bad things dat go on round here have him behind dem.' But she refused to say more. 'No,' she insisted. 'Better you not know. You not want to get mixed up in such things.'

Privately Dougal agreed, but he felt angry at the casual assurance with which he had been warned off. 'Regina,' he said, 'I want to go ahead with plans for opening up the hall as a drop-in centre. I'd like you to organise a rota if you will, of people who might be willing to man it. I'll be around of course, so no one need be afraid.'

Regina looked sceptical. 'You tink jus' because you dere, nothin' bad goin' to happen?' she asked.

'No,' said Dougal, 'not exactly. But I still think we've got to try, and I think once they all see that we're not a threat, and that we actually do want to help, they won't be so hostile. I'm going to get some flyers printed and stick them up in the shops.'

6

Father Goody, respected canon of Carbery Cathedral, slammed his fist down hard on the table and glared round at his assembled staff. 'What do you mean no one's done anything yet?' he thundered. His head was still hurting from over indulgence in spirits (not of the holy kind) the night before, and he was in a mood to take it out on anyone unwise enough to get in his way. He sucked in his cheeks, a habit he had when cross, and then blew heavily. 'The conference is due to start in six weeks' time!'

Brian winced and then looked flustered. 'Well it's just that it's always been Dougal's job,' he explained.

Beverley, the new female appointee, looked sour. 'I don't think we should be hosting something like this anyway,' she announced.

Father Goody ignored her. They were discussing the annual 'Restore' conference that Walsingham had hosted ever since the movement first began, some three years before women were first admitted as priests. Now he looked annoyed. 'Since Dougal is no longer here,' he snarled, 'did it not occur to one of you numbskulls that someone else should have taken on the job?'

Eight wounded faces stared owlishly back at him and Beverley, who rather thought this summed up the organizational aptitude of Walsingham, was unwise enough to snigger. Father Goody rounded on her, 'Beverley, as our newest member of staff, I hardly think your input is very useful here. Kindly be quiet. Unless that is,' he added sneeringly, 'you are offering to take on the duties yourself.'

Beverley flushed but subsided, and William interposed, 'The problem is, Tim, that none of us thought about it. We've always just been so used to everything happening. Dougal used to organise all this kind of thing. And he used to arrange all the speakers and advance publicity every year, and then just send out the bumph when we needed to register. We rather thought we did our bit just by turning up.'

Father Goody breathed heavily and muttered something under his breath. Aloud he said, 'Am I to take it then, that we don't even have any speakers.'

There was an embarrassed silence. 'Well, Oswald's offered to do one on the 'Maleness of rite' ... and I suppose I could do something on Carthusian liturgy,' faltered William.

'And I'd be happy to do one on gender issues and orthodoxy,' broke in Brian.

Beverley could contain herself no longer. 'I've never come across such a half-baked load of rubbish,' she exploded. 'How can you even begin to think of attracting women to the college when you're holding things like this? It's disgusting. And what's the point? This conference is offensive, not just to women in ministry, but to women as a whole. And as for the lectures you're proposing! Honestly, I've never heard such a load of tripe in my life!'

A glassy expression settled over Father Goody's face. 'Yes, thank you, Beverley,' he said. 'I would agree the topics are not perhaps quite as inspiring as they ought to be.' He turned his attention back to the others who were now, to a man, sitting forwards on the edges of their seats.

'Well, I'm very sorry,' fluttered Brian distractedly, as the principal's eye settled on him. 'It was all we could come up with at such short notice.'

Father Goody banged shut the file in front of him on the table. He had evidently decided he had had enough. 'You have exactly one week,' he said nastily, 'in which to find five speakers with at least something halfway interesting to say, and to send out flyers and registration forms to all members. And you, Beverley,' he added, fixing her with a glare, 'since you apparently feel so strongly on the subject, and to show that I at least am *not* prejudiced against women, you can organise room allocation for the three days involved, and perhaps arrange for some of your friends to come along too. By which of course I mean,' he added, glancing at her face, 'women who take an orthodox view of priesthood and who are in sympathy with our aims here at Walsingham.'

He gathered together his papers, cast one last look around, and swept out. A buzz of excited chatter broke out as the door closed on his retreating back, and Beverley stared at the white wooden panels mulishly. She rather thought she had had enough of this. She determined to do exactly what Father Goody had instructed her and arrange for some of her friends to come along.

*

'Exactly what is this, Nicholas?' asked the Bishop a week later, frowning.

Nicholas glanced casually at the letter the Bishop was holding out to him. 'Oh, it's the annual conference at Walsingham, Bishop,' he said. 'You must have heard of it. They get together every autumn to bemoan the fact that women have got the vote, and exchange patterns for cassocks.'

The Bishop looked at him. 'I do not think this is a joking matter, Nicholas,' he said severely. 'Such gatherings spread disunity, and it is my private opinion that these men ought now to accept the authority of the Church, or leave. But they should not persist in causing trouble like this.'

Later, over a lunch of homemade lentil soup and wholemeal scones, he said to his wife, 'My dear, I had high hopes after my warnings to Walsingham that all of this anti-women business would cease, but only this morning I have discovered they plan to host another inflammatory conference within the month.'

Myra smiled. She too had received a letter. From Beverley. 'Please,' Walsingham's newest patristics tutor had written, 'do come along. You've no idea the strength of feeling against women that there is here. To hear them all speak in the common room you'd think we were some kind of sub-species, and certainly not redeemed. To this lot, Eve not only gave Adam the apple, but she cultivated it first. And yet half of them act like they want to be women anyway; some of them even wear make-up. Please do come. I realise of course you won't want financially to support something like this, but I'm sure it will be worth it if enough women can infiltrate it to stage some sort of protest. In fact, with enough of us, we could disrupt the whole thing.'

Now Myra said tranquilly, 'I really wouldn't worry, Hubert, if I were you. These things have a way of sorting themselves out in time. By the way, dear,' she added, 'I'm planning on going to visit my sister in about a month's time. I shouldn't be long, only about three days.'

'Really?' said the Bishop, surprised. Myra and her sisters had never seemed to him to be very close. In fact their general coolness towards one another had rather worried him in the past, and he had tried energetically to encourage his wife to go and visit, or even invite them to spend a few days at the rectory. Relations, however, had remained almost non-existent, apart from the obligatory exchange of cards at Christmas and in recent years he had rather given up. Now he felt rather encouraged by this unexpected display of sisterly fraternization.

'Which one?' he enquired.

'Evadne.'

The Bishop smiled warmly. 'That's lovely, dear. I hope you have a very pleasant time.'

Dougal also received notice of the conference. Brian sent him a handwritten note. It arrived when he was feeling rather low. He had been out on his rounds again the night before but, as usual, had met with almost no response. The girls now at least greeted him, but they seemed totally disinterested in anything he might say, and brushed him aside as soon as anyone more interesting appeared on the horizon. He could not imagine what it was he was doing wrong, but the net result was that he felt profoundly depressed. He was beginning to wonder whether his soul-stirring sense of call had actually been no more than his overworked imagination. And that in turn had led him to wonder whether he should, as Amanda kept urging him, find something more suitable.

Into this state of emotional turmoil Brian's note came, therefore, as something akin to spiritual manna. A kind of tenuous lifeline threading back into his past life. Looking at it, propped up against the sugar bowl in his newly painted kitchen, Dougal shuddered and then felt a kind of aching sadness, thinking of all that he had lost. It struck him that at that precise moment there was nowhere he would rather be than back with his brother priests within the safe confines of Walsingham. He had been a fool ever to think he might have been called to St Prosdocimus for a purpose. All it had been was a rather severe lesson in humility and Amanda had been right.

The thought of Amanda made him suddenly wonder how she was getting on. With a jolt, he realised it had been ages since he had last seen her. He could not even remember when they had last spoken on the phone. The fact that Amanda could equally well have made the effort to get in touch did not occur to Dougal. Rather, it suddenly hit him that he had been neglecting her.

Brian's note, bland and slightly yellow, with the impossibly neat little spidery writing, stared up at him. It acted as a kind of spur. He had been so caught up in this stupid vision, he thought, that he had allowed it to swamp him, to blot out everything else. But no longer. Glaring at it, as if it had given voice to some kind of accusation, he came to a sudden decision. He would stop all this garbage. He would take up again the threads of his life before it was too late. He would regain control. And first and foremost, as witness of that, he would phone up Amanda.

He went through to the study and dialled her number. When he got through, however, the answerphone came on. 'Hello,' bubbled Amanda's voice cheerily, 'it's me, but I'm not here. Assuming you haven't got the wrong number (loud giggle), leave your name and all that kind of stuff and I'll get back to you.' There was a long beep.

Crestfallen at not finding her there, Dougal cleared his throat and prepared to leave a message. 'Hello, Amanda,' he began, 'it's me, I ...,'

He was interrupted by a funny kind of click and then a voice shrieked, 'Dougal, hi! Oh blast, I can't turn this thing off, hang on a sec.' There was a high-pitched stuttering whine followed by three more bleeps, and then the line abruptly cleared. 'Sorry,' apologised Amanda, 'I had it on answer/fax. It doesn't like changing once it's started.'

'Were you just on your way out?' asked Dougal, surprised.

There was a slight pause and then, 'Oh no,' Amanda assured him. 'I just tend to leave the answerphone on all the time these days, that's all. Then if it's someone I don't particularly want to talk to, I can ignore them.'

Dimly Dougal felt that there was something about this that was not quite right. He felt it lacked courtesy. Also he had never known Amanda do it before, and he felt taken aback. He stifled his reaction, however, and said, 'I thought you might like to do something this weekend.'

It felt to Dougal as if, for the briefest of seconds, Amanda hesitated and then she said, 'Oh Dougal, that would be wonderful ... but I've arranged to go down to Henley this weekend.'

She did not say with whom, and for a second Dougal had the peculiar but distinct impression she did not want him to ask. But then she went on rather hastily, 'It's an old schoolfriend actually. Her family lives down there. They're having some kind of bash and I haven't seen them all for ages, so Mirielle asked me to stay over.'

Dougal felt obscurely hurt but, with his refound clarity, he told himself he quite understood. 'I ... I don't suppose I could come?' he ventured.

Amanda's response was immediate. 'Dougal, darling, any other time of course you could, I'm sure. But this is a formal twenty-first and the numbers are all fixed. I couldn't just ask if you could come along too.'

'Ah,' said Dougal, in a small voice.

'Perhaps the weekend after?' said Amanda brightly.

'Yes,' said Dougal. 'That would be nice.'

Five minutes later, when he rang off, he felt even more depressed than ever. He could not put his finger on it, but it felt to him as if there were some kind of invisible barrier between them, almost as if everything they said had to go through a kind of filter. And then it occurred to him that, if there was any kind of uneasiness, it was probably all due to him. He realised he had been selfish and inconsiderate towards her over the past few weeks. He had ignored almost everything she said, expecting her simply to fit in with what he wanted, and paying not the slightest attention to her complaints; indeed there had been so many, it had been easier simply to blot them all out. But it had all got to change. And with that resolution, he went and filled out the reply form for the Restore conference.

He was just signing the accompanying cheque when the doorbell rang. 'Yes,' he said, going and opening the door and pinning what he hoped was a friendly expression on his face. 'Can I help you?'

The man standing before him was a complete stranger. He was aged about forty, Dougal judged, slightly overweight, and wearing jeans and a tweed jacket. 'Reverend Sampratt?' he asked.

'Yes,' said Dougal.

The man fished in his pocket and brought out a card. 'My name's Rob Fisher. I'm a reporter for the *Carbery Times*. We had a tip that you're doing something a bit unusual down here.'

Dougal was surprised. 'Er ... no,' he began, wondering what on earth the man was talking about.

But the man ignored him. 'We've had information,' he continued, consulting a notebook, 'that you're getting up some sort of initiative to help local prostitutes and drug addicts.'

Dougal felt himself flush. 'Well,' he began.

'May I come in?' asked the man and, without waiting for Dougal to respond, he pushed his way past and walked through into the living room. 'They're alright, these places, once you get inside, aren't they?' he remarked.

Dougal's brain was whirling. The attention of the *Carbery Times* was, he felt, the last thing he needed – especially in view of the decision he had made not five minutes before. 'May I know who your informant was?' he asked.

The journalist flung himself uninvited onto Dougal's sofa and stretched, 'Not entirely sure really,' he said conversationally. 'My editor passed it on to me. I think some bird phoned or something, but he didn't say. He just said to come down and check it out.'

'Well, I'm afraid you've been misinformed,' said Dougal stiffly.

At that moment there was another ring at the door. Three to be precise, and then the letterbox was pushed open and a shrill voice called, 'Yoohoo, Father, it's me. Maisie. I've come to tell ye fortune.'

For perhaps two seconds Dougal and the reporter stared at each other, and then Maisie rang the doorbell again. 'I think you'd better get that,' remarked the journalist, taking out a pen and smiling broadly. 'Sounds like a determined lady you've got out there.'

Trying to work out what on earth to do, Dougal again went and opened the door. But any hopes he had been nurturing that by day Maisie might be more restrained in her attire, evaporated. She was dressed as ever in a thin band of black lycra skirt and her fishnet-clad legs seemed to go on for ever. The tee shirt she wore on top was short and very tight, and bore the inscription 'Bad Girl!' in huge silver letters across the front. 'Hiya,' she said. Without waiting for any kind of response she swept past him, waving a pack of cards in his face and announced gaily, 'I've brought me tarot cards. I said I would.'

Dougal tried to stop her. 'No,' he began. 'It's very kind. But it's not convenient. Not at the moment.'

Maisie ignored him. 'Don't be silly. It's no trouble. I like it.' She pulled up short, taking in the man sprawled across the sofa. 'Oh, you are busy!'

Startled by the interruption, the journalist rose to his feet, and then stared at her appraisingly. He looked beyond her to Dougal. 'Very nice,' he remarked. 'One of your choir girls, I suppose?'

Dougal could have hit him, but Maisie seemed completely unabashed. 'Look I'm sorry, I didn't realise. I'll come back later, shall I?'

Seeing Dougal's unease, a look of calculation swept across the reporter's face. 'No, don't do that,' he said, interposing himself swiftly between her and the door. 'I have the feeling you might be one of the people I'm here to see the vicar about.' He flashed his card before Maisie's eyes. 'I'm from the *Carbery Times*. I've come to do a piece on this new centre the reverend's setting up.'

Comprehension dawned on Maisie's face. 'Oh that,' she said

conversationally. 'Yeah, I know all about that. We all do.'

'All?'

'Me and the girls. Father D says it's for us.'

She settled herself comfortably on the far side of the sofa, and Dougal found himself praying earnestly that she would pull down her skirt. Unfortunately, however, the Almighty appeared to be busy elsewhere, and Dougal's prayer went unanswered. For perhaps five seconds, Rob Fisher stared at Maisie's legs as though his eyes would drop out and then, recollecting himself, he swallowed, settled himself opposite her and prepared to write.

'When's it open?' he asked.

In vain Dougal tried to shut her up but, off-duty, he discovered Maisie possessed a wholly unsuspected loquacity. More than that, he was absolutely amazed by all she had apparently taken in. She told Rob Fisher all about how Dougal went round the streets at night, talking to them about Jesus; how he tried to befriend the street kids, and how the church was now to have a drop-in centre where they could all go anytime. Rob Fisher could hardly write fast enough.

'Where?' he asked.

'The 'all, I think,' said Maisie blithely, totally oblivious of the discomfort she was causing.

'And you say it hasn't opened yet?'

'No, not yet,' agreed Maisie vaguely. 'I think it's opening this weekend. That's what the leaflets say anyway.'

'Leaflets?' Rob Fisher's nose twitched, and Dougal thought how uncanny a resemblance he bore to a rat.

He made a choking sound but it was too late. Maisie was already scrabbling in her bag. 'Yeah. I've got one here, I think,' she announced. 'You can 'ave it if you want.'

To his absolute horror Dougal realised she had found it and was handing it over. A couple of days ago and he would have been delighted at this tangible evidence that his efforts had, despite all appearances to the contrary, borne fruit, but not now. 'No,' he said in strangled tones. 'Don't give it to him. I mean, it's not right.'

They both turned and stared at him. 'What d'ya mean?' demanded Maisie. 'Is the date wrong or something?'

Dougal had a most unpleasant singing in his ears. He felt trapped. 'Yes ... no,' he began. 'That is, the date's right. I just don't think we ought to have publicity.'

The reporter turned injured eyes on him. 'Why ever not?' he asked in an innocent tone.

'Ah,' said Maisie, and smiled. 'Isn't that just so like 'im! He's so humble.' She turned back to the reporter and gave him the most brilliant of smiles. 'That's Father D, for you,' she announced. 'He does so much, but won't take a word of thanks.' Then she leant forward confidentially and Dougal heard her whisper, 'You know what? I think he's a saint!'

There seemed no stopping her after that. With horror, Dougal heard his nightly, and up to then wholly unsuccessful, forays embellished into almost canonical progressions of triumph. She gave the impression of eager vagrants lining the streets, waiting to be blessed by the passing of his shadow; of rejected and forgotten working girls, thirsting for a word of redemption. Dougal had had no idea Maisie possessed such a vivid imagination. 'No,' he kept stuttering, 'it's not true. None of it.'

But Rob Fisher ignored him. 'Will you all be there?' he asked, 'Saturday night?'

Maisie dimpled. 'Course,' she assurred him. 'You can take our photos if you like.'

By the time they left Dougal felt shattered. He felt as if he was the victim of some bizarre and cruel cosmic joke. Only hours before he had felt devastated by the knowledge that no one at St Prosdocimus wanted or would use the centre. Now he was totally blasted by the horrific thought that they would. Once Rob Fisher had left, Maisie had again offered to read his cards, but he was able to fend off that suggestion. 'The one thing I really don't wish to know just at the moment,' he said hollowly, 'is my future.'

Maisie looked at him speculatively and then smiled. 'Don't worry,' she said reassuringly, misinterpreting him. 'I'll make sure there are people there. I'll get the girls together.' She pushed past him as he opened the front door and then, at the last moment, suddenly turned and pressed her body up against his. She was a tall girl and Dougal felt the hard points of her nipples squashed against his chest. A cold sweat broke out across his brow. 'You'll be famous,' she whispered. Her body shivered against his and she ran her hand down his front.

Dougal gulped. 'No,' he said, embarrassed, trying to push her away. 'That's not the point.' He tried to step back but, in the narrow confines of the hall, found he could not move.

Maisie laughed softly. 'You really are an innocent, aren't you,' she said. It was a statement. But to his acute discomfort she made no attempt to withdraw herself. 'Tell you what, I'll give you a freebie, if ye like.'

Never in all his life before had Dougal had such an offer. He was shocked. But even worse he suddenly discovered he would rather like to accept. There was something rather attractive about Maisie. Horror overwhelmed him. How on earth could he be so callow? He was engaged to Amanda. 'No, Maisie,' he gasped, making an even more determined effort to push himself away. 'It's very kind ... but I don't do that sort of thing.'

'D'ye mean ye're gay?' demanded Maisie, evidently disappointed.

'No!' spluttered Dougal, even more flustered. 'I mean I think sex outside marriage is wrong.'

He finally succeeded in thrusting her away and, finding herself deposited none too gently on the doorstep, Maisie looked at him and then pouted. 'Funny bloke,' she remarked. 'Thought ye might like it.' She shrugged. 'Well if ye ever change ye mind ...' Then she turned and began to walk slowly down the path, but at the gate she paused and looked back. 'I'll still bring the girls on Saturday.' Then she winked broadly and was gone.

*

'So exactly what is it you have in mind?' the Bishop's wife asked into the phone.

At the other end of the line Beverley laughed unpleasantly. 'Well,' she explained, 'as I said in my letter, I've been told to try and get some women to come along, so that's exactly what I'm doing. I thought we could actively demonstrate at all the meetings and ask questions. You know the sort of thing. I've just felt so outraged by the attitudes here over the past few weeks that I felt we had to do something as a mark of protest.'

Down the phone, Myra heard anger bubble through the younger woman's voice and felt a twinge of sympathy. Her vocation now of course was simply to be dear Hubert's wife, but still, if things had been different ... The thought trailed away in her mind, unspoken. To have wished for anything different would have been disloyalty and Myra was, above all else, loyal. She would not repine for insubstantial might-have-beens. Still, these men, with their convoluted and what often seemed to be specious theologizings, exasperated her. She thought it abhorrent that they should be allowed to insult women so.

'They're all such hypocrites,' Beverley was going on. 'They bang on and on about unity, and yet now they're saying that unless the Church changes its mind and reverses the legislation permitting women to be allowed into holy orders, they're going to form a breakaway group. A true Church!' Her anger erupted, 'And as if that weren't bad enough,' she fumed, 'half of them are practising homosexuals anyway. You should see the lace on their cottas! I sometimes think the main reason they don't like women is simply that they're jealous.'

Dragging her thoughts back from her own private reverie, Myra felt slightly alarmed. She had long wondered whether Walsingham was quite the healthiest of atmospheres for Beverley. 'I do think, dear, we have to be a bit careful here,' she said cautiously, attempting to pour oil on what were quite patently troubled waters. 'Demonstrating for women's rights is one thing, but we don't want to be categorised as anti-gay now, do we?'

'Why not?' exploded Beverley, now thoroughly roused. 'You've no idea what they're like here!'

But Myra would have none of this. She was perfectly prepared to do all she could to further the cause of women's rights, but she was not prepared to allow herself to be dragged unthinking down the labyrinthine paths of bigotry. 'Because,' she said quietly, 'if we go to extremes and get diverted from the main issue, no one will listen to us.'

Beverley breathed heavily, but even she was forced to admit the logic of this. She restrained herself with difficulty. 'I suppose so,' she said grudgingly. Then, with rather more warmth, 'Of course you're right, but it makes me so angry. And why on earth priests with homosexual or lesbian tendencies should feel they have the right to an active sex life when extra-marital sex is denied the rest of us, I'll never know!'

Myra reflected, not for the first time, that Beverley was still very young. Staunch evangelical that she was, she privately agreed with her completely, but she had long ago learned that some issues were better approached from the side. 'If we can just get back to the matter in hand, dear,' she suggested, 'exactly *what* are you proposing we do?'

Beverley thought for a minute. 'Well, tee shirts for a start,' she said. 'I thought we could have them printed with slogans like, 'Women are redeemed too' or 'The snake was male'. And I thought we could have banners and get the local media along. That way, who knows, we might even make the national news.'

'Perhaps we could set up some alternative workshops,' suggested the Bishop's wife reflectively. Then she added, 'Only on no account must Hubert find out I'm involved in all of this. He disapproves of Restore too, of course, but he would be deeply upset if he thought I were actively involved in plans to disrupt their conference.'

Beverley digested this. 'Alright,' she said, 'but how many others do you think you can get to come along?'

'So far I've got twelve names. How big is the conference?'

'At the last count they'd got a hundred and sixty down. But some of them are the most incredible old fossils. One man has been on the retired list for thirty years.'

A photograph on the desk, of Hubert in his investiture robes, caught Myra's eye and she smiled. 'Good,' she said seraphically, 'at this rate, give them a few years and there won't be many left anyway. Our task is clearly to stop them proselytizing the young.'

'Yes,' said Beverley. She did not sound overly convinced. 'But there are a good number of younger priests too,' she said. 'And I noticed Dougal Sampratt's name is down. I think he's someone we should worry about. He's very influential.'

'Really?' Myra cogitated. 'Well then,' she said at last, 'perhaps we ought to concentrate our efforts on persuading him that his fears have been misplaced.'

7

Nicholas picked Amanda up promptly at ten. 'How far is it?' she asked, sinking backwards into the low seat and swinging her legs elegantly across.

He looked at the legs appreciatively. 'Not far. Only a couple of hours. But there's no rush.' He smiled. 'I told Ma and Pa we'd be there by six. I thought we could make a day of it. You know, stop off for lunch somewhere. There's a glorious little pub I know down by the river. I thought we could enjoy ourselves.'

They threaded their way through the London traffic. Nicholas drove fast, she noted, and he took risks. Amanda, always slightly apprehensive when driven by anyone other than Dougal and her father, felt nervous. But after a while she realised that his risks were calculated and she began to relax. Leaning back, she closed her eyes and fell into a doze.

She was awakened about an hour and a half later. 'We're here,' Nicholas announced, giving her leg a shove. She jerked into consciousness, just as he ploughed to a stop with a flurry that sent gravel scattering in every direction.

'What?' she asked blearily, uncertain for a second where she was and staring round uncomprehendingly.

'The pub I mentioned, sleepy head. You've been out for the count.'

'I was tired.'

He rammed on the hand brake and stretched. 'I know what'll wake you up. Why don't we have a walk? We'll eat after.'

Amanda, always slow to wake up, explored the suggestion. 'Maybe,' she said tentatively. She clambered from the car and stared round. To her intense surprise she discovered a view of almost postcard prettiness. They were deep in the countryside it appeared, and the little pub in front of them had a thatched roof and leaded windows. It nestled into the side of a long, thickly wooded hill, and in front of it ran the river Nicholas had spoken about, with a couple of swans and assorted ducks paddling lazily around. Beyond that, she saw a large square of village green, with a cricket pavilion off to one side, and a huge gnarled old oak off to the other, its spreading branches extending out in a kind of rustic blessing. 'How pretty,' she said dryly.

He nodded, giving a self-satisfied smile as if he had somehow put it there. 'Yes. Thought you'd like it. And the view from the top of the hill's superb. It's a nature reserve, you know.' He said this last as if she might somehow be expected to know the location of every reserve in Britain. 'It's owned by the Forestry Commission. When you walk through it, all you can hear are the birds. That and the silence. It's like being in another world.'

'Hu ... um,' said Amanda. She did not know why, but something in his tone was annoying her. She glanced down at her extremely expensive sandals and remembered she did not like country walks. 'It's not too rough is it?' she asked dubiously.

Nicholas laughed as if the suggestion was somehow ludicrous. 'Course not. You'll love it ... Trust me.'

Without more ado, he set off briskly towards the footpath leading up the hill. She stared after his retreating back and then, after a second, followed in his wake. At the stile that led into the reserve he took her hand to help her over. Once on the other side she expected him to let go but, as if it was the most natural thing in the world, he retained it and, hand in hand, they began to walk slowly up the hill. Amanda had the peculiar sensation that matters were passing beyond her control.

As they reached the first thin straddling of trees, just as Nicholas had promised, the silence seemed suddenly to roll down and envelop them. It was so total and so unexpected that for a second Amanda felt startled, and she checked, an eerie sensation that she had indeed passed into another world coming over her. Uncertainly, she turned and looked back and saw far below them the pub, with Nicholas's car drawn up skew-whiff alongside the green. At the same moment a figure came out of the door of the pub itself. A young man carrying a crate. He tossed it to the ground, almost negligently, and then turned and went back in.

'It's beautiful, isn't it?' said Nicholas, watching her. She had the oddest feeling there was something speculative in the look.

She was unnerved. 'Y ... es.'

He stared at her a moment longer. 'Come on.' He drew her into the shadow of the trees. It was dark and there were strange little rustlings in the undergrowth. She thought they were going to walk on, but instead he twisted suddenly and caught her to him, and the next second she found his mouth clamped over hers. She was so surprised that for a moment she half staggered and would have fallen, but his arms came up and around her, holding her, and his tongue pushed against her mouth. For a second she stood, rigid with astonishment, but the next second his tongue had forced her lips apart and she found her own arm reaching up and around his neck, pulling him closer. It was all the permission he needed. With a low moan he forced her gently back and down onto the ground, drawing up her skirt with one hand and running his other between her thighs. Amanda was lost. Never for one moment did it occur to her that what she was now doing was wrong. Dougal was so far removed from her thoughts that, just at that moment, he might have been on a different planet. He might not even have existed.

Later, as they lay in exhaustion, Nicholas said, 'You're not seriously going to marry Dougal, are you.' It was a statement.

'What?' She went rigid as memory flooded back, and the full force of what she had just done hit her.

But Nicholas seemed oblivious. He reached across and pulled her to him. 'I said you're not going to marry him.'

Amanda had the distinct and rather unnerving impression that she had gone mad. She must have done. Why else should she just have made love in the middle of a forest, to someone other than her fiancé, and in full view of anyone who might be passing? 'Why not?' she asked, feeling suddenly sick.

He stared at her for a long moment and then said quietly, 'Because you're going to marry me.'

*

Back at St Prosdocimus, Dougal was beginning to feel decidedly ill. His head ached and there was a queasy feeling in the pit of his stomach, which was not helped when he received a card in his morning post from Maisie. 'Gud luck, Father,' she had written, 'me and the girls will all be their (Maisie apparently had some problems with her spelling). I've bought a new top!' Dougal quailed, remembering her last appearance, and then discovered he had an urgent need for the lavatory.

Regina appeared at eleven. 'We all set,' she announced. 'De women's group been bakin' buns and makin' sandwiches all mornin', and de rotas all arranged up till midnight.'

She beamed, clearly expecting approval, and Dougal managed to summon up a weak smile. 'You know we don't have to do this ... ,' he began.

Regina stared at him.

'That is,' he went on hastily, 'I know the reservations you've all been having. I really don't want to lead you all into something you don't fully support.'

The black woman's brow cleared. 'Oh, Dougal,' she said, a huge grin breaking across her face, 'You not got no call to worry. It's true we were a bit shook up when you first suggested de idea, but we all bin prayin' about it since, and we now convinced dat dis is de will of God.'

Dougal swallowed. He wished he was as sure, but unfortunately he was beginning to suspect he was the victim of some kind of divine practical joke. A rising tide of panic momentarily prevented him from replying.

'It's alright,' Regina said again, misinterpreting his silence. 'We know that you deeply carin' for all of us. We're behind you. We want to serve de Lord too.'

At midday, in growing misery, Dougal went over to the church hall to survey progress. He found it positively seething with activity and he stared round in amazement. He had had no idea St Prosdocimus had so many members. As he stood in the doorway, a brawny West Indian staggered past, sweating beneath the weight of a large trestle table. 'Mind yourself, Reverend,' said the man cheerfully.

Dougal skipped aside. He had not the slightest idea who the man was. 'Have I met you before?' he asked.

'No,' said the man cheerfully. 'I'm Pentecostal.' Then, seeing Dougal's look of total bewilderment, he added, 'Regina's bin along and told us what you doing. We think it's marvellous. The church goin' out into de world! Pastor Jethro say we ought to help. So that's what we're doin'. There are quite a few of us here, and Pastor Jethro's comin' along to the service tonight.'

'Ah,' said Dougal. He didn't even know who Pastor Jethro was, but it seemed somehow rude to mention this fact.

He went back to the rectory and discovered the light flashing on his answerphone. 'Dougal,' wailed a distraught voice as soon as he flicked it on, 'It's Brian. I've simply got to speak to you. You wouldn't believe what's been going on since you left! Unless I hear otherwise, I'll drop round this evening after supper.' There was a pause, and then he added plaintively, 'Please, please, do be there!'

'Oh my God,' said Dougal, unable to help himself. From the opposite wall of the study a large picture of the good shepherd, tastefully placed there by Regina, smiled at him mournfully. 'It's no good looking like that,' said Dougal sourly, staring at the picture. 'And I'd have thought you could have had a little sympathy. After all, they crucified you!' The halo round the figure's head seemed to glow gently. But it was not a very comforting glow. 'It's bad enough with the centre opening tonight,' Dougal exploded wrathfully. 'I can't cope with Brian too. You know what he's like!'

Dimly it occurred to him that it was perhaps rather odd to be talking to a picture, and he wondered briefly whether he was going mad. But on reflection he thought that was unlikely. Insanity would have been too easy, and he was beginning to feel there was something cruelly perverse in life that would not allow that refuge. Dismally, he dialled Brian's number at Walsingham but, as he had anticipated, there was no response. A cold sweat broke out on Dougal's brow. Quite apart from the fact that he felt unable just at that moment to cope with Brian, the last thing he wanted was for his former colleague to witness his humiliation.

With a growing sense of futility, he tried the college housekeeper, the bursary and then the student common room. All alike remained dead. Finally, with deep reluctance, he tried Father Goody's number, and was rewarded at last by an answerphone. 'You've got through to Father Goody's office,' came the disembodied voice of a secretary. Somehow she managed to make it sound as if the caller had got through to another sphere. 'Father is either not in his office, or is attending to another call. Please leave your name, number and a message, and someone will get back to you as soon as possible.' Dougal had the irreverent thought that trying to speak to the principal of Walsingham was like trying to make an appointment with God, but the phone was beeping and hastily he said, 'Yes, hello ... It's Dougal Sampratt here. I wanted to leave a message for Brian ...'

As he replaced the receiver, he was left with the pleasing knowledge that a message for someone else left on the principal's phone would provoke extreme displeasure. But hot on the heels of this rather unchristian sentiment came the realisation that Brian was extremely unlikely ever to receive the message and, miserably, Dougal resigned himself to the inevitable. There was not, he thought, much else that could go wrong.

The centre was to open at nine, after a short service of prayer and praise over in the church which, Regina had assured him, was absolutely essential to the success of the enterprise. 'We got to fight back the attack of Satan, Dougal,' she had said. He goin' to try and attack something like this and stop us, or bring us into disrepute, so we got to have some prayer cover here.'

By seven Brian had still not arrived. Unsurprised, Dougal left a hastily scrawled message pinned to his front door and, praying that his friend would not arrive while the service was still in progress, went over to the church.

It was growing dark, with a chilly feel to the air, and beneath his jacket Dougal felt himself shiver; though whether with cold or terror, he was unsure. With each step he took, his heart became more leaden. He felt as if some huge dark weight was almost physically pressing down onto him, crushing him into the ground, and it was all he could do to stop himself from turning round and taking to his heels. But the thought of Regina restrained him. He knew she would be devastated if he failed to appear. But with each step he took he became more and more convinced that the whole idea was a manifestation of idiocy, and that it would serve only to make him look stupid. Glumly, he began to realise that his career in the church, in the sense of holding any position of importance, was at an end. He would be a laughing stock after this. Ahead of him loomed the concrete walls of St Prosdocimus, the barbed wire that had been placed around its perimeters glinting dully in the streetlights. Like a metal crown of thorns, Dougal thought feverishly. He suppressed a hysterical desire to laugh, swallowed, squared his shoulders, and walked in.

Ten minutes later he found himself, fully robed and standing in the patch of light that fell from the doorway to St Prosdocimus, greeting people and trying vainly to keep his shaking hands under control.

The congregation filed slowly in. Once again Dougal felt surprised. There were more people than he had ever seen there before, and there was an air of suppressed excitement about them, as if they felt they were engaged in something momentous. Then a small music group arrived and, without being asked, set up their equipment in a cleared space to the left of the altar. Dougal had not the slightest idea who they were.

'My grandson,' whispered Eliston proudly, going past just at that moment and catching Dougal's amazed look. 'He's a student at the Royal Academy. He offered to come along and play. The other two are his friends.'

'Good heavens,' said Dougal.

Eliston took this as a compliment. 'Don't mention it,' he said. 'They're good Christian boys, despite the way they dress!'

At that moment the boys in question broke into a spirited and very noisy rendition of a Graham Kendrick song, and Dougal gulped. 'Please, God,' he prayed, 'I know we seem to be having some difficulties at the moment, but whatever you do *don't let Brian come yet!*'

It was his one prayer of the day that seemed to be answered. One minute to the hour, as Dougal scuttled up to the altar in readiness to start the service, Brian had still not arrived.

The singing began. The congregation rose as one to their feet, arms upraised and, to Dougal's astonishment, launched into what sounded like a rather startling battle cry, liberally sprinkled with Alleluias and shouts of praise. Dougal had never heard anything like it. Then, when they stopped, as if from nowhere, the mysterious Pastor Jethro appeared and launched into a throbbing word on the fall of the idol Dagon. At least, Dougal assumed it was Pastor Jethro, from the response of the congregation. Helplessly he looked around, but it was no good. The service seemed to have taken on a life of its own.

More music. Then prayer. Things got worse. To his chagrin, Dougal found he didn't actually lead the service at all. Rather it swept past him, like a wholly unexpected tidal wave and then, when it was spent, dumped him willy-nilly on an alien shore. 'You'll be alright now, Dougal,' Regina assured him at the end, as she bustled past him on her way out. 'De Spirit here tonight. He not allow nothin' bad to happen to you.'

Unfortunately, Brian was apparently outside this sphere of heavenly influence. Just at that moment he was getting out of his car. He had parked on the far side of the square facing the vicarage and he walked across the threadbare grass, fastidiously picking his way round the crumpled cans and dog mess, and came to a stop in front of Dougal's front door. 'Oh dear,' he tutted, putting on his spectacles and peering at the note Dougal had left. He peered at his watch. Eight forty-five. The note said that there was a service starting at eight over in the church, and that Dougal would then be in the church hall after nine. Brian did a quick calculation. Unfailingly punctilious in matters of liturgy, he abhorred the idea of barging in on a service just as it was drawing to a close, but that left all of twenty minutes before he could catch up with Dougal in the hall.

Brian peered around, trying to decide what best to do and blowing softly between his teeth. His eyes alighted on the pub on the corner. The Wigspittle and Pole was as unprepossessing as its name but, just at that moment, it appeared to him to offer a haven. Pulling on his gloves more tightly, Brian gave a low explosive sigh of satisfaction, and set off towards its pale light.

8

Over in the church, and feeling a complete failure, Dougal disrobed. He had hoped to have some moments of quiet alone in the vestry before going on to the hall, but St Prosdocimus did not go in much for quiet. They did not go in much for privacy either. As he removed and hung up his hood, prior to unbuttoning his cassock, the door swung open and a sea of excited faces stared in.

'Hurry up, Dougal,' said Eliston. 'Regina's already gone on ahead. She'll be wonderin' where we all are.'

Behind the group clustered around him, Dougal made out the face of Rob Fisher. The journalist made a thumbs-up sign, and then yanked at a camera hung from the neck of the man beside him. He winked and, with a sinking feeling, Dougal realised that, true to his word, Rob Fisher had brought along a photographer.

They began to walk in a body across to the hall, and the journalist insinuated himself at Dougal's side. 'Good turn out,' he remarked. Dougal noticed he was panting slightly. 'We were a bit too late to get photos of the service, but it looks like we'll get some pretty good shots now.'

Dougal grunted non-committally and wondered if Brian would be waiting for him yet. He hoped not. He could imagine what he might say afterwards, back in the privacy of the Walsingham common room. They went in, and were immediately engulfed in a wave of heat. The air felt thick, heavy with a mixture of cheap perfume and smoke. It was so unexpected that Dougal half reeled, and then his eyes adjusted to the rather dingy light (which was all the hall could achieve) and he made out the figures waiting inside.

His first impression was of a sea of scantily clad, smoke-wreathed forms who looked like they would have been entirely at home in the *Folies-Bergère*. 'Good Lord,' he said, unable to help himself. 'Where on earth have they all come from?'

'I brought them, Father,' trilled a cheery voice. A figure detached itself from the shadows at the side and Maisie undulated forwards. The movement could hardly be described as a walk, because the stacked heels she was wearing were so high she seemed in imminent danger of toppling over. Dougal swallowed and cast a nervous glance at Rob Fisher, and his heart sank as he saw the journalist pull out a notebook and begin to write.

Maisie, however, seemed oblivious. 'I told you I would, didn't I?' she demanded, sticking out her chest. 'We don't usually start working till around ten.' She grinned at Dougal pertly. She had decided she rather liked the priest. 'So you could say, in a manner of speaking, we're all yours.'

Dougal was spared the necessity of replying by Regina, who just at that moment steam-rollered her way forward and planted herself firmly in the way. The churchwarden obviously considered there were some temptations to which her priest should not be subjected. 'Cover yourself up, girl,' she commanded peremptorily. 'Ain't you got no shame? You talkin' to a man of de cloth here. You ain't got no call to flaunt yo'self like that. He not one of yo' customers.'

Maisie sniffed, her good humour unimpaired. 'He doesn't mind,' she assured Regina airily. 'He comes to see us every night.'

Rob Fisher scribbled feverishly on his pad. There was a blinding flash of light, and the camera clicked several times in rapid succession. ''Ere, stop that!' said Maisie. 'I'm not ready yet.'

'Oh yes you are, love,' said Rob Fisher. 'Believe me. More than ready.' As the eyes of everyone readjusted, he eyed her hopefully. 'Would you mind answering a few questions?'

Maisie looked delighted. 'Course not,' she said.

Before Dougal could intervene, the reporter had drawn her away to the side. He turned back and discovered Regina glaring at him belligerently. 'This not good, Dougal,' she said reprovingly. 'Dese girls actin' like dey own de place. And de boys are even worse. Dey droppin' ash on de floor.'

Dougal shrugged helplessly. 'But this is what they're like,' he said. 'It's one of the reasons we're trying to help them. Because they don't conform.'

Regina's ample bosom swelled in a manner reminiscent of Maisie, but somehow the effect was not the same. 'Well dey goin' to conform if dey comin' here,' she announced indignantly. 'I'm not goin' have dem messin' up de hall.' And before Dougal could stop her, she had swung round and shouted loudly, 'Smokin' is de work of de devil. If you want to smoke, go outside. And don't drop ash on my floor!'

There had been a low hum of conversation, but now a stunned silence fell, and then one or two of the girls began to laugh. But for Dougal the effect was good. Regina's words seemed to act on him as a kind of trigger, sweeping away the paralysing sense of helplessness that had been gripping him. Almost without thinking, he found himself suddenly moving forward. 'That's quite enough,' he called loudly. 'Regina's quite right. We want to welcome you all here tonight. We are very glad to see you, and we hope you're going to use this centre a lot from now on. We're here to give you a friendly welcome. Warmth. A cup of tea and food. A listening ear if you want. We want to help in any way we can. And I do emphasise that.

'But there are some ground rules that have to be observed if this place is going to work. Number one is that any drugs or drink that any of you are carrying have to be checked in at the door. You can pick them up on the way out, but you are not to use anything like that in this hall, and anyone doing so will be thrown out. Because this has got to be a safe place for everyone. Number two is that no one within these walls is allowed to ply their trade. Whatever that might be.'

'Does that include you, Father?' called a voice.

Dougal ignored it. He peered round at the rows of heavily painted faces all turned towards him, and with difficulty repressed a shudder; not of distaste, but of pain. To his eyes some of the girls looked unbelievably young, but one or two looked raddled and old, as if somehow a light had been extinguished inside them. For a second he thought he could not go on, but then he took a grip of himself. 'We are a Christian group,' he said loudly, 'and we live by what's laid down in the Bible. No one is going to try and pressure any of you into believing what you don't want to, but as we want to try and help you, so please try and respect us.' He faltered then and, unable to help himself, glanced quickly round to check their response. Regina, he noted, was now beaming and over at the side he saw Rob Fisher still writing away. But the face that suddenly loomed from out of the surrounding gloom and caught his attention was that of a young girl, about twenty he guessed, standing staring at him from some ten feet away. Her long red-gold hair cascaded in tumbling curls over her shoulders and down her back, but the eyes that surveyed him were cold, staring at him measuringly. She seemed somehow slightly detached from the others, and Dougal had the oddest sense that he was being judged; whether he passed muster or not, he could not tell. Then someone said something to her and she turned her head slightly and replied, her eyes still fixed on his face.

She was one of the most beautiful creatures Dougal had ever seen, with classic features chiselled and smooth, and wide set eyes staring fearlessly out on a tough world. But, to Dougal, there was something indescribably angry and bitter about her. The lips were full and generous, it was true, but there was a kind of hard set to them, a shadow almost.

He made a move to step forward, wanting to know more about her, but the crowd that had accompanied him from church suddenly surged forward, and he found himself surrounded. Then the next moment the girl had moved away.

The other women settled themselves obediently down at the tables and Dougal began to move around saying hello. Most of them he found he already knew, by sight at least, but some he had never seen before. And then it was borne in upon him that, though there were a few boys there, most of the lads he had come across on his nocturnal perambulations, were not. He mentioned this to one of the girls and she said vaguely, 'Oh no, they won't come. They all know about it. Maisie did tell them, and we've all seen the leaflets of course, but most of them say you're a wanker. To be honest, Father, they don't like you.'

Totally irrationally, Dougal felt rather hurt, but then he reflected that if they really were that antagonistic, it was probably better that they were not there. They would have caused trouble. And then, suddenly, as his mind was trying to work out various strategies of approach that might in the future win them over, he found himself face to the face with the young woman who had caught his attention before. 'Hello,' he said, trying to smile reassuringly. 'Who are you then?'

The girl regarded him almost insolently through narrowed eyes, blowing a cloud of smoke into the air. 'Pepper,' she said languidly. 'I'm Pepper.' She was sitting half sprawled along a bench, arm looped over the back, one leg upraised over the seat, and she made not the slightest effort to move so that he could sit down.

Dougal looked at her, feeling puzzled. 'Well, it's very nice to see you,' he began, then stopped, realising how lame that sounded. 'Have we met before?'

She shrugged. 'Not exactly. I've seen you, but we haven't spoken. I was busy.'

He digested this, knowing full well what she meant. All around there was the steady buzz of conversation and the chink of cups against saucers. He noted that Rob Fisher and his photographer were still busy and that Regina was bustling around between the tables, carrying plates of untouched buns. She looked cross. 'I don't think you like me very much, do you?' he asked, turning back.

'Not a lot.'

He made a move to sit down and, very reluctantly, she withdrew her leg. 'May I ask why not?'

It took her a while to answer. Her glance flickered away from him and around the room, and he noticed that her mouth, if it were possible, had grown even harder. Then she suddenly swung back, almost violently, and stared him straight in the eye. 'I don't like any blokes actually.'

Dougal blinked, rather surprised. 'Oh,' he said. And then, unable to think of anything else, 'Any particular reason, or is it just a general dislike?'

It took her a long moment to reply, and when she did her voice was harsh. 'Do you know how old I was when I started on this game?' she enquired conversationally.

He shook his head.

'Eleven. And do you know who put me on it? Me step-dad. 'E even initiated me.' She turned away again. 'Kind of 'im, don't you think?'

Dougal found he didn't know how to reply, but Pepper had apparently not finished. 'And do you know what 'appened then?'

Again he shook his head.

'I got bleedin' pregnant, an' 'e made me 'ave an abortion.' Through the smoke he saw her face contort. 'Not even a bleedin' teenager!' She suddenly flung down the cigarette in disgust, and then rounded on him. 'And you want to know why I don't like your lot? Because you're hypocrites, the lot of you!'

This last was spat out and, in spite of himself, Dougal felt stung. 'I'm very sorry that happened to you,' he said levelly, not moving, 'but not all men are like that, you know.'

'No?'

'No.'

She got up as if she could suddenly stand no more. 'Well you're going to have to bleedin' prove it!'

Over in the Wigspittle and Pole, Danny and his friends had been drinking since the end of that afternoon's football match, and were now on their sixth pint. They had been sitting discussing Dougal's new project for the last couple of hours, growing increasingly irate the more they drank, and Biff had just expressed the view that Dougal was too fuckin' full of it and that the centre was shit. Now they looked up as the door opened and a small gust of cold air blew in, fluttering the leaflets Dougal had left on the bar. Brian's stiff three-inch collar drew their eyes like a magnet. 'Blimey,' remarked Darren, 'do you think 'e's come over to get us?'

'A pint of your best please, landlord,' called Brian loudly, totally oblivious of the interest he was arousing, and mincing his way forward towards the bar. Once arrived, he turned and gazed round, pursing his lips delicately. He could not say he was overly enamoured with the interior of this particular hostelry. Its decor was a depressing beige colour, and the bar looked as if it had somehow been temporarily deposited in the corner, to await proper positioning later when the decorators should arrive. Brian, who was fastidious about this sort of thing, looked about critically. He had just decided that the interior was perhaps beyond redemption, even for a man of his talents, when Danny lurched to his feet, staggered over, and planted himself firmly in front of him.

Danny's self-image had suffered rather over the past few weeks. He had very publicly sworn revenge on Dougal, but he was actually rather frightened of the big priest and had been unable to think of anything effective to do. Swiping his milk from the doorstep every morning, though pleasing because of the irritation it produced, had quite patently not fitted the bill. Consequently, Danny's standing with his mates had been severely impaired and it had been borne in upon him that, if he did not do something soon, his credibility within the group might well be damaged beyond repair.

Becoming aware of his rather smelly presence, Brian blinked. 'Ah, good evening,' he said, unnerved and attempting a weak stab at jocularity. This, however, failed, because to Danny he sounded like an effete pansy. Which, of course, was what he was, but that was hardly likely to ensure him a warm reception in the Wigspittle and Pole. Danny, a card-carrying member of the National Front, sensing the presence of a hated and weaker enemy and correctly divining that his presence was in some way connected with Dougal, decided to regain some of his lost standing.

'You lookin' for someone?' he enquired sweetly. 'Can I 'elp you?' He thrust his beery face close to Brian's and, beneath the hot inrush of his foetid breath, the priest recoiled.

'Er ... no, thank you,' said Brian. 'It's very kind, but I'm ...'

'I s'pose you're a mate of that pouffy priest over at St Prosdocimus,' said Danny loudly, rather enjoying the effect he was having.

He took a step forward and leant even closer and Brian, unable to help himself, skipped two paces back. 'Well ...' tried the priest again, trying to decide how best to handle the situation and failing dismally.

But Danny was not interested in anything he might have to say. He lovingly entwined a hand around Brian's lapels, just as the barman deposited a brimming glass down on the counter behind them, and shoved hard. A little puddle of beer slopped messily around the base. 'Leave off, Danny,' said the barman, who was used to this kind of thing. 'Let the bloke pay.'

Surprised, Danny released his grip and Brian, finding himself unexpectedly free, hastily scrabbled in his pocket for change, and again moved away. 'Thank you,' he bleated, panting slightly and banging a handful of coins down on the bar. He stared forlornly at the door, trying to calculate his chances of escape. Unfortunately, however, Danny was directly in his path.

The barman, following the train of his eyes and sizing up the dilemma, shook his head sympathetically. 'Give it a rest, Danny,' he again admonished. 'Look, the bloke's even bought you a drink.'

Danny, at the best of times not noted for intellectual agility and now even further hampered by the six pints he had imbibed, blinked in surprise. ''As 'e?' he asked.

'Yeah,' assured the barman. 'Look, it's be'ind you.' He winked at Brian, who stared at him with the kind of rapt expression more normally associated with artistic depictions of unexpected heavenly visitation. 'I'd go, mate, if I was you. Now!' hissed his saviour.

Danny slowly heeled round, staring at the bar, brow knit as he strove to come to terms with this new development. 'There is a drink,' he said wonderingly.

'Told you so,' said the barman.

He again jerked his head towards Brian, who seemed almost catatonic with terror. 'Where's the church hall?' whispered the latter, struggling manfully to regain control of his legs.

Danny lunged at the glass. In his befuddled state he appeared to be having some difficulty negotiating the task of getting it to his lips. More beer spilled.

'Out the door, across the green and turn left,' muttered the barman. 'Next to the church. You can't miss it.' To Danny he said loudly, 'That's right, mate, drink up. Down in one!'

Brian needed no further urging. As Danny finally succeeded in welding his lips onto the glass and pouring half the contents down his front, he skipped around him and began a rapid trot towards the door.

''Ere!' shouted the others, who had been watching the encounter with interest. ''Ere, Danny, 'e's gettin' away.'

There was the sound of chairs being pushed back and of feet scraping on the floor. Danny, who had discovered he did not like this particular brand of beer and was wondering why he was so wet, stared round in surprise. Brian did not look back. He thrust aside a chair, half fell over a table and then, three paces from the door, broke into an unseemly run. Behind him feet pounded across the floor. Brian shot through the double glass doors and out into the darkness of the street like a bullet from a gun. Once outside, he paused, unsure for a second of his bearings. Behind him Danny, who had finally realised that his prey was escaping, exploded onto the street.

'Help!' shrieked Brian. 'I'm being attacked. Help!' His voice was swallowed up into the dark void of the night.

'Gotcha!' shouted Danny, lurching drunkenly towards him. The others tumbled onto the street in his wake.

'Oooh!' screamed Brian again. Without more ado he took to his heels and raced across the green, praying there would be no more yobs in his path. Danny and the others belted after him. In normal circumstances Brian, portly and more used to a dainty saunter, would have been no match for them at all. But tonight, handicapped as they were by the mixture of drink and drugs that they had consumed, they lurched drunkenly in his wake, bumping into each other and falling over their feet.

Ahead of him Brian saw the church. His lungs almost exploding, he redoubled his efforts and hurtled towards the smaller building at its side. Safety! Just as he reached the small path that led down to the main building, Darren reached out a hand and almost caught him. Brian thought he would faint. He twisted away and pelted on. If only someone would come out. And then, ahead, the door *did* swing back and Dougal himself appeared, framed in the light. There was another man beside him. He deposited something beside the door and then turned as if to go back in.

'Dougal!' screamed Brian. 'Help!'

With one last supreme effort, he catapulted forward, flinging himself into Dougal's surprised arms. To his intense surprise lights seemed to flash. For one horrified second he thought he was going to have a heart attack, but then the footsteps behind him skidded to a halt, and suddenly a whole mass of people poured out of the hall and onto the street. A great tide of black rose around Brian and he clutched at the doorframe, fighting for breath. 'They're chasing me,' he began.

But he was addressing empty air. Dougal, taking in the situation at a glance and already feeling upset after his conversation with Pepper, strode forward and raised his fist menacingly. 'Take one step nearer,' he thundered to the thugs, 'and I'll make sure it's your last!'

'Oh, Father,' came Maisie's voice adoringly. 'Ye so brave!'

'Terrific!' said Rob Fisher. 'Here, Dave, you are getting photos of all this?'

9

'Battling Priest Declares War on Vice'. During the following week the papers were full of it. The *Carbery Star*, which came out on Monday, had a picture of Dougal emblazoned across its front page, with the exhortation, 'Attaboy Rev!' splashed across the bottom. By Wednesday the report had made the inner pages of a couple of tabloids, and on the Thursday the broadsheets also picked it up.

Sitting in his study on the Friday morning, carefully going through the papers for the past week as was his wont, Bishop Hubert was riveted. 'Nicholas,' he called in excitement. 'My goodness! Have you seen this?'

Nicholas's bland face appeared in the open door. 'What, Bishop?' he enquired.

Bishop Hubert pointed at the paper spread out on his desk. 'This,' he said, almost beside himself. 'Merciful heavens! This is just what the diocese needs.'

Alarm bells sounded in Nicholas's head, and he came forward slowly and peered over the Bishop's shoulder. He found himself staring at a large picture of Dougal, fist upraised and looking like some kind of Old Testament prophet. Lower down, on the left, he saw a smaller inset of Brian, clutching Dougal's other arm and looking distractedly back over his shoulder at what appeared to be a mob of ill-intentioned youths.

Nicholas could not help himself. 'Oh God, he's not at it again, is he?' he said.

Luckily the Bishop was so engrossed he did not hear. 'It's absolutely amazing, Nicholas,' he was saying. 'I knew he was the right man for the job. Something told me. But to have made such a mark so soon.

It's unbelievable.'

Nicholas agreed.

'And look,' went on the Bishop. 'There's that young man from Walsingham helping him. You know,' he turned and looked at Nicholas seriously, 'I really believe I misjudged that young man. When I met him at Walsingham I thought ... well I won't repeat what I thought. But suffice it to say, I did not form a very good impression. But this article says he's involved with Dougal in this project. Apparently he's been out on the streets too.'

At the latter news, Nicholas was not the slightest bit surprised. Through the Bishop's excitedly flailing arms, he tried vainly to read exactly what the article said. 'What is it they've actually been doing, Bishop?' he asked at last, failing dismally.

'My dear boy, it's amazing.' Bishop Hubert's upturned face, slightly pink, took on the glow of one of the Botticelli cherubs Nicholas hated so much. 'Apparently Dougal has started some kind of initiative to clean up the estate around St Prosdocimus and to help the prostitutes and drug addicts. He's set up some kind of drop-in centre in the church hall and, according to this report, he's doing enormous good. The young people seem to be flocking to it in droves.' A dreamy look settled on the Bishop's face. 'This is just the sort of thing the diocese should be involved in. We must throw our full weight behind Dougal and demonstrate our support.'

Nicholas rather thought he would like to throw something at Dougal too, but he carefully schooled his face into an expression of benign interest. 'Really?' he said, his brain working furiously. Needless to say, he did not like this development. First, he did not wish Dougal to appear as anything other than a nonentity and, second, he disapproved of anything manifesting an excess of religious zeal. He thought it was un-Anglican. He moved round the Bishop in order to get a clearer view, and scrutinised the article carefully. 'Ah, yes,' he said, after a pause.

He allowed his tone to convey just the right amount of judicious reservation, and Bishop Hubert blinked. 'Is something wrong?' he asked, a slight frown appearing on his brow.

'Oh no, no. Of course not, Bishop,' assured Nicholas. Then he pursed his lips, eyes still fixed on the paper, and shook his head reluctantly. 'I't just that ...' He trailed off.

'What?' demanded the Bishop, beginning to get worried.

'Well ... I don't know. It's just that ... well this bit here.' He pointed with his finger to the short paragraph describing how Dougal had begun to go out onto the streets at night to befriend the street girls. Again he shook his head, allowing himself just the slightest trace of solicitous concern. 'I just wonder if Dougal is not perhaps being rather ill-advised.'

The Bishop, totally lacking in guile himself, looked puzzled. 'How do you mean?' he asked, his brow clouding.

'Well ...' Nicholas permitted himself the quickest of glances. The sort of glance that said, 'I, a man of integrity, do not wish in any way to prick the bubble of your joy, or cast unfounded aspersions upon the reputation of another. But decency requires me to speak.' He cleared his throat. 'I am not entirely convinced that frequenting the haunts of known prostitutes every night is the best way of going about helping them. Such behaviour might be open to misconstruction. Not,' he went on hastily, seeing the look of outrage that spread across the Bishop's face, 'that there is anything at all improper in Dougal's motives. But we've had so many damaging scandals over the last few years – and Dougal is human after all. What if he should find himself in a compromising situation? After all, current guidelines already advise against even being alone with a member of the opposite sex, for fear of any accusations that might be made.'

Nicholas was rewarded by seeing the tiniest trace of fear lodge at the back of the Bishop's eyes. 'But he's trying to save these women,' interrupted his superior plaintively. 'Surely no one could attribute ill motives to that?'

Nicholas looked dubious. 'Not you or I, Bishop, certainly. But with individuals who are maybe looking for scandal ... and who would like nothing better than to discredit us. Who knows?'

His words hung on the air and the Bishop flinched. 'I'm sure you're wrong, Nicholas,' he said firmly, turning and staring back down at the paper. But the set of his shoulders looked unconvinced and Nicholas smiled grimly.

'I'm sure *you're* right, Bishop,' he murmured.

His mind now torn by doubt, the Bishop stared at the offending paragraph. 'But this is good,' he repeated.

Nicholas said nothing.

'Isn't it?' Obviously wrestling with the conundrum, the Bishop tapped his fingers distractedly on the desktop. Then to Nicholas's amazement and annoyance, his brow suddenly cleared. 'Of course you're absolutely right,' he said. 'People who are ill-disposed towards us will naturally try to discredit us in any way they can. That is the battle that we have with the world.' He beamed happily, as if the matter had just become crystal clear. 'But we must not allow fear of what *may* happen to disable us from tackling what lies directly in our path. What Dougal is doing now is having the most tremendous impact. Rather than trying to stop him in this mission for fear of possible misunderstanding, we must try and ensure that nothing goes wrong. He must have adequate support and guidance.' Decisively he pushed back his chair and rose impetuously to his feet. 'Nicholas, I am truly grateful to you for having the courage to point out possible hazards to me. I really believe you were inspired by the Holy Spirit to alert me to possible dangers, and my duty is now clear. I want you to arrange an episcopal visit. I want to see that centre for myself, and I want to tour the streets. I want to make it absolutely clear to the world at large that Dougal is doing this with the Church's blessing, and that we are fully behind him.'

It was Nicholas' turn to blink. This was not quite the outcome he had been working towards. 'But, Bishop,' he began feebly.

'Oh I know what you're going to say, dear boy. My schedule! But I really believe this is important enough to lay aside other less pressing matters. Dougal must know that he has the Church's blessing and support.'

Nicholas was seething, but having gone so far, there seemed very little he could do. 'I really think he's potty,' he complained later to Max, the diocesan training officer who inhabited the office next to his. 'He reads all this garbage about St Prosdocimus in the paper this morning, and now he's got this bee in his bonnet about going down there and doing a walkabout. I ask you! I think he believes that berk Sampratt is the reincarnation of Mother Teresa or something. We'll be having miracles next. That or they'll be attempting to walk on water together.'

Max looked gloomy. 'Tell me about it,' he said. 'Hotrod Hubert has got this vile scheme to teach every child in the diocese under the age of five to recite the Magnificat. He's got me drawing up training packs for play schemes and nursery groups. He said we ought to use cartoons.' His expression became even more sour. 'But at least we haven't started on that awful triplet evangelism plan yet. Honestly I'm dreading that. The amount of work if it ever happens doesn't bear thinking about!' He looked at Nicholas in sudden fear. 'You're not going to tell me that's going ahead, are you?'

'No.' Nicholas shook his head. 'Not if I can help it. I've managed to tie that up in a clergy deployment survey. I'm hoping he's going to forget about it, though he does keep making the occasional bleat.' His brow furrowed. 'But to be honest, I'm much more worried by this Sampratt thing. The man's a complete idiot. He could cause enormous damage if he goes on the way he is at the moment. The trouble is, he's a loose cannon, but the papers seem in danger of making him into a saint.'

Dougal's unexpected notoriety was not the only reason Nicholas was feeling cross with him. After his last weekend with Amanda, when they had consummated their passion beneath the pines, he had rather imagined that his rival had been effectively dealt with and that the field was now safely cleared. But ever since Amanda had been showing an alarming tendency to dissolve into tears. 'I just feel so guilty,' she kept wailing. 'I don't know how to tell him.'

Nicholas had felt thoroughly exasperated. 'Just tell him that you never loved him in the first place and that it's all over,' he said sourly.

But Amanda looked confused. 'I did love him once,' she said, in an uncertain voice. 'I know I did.'

Nicholas, not by nature an overly jealous man, had felt a sudden stab of quite irrational and violent rage. 'We're meant for each other,' he protested loudly. And then, when she still looked ambivalent, he reasserted his claim in the only way he knew how. But still, despite all his urging, she had refused as yet to tell Dougal that the engagement was off. As a result, to see his rival being fêted so unexpectedly and enthusiastically in the national papers, was salt in poor Nicholas's wounds. He hated the man. He wished he could get rid of Dougal once and for all. And then, as he sat at his desk balefully chewing his pen, a thought occurred to him. He could. He could engineer precisely the situation that he had been speaking about to the Bishop. Somehow he had got to make it appear that Dougal was a pervert, who had embarked on his so-called mission not from any desire to help the sexually disadvantaged, but because of his unbridled lust. A savage look came over Nicholas's face. If he could accomplish that, not only would Dougal's career in the Church be at an end, but Amanda would never look at him again. Then another thought suggested itself to him. He might even, he thought, if he played his cards very well, get rid of hated Hubert too. An evil smile on his face, Nicholas picked up the phone and dialled Dougal's number.

Over at St Prosdocimus, Dougal was equally a prey to strong emotions. He too had seen the papers, and he was utterly appalled. He had the horrible feeling he was caught by something from which he was not going to be able to break free. Since Monday his phone had not stopped ringing and a little clutch of photographers had gathered around his front door and the church. Yet paradoxically, since the opening night, no one had been along to the centre. Maisie, it was true, had looked in, but that had been merely to tell him that Carl, the area pimp, was not pleased. 'He doesn't want the area cleaned up, Father,' she announced. 'He was really cross when he saw the papers. He said that kind of publicity might be bad for business. He said he was going to come and see you.'

At the time this information had not greatly added to Dougal's peace of mind. There had seemed to be an implied threat, and Dougal had heard tales of Carl's exploits, none of which had been particularly pleasant, from parishioners. But the visit had not so far been made and, as the days passed, almost unconsciously he found his anxiety on this particular score receding, his mind dominated by other more pressing concerns.

Chief among these was Brian. His friend had been almost beside himself on Saturday night, so overcome with terror that it had been all he could do, once Danny and his drunken cronies had withdrawn, to walk into the centre unaided. Once seated, Dougal had instructed Regina to ply him with strong tea, but Brian had refused, staring at Dougal accusingly and looking as if he was about to choke. When he had recovered his breath sufficiently he had hissed, 'You should have warned me, Dougal. You should have said this could happen.'

Dougal shrugged helplessly. 'But, Brian,' he said, 'how could I possibly have known?'

'Known?' spluttered Brian, aghast. 'Known? You must have known the type of parish you're in. You should have told me about these yobbos.'

It occurred to Dougal that Brian was being rather unfair. 'But I couldn't have known you'd go to the pub,' he pointed out reasonably. 'And you know for yourself what kind of an area this is. You saw when you came along to the induction. You could just as easily have seen for yourself that this might happen.'

But Brian was beyond reason. Never in all his life had he encountered such naked aggression. Snide comments he had had in abundance, but never before had he had anyone threaten to dismember him. He was not even sure why he had been attacked; whether it was because he was a clergyman, or because he was gay. But whatever, deep in the inner recesses of his sensitive soul, it had disturbed him. 'No,

Dougal,' he said with dignity, tottering to his feet. 'I did not realise. I had no idea that there were such animals down here.'

So affected was he, that he completely forgot why he had come, all thoughts of Walsingham, the Restore conference, and the problems it was causing, totally blasted from his mind. 'I can't talk about anything now,' he said distractedly, when Dougal tried to broach the reason for his visit. 'I'm far too upset.' And with that he had staggered to the door, poking his nose out into the night like a frightened rabbit scenting for a fox.

'I'll go with him, shall I?' offered Eliston, watching the proceedings with interest. 'I will see de gentleman back to his car, if you like.'

Unable to leave his post, Dougal accepted gratefully, but as he watched Brian totter down the street, clutching the elderly churchwarden's arm, he felt as if another nail had been hammered into the once smooth patina of his life, splintering its outer shell and cutting him off from all he had known before.

'Dougal,' said Nicholas's cloying voice down the phone, 'Nicholas de Vere here. The Bishop has seen the papers and he asked me to give you a buzz.'

Dougal felt a stab of apprehension.

'He'd like to come along and see your centre for himself,' went on Nicholas. 'He said he wanted to look into it.' He kept his voice deliberately neutral, hoping Dougal would misunderstand. But it was no good, for the present the Bishop's enthusiasm could not be disguised. He sighed and then said sulkily, 'Actually he was rather pleased. He said this kind of initiative is just what the diocese needs.'

'Did he?' said Dougal, surprised.

Nicholas grunted. 'He wants to come and do walkabout. You know the kind of thing. See the natives.'

Dougal digested this. 'Well, there's not really that much to see yet,' he said apologetically.

'Uum, yes, well ... Your modesty becomes you, but I'm sure you'll dredge up something. When could you offer him? I can make a window in a couple of weeks' time if that's any good.'

Dougal thought rapidly. 'Not two weeks,' he said. 'I'll be at the Restore conference then. How about the week after?'

Nicholas sighed, as if the suggestion personally caused him the most inordinate amount of bother. 'Oh, I suppose so,' he said. 'Thursday might be the least trouble.'

Dougal felt puzzled. Nicholas's total lack of enthusiasm was all too clear, but he could not for the life of him understand the hostility he seemed to be picking up. 'Okay, fine,' he said. Then, 'Is anything wrong?'

At the other end of the phone Nicholas scowled. 'No, of course not,' he replied, teeth gritted. 'What could possibly be wrong? Just a heavy day that's all.' He pulled the diary towards him and picked up a pen. Almost cringing, he crossed through the entry for the meeting with industrial chaplains and the Bishop's council already entered for the Thursday, and wrote over the top 'St Prosdocimus', heavily underscored. 'Ten o'clock do you?'

'Of course,' said Dougal. 'That'll be fine. Should I lay on lunch?'

'Yes, dinner too, I suppose,' said Nicholas gloomily. 'The old boy wants to come out on rounds with you, and see the centre in operation at night. Shouldn't be surprised if he'd do a service if you wanted too. Drum up the troops and all that.'

'I see. Yes,' said Dougal. 'That would be good.'

When he put down the phone some five minutes later, he felt heartened. If the Bishop really was as pleased as Nicholas seemed to be implying, then perhaps things were not such a disaster after all. His gloom receded slightly and, in a spurt of new found optimism, he thought suddenly of Pepper.

Ever since the Saturday night, after she had spat her story at him, he had been unable to get her out of his mind. She was exactly the type of girl, he thought now, that he had been put there to help. Staring at himself rather pompously in the mirror as he combed his hair and put on his scarf, he suddenly thought how splendid it would be if he could save her. If he could demonstrate to her that someone at least cared. With that ennobling thought, he gave one last tweak to his collar, picked up his Bible and then, whistling softly, headed determinedly for the door.

10

Amanda stared miserably into her cup of gently steaming coffee. 'You just don't understand, Jill,' she complained bitterly. 'I'm so confused. I just don't know what to think anymore.' They were sitting in a little cafe tucked away at the back of Selfridges, and Amanda had taken an extended lunch break.

'But what's the problem?' asked her friend. 'It's simple isn't it? You just have to choose.'

Amanda frowned and dribbled a thin trail of sugar across the table-top with her spoon. 'No, it's not simple at all,' she said reprovingly. 'It used to be. Before Dougal started behaving so peculiarly and before I met Nicholas.' She grimaced. 'You know, I thought I'd got everything planned. I thought I'd marry Dougal, and that he'd do a short stint as a parish priest somewhere nice. And then he'd become a bishop. And I thought I'd run the house for us both, have four kids ... and go and speak at conferences for clergy wives.'

Jill was becoming rather bored. It seemed to her she was always listening to Amanda's problems these days, and she rather wanted to talk about some of her own. Added to which, she only had another half hour, and then she had to be back at work. 'Well then, do that,' she said with some acerbity.

'But I can't,' wailed Amanda. 'Nicholas says *he* wants to marry me, and that I've got to tell Dougal it's all off.'

Jill, who had not yet received any proposal of marriage, glared at her. 'Then marry Nicholas,' she said tartly.

'But is he dependable?' Amanda launched off, yet again, into her own little world. 'The sex was good,' she said reflectively. 'Well amazing actually.' Jill looked as if she would hit her. 'But maybe it all happened a bit too easily.' She looked up, staring through Jill as if she wasn't there. 'I mean, I had to wait months with Dougal before he'd even kiss me properly, and then the angst! He made it sound as if we were committing a mortal sin.'

Jill, who disliked being treated as if she was part of the wallpaper, yawned. 'Perhaps he's gay,' she suggested unsympathetically.

Amanda was shocked. 'Of course he's not,' she said. 'He's just very moral that's all. After all, he's a priest.'

'So is Nicholas.'

Amanda digested this. 'He says he loves me.' She transferred her gaze to the plate of limp salad in front of her and sighed. 'The other question of course,' she went on musingly,' is which one of them's going to go furthest.' Jill was now becoming seriously angry, but Amanda was oblivious. 'A few months ago I'd have said Dougal. No contest. Then I thought for a while, going to that dreadful St Prosdocimus place, that he was having some kind of nervous breakdown and was a no-hoper. But with all this stuff in the papers over the last few days ... I'm wondering if I haven't actually underestimated Dougal. Maybe he's going to pull it off after all. Everyone seems to be talking about him.'

Jill decided she could stand no more. 'Yes, well,' she said crossly, 'fun though this is, I've got to get back. Some of us have to work for a living.' She rose to her feet, pushing back her chair so that it scraped noisily across the floor. 'Just wait and see what happens,' she advised. 'It'll sort itself out.'

It began to sort itself out three days later. Amanda's period was late. She bought a kit, and discovered she was pregnant.

*

Back at Walsingham, Brian was still enjoying the attention his near brush with death (as he maintained) had produced. 'My dears,' he proclaimed loudly, holding court in the common room, 'they're no more than a bunch of homophobes down there. And Dougal!' He rolled his eyes dramatically. 'You've no idea how much he's changed.'

'A pity some of the rest of you haven't too,' remarked Father Goody acidly, coming into the room just at that moment and overhearing the latter part of Brian's remark. His gaze swept round. 'Has anyone here seen Beverley?'

They all shook their heads and Father Goody glowered. 'That woman has a remarkable facility for never being there when you want her, and always being there when you don't,' he remarked to no one in particular. His eye came back to Brian and he glared at him. 'May I take it all the arrangements for the Restore conference are now in place?'

Brian gulped. 'Well, most of them,' he said.

'Most of them!'

'Yes, well .... there are just a few loose ends to tie up.'

'What kind of loose ends?'

Father Goody came farther into the room and Brian squirmed. He had been hoping to avoid this conversation. 'Oh, you know the sort of thing,' he said vaguely. He discovered he was suddenly feeling rather hot and ran a finger round the inside of his collar.

'No I don't. Tell me.'

Brian looked at William helplessly, and William suddenly discovered something of enormous interest outside the window. It was clear no one was going to come to Brian's aid. 'Well,' he began again, rather resentfully. He really didn't see why it all seemed to be falling on him. 'I've managed to fix up this priest from South America, who's running a campaign over there to have Mary proclaimed as co-redemptrix, as our main speaker. His argument is that if Mary's equal in status in Christ, that gives divine sanction to the role of women as wives and mothers, and precludes their involvement in anything else.'

'Really?'

Father Goody looked interested and Brian relaxed slightly. He felt if he could only focus the principal's interest on this and divert any enquiry away from speakers for the plenary sessions, who had all so far failed to materialise, he might be able to come out unscathed after all. 'Yes,' he said, with a great deal more enthusiasm than he actually felt. 'He maintains that if Mary really does have this standing, then its the clearest indication that God never did intend women to hold more obvious positions of authority, and that clearly means they can't be priests. That Mary was content to be only a mother means that all women should be happy with that role.'

Right on cue, Beverley appeared. 'Rubbish,' she said loudly. 'I think that kind of arguement's blasphemous.' She stared round menacingly, as if challenging anyone to disagree. 'Christianity is based wholly upon the belief that Jesus is the Son of God, and he is our redeemer. Mary is simply his earthly mother. To maintain otherwise is tantamount to heresy. We'll be calling her Mother Earth next, or some such rubbish.'

An astonished twittering broke out and Brian looked at her, wounded. He couldn't for the life of him see whether it mattered if

Mary was called God or not. He rather liked the idea of a Queen of heaven. It made him feel all cosy.

But Beverley was still bristling with outrage and Father Goody, never one to refuse a challenge, rounded on her. 'I seem to detect a certain inquisitorial strain in you, Beverley,' he said. 'I thought we'd left this unwillingness to listen to arguments other than our own back in the dark ages.'

Beverley went pink. 'I haven't noticed much openness round here,' she snapped, stung by the injustice. 'Besides, this is actually a central tenet of our faith that's under attack. We might as well all become Buddhists at this rate.'

Father Goody rather unkindly wished that Beverley would. He did not, however, give voice to this thought. 'The rich tapestry of Anglicanism,' he said loftily, 'is broad enough to encompass many differing strands of thought. I think Brian's speaker sounds most interesting, and I do not think he is about to rend a hole in the fabric of Christianity!' And with that he swept out, entirely forgetting that he had been looking for her in the first place to discuss some timetable changes.

As the door swung to on his back, Brian breathed an audible sigh of relief. On balance, he felt he had got off rather lightly. He had been dreading all week telling Father Goody that his two main speakers, Father Martinez from Brazil, and Brother Luigi Pascale from the English College in Rome, were refusing to acknowledge each other. Beside that, Beverley's outburst seemed mild. She was not, however, looking very mild just at that moment. 'You're not serious, Brian?' she demanded, rounding on him again. 'You're not really going to have that twerp here as the main speaker?'

'He was the only one who would come at such short notice and for the whole conference,' said Brian defensively.

'But he's a heretic,' said Beverley, looking as if she was about to explode.

William sniffed. 'I'd be a bit careful who you're calling a heretic, ducky,' he said.

The atmosphere at Walsingham was growing increasingly bad. A state of open war now existed between Beverley and Brian, so bad that even the students began to pick it up. Father Goody, always remote, took to locking himself away within the confines of his study, and drinking rather more than usual. He was, he acknowledged, fed up with them all.

His drinking was actually becoming a problem. Father Goody had always enjoyed the occasional tipple, and had long kept a bottle of whisky in the bottom drawer of his desk. It had been his habit to have a quick snort, as he termed it, before dinner every night. He had found it lubricated the not always easy wheels of intercourse with students. Now, however, he found himself resorting to it rather more frequently, and once he turned up tipsy to a lecture.

The trouble was, over the last few months, matters seemed to have been creeping away from him. It had all started when the last bishop had abandoned his wife of twenty-five years and taken off with another woman, announcing he was going to look for the long lost son he had had with her. Looking back it had been then, Father Goody decided, that there had been a sea change in the general climate. Suddenly people had started to ask embarrassing questions, questions about things like spiritual discipline and standards of morality, and at Walsingham they had seemed to come under special scrutiny. Father Goody had heard, that a report on the college had been presented to the House of Bishops accusing them of sexual laxity and depravity. But though he had not seen it, he had certainly felt its effects.

Even before Bishop Hubert had been appointed, a commission of inquiry had been set up, and it had been all Father Goody could do to stave off immediate closure. Then criticisms had been made about the college's stance against women, and the general intransigence of members of staff. Before that particular onslaught Dougal had, as it were, been the sacrificial lamb. In the event it had been an easy choice, because Father Goody did not like him. He was too much of a Puritan. But in the aftermath, the necessity of appointing Beverley had been a pill he had found almost too bitter to swallow. At the time she had seemed the least offensive of a highly unpalatable bunch of candidates. But, if Beverley had been the safe choice, Father Goody shuddered at the thought of what the others might have been like. The woman, he felt, was a menace, bellicose and confrontational, and it slowly dawned on him that he did not like the Church any more. It was no longer the institution to which he had pledged allegiance as a boy, and which he had always thought of as a rather exclusive all-male club; a sort of ecclesiastical Athenaeum.

He began to think that once the Restore conference was safely over, he would begin to cast around for another appointment. Something prestigious, but not too arduous; the fitting culmination to his working life. Meanwhile his drinks bill escalated, and staff and students alike began to comment on the unsteadiness of his gait.

Dougal was oblivious to these developments. The attentions of the press had tailed off after a few days, and once again life had resumed its rather turgid course. He said Matins first thing every morning, then went back to his study and read the Bible and prayed. Then, as often as not, he rather haphazardly attempted a few visits to otherwise invisible parishioners, and on Tuesday and Thursday mornings he set up a playgroup for the under-fives. At nights his life similarly evolved into a pattern. First, at around nine o'clock, he would call in at the centre to make sure it was adequately manned, and then he would set out on what he was increasingly coming to see as his rather futile street patrol. He bumped into Maisie several times, but of Pepper, though he looked for her, there was no sign. And then one night he found her.

She was standing under the third lamp post along from the end of the road, just across from the church, and smoking a cigarette. 'Hello,' he said, wandering up, and conscious that he was walking rather too fast because he was afraid she might disappear.

She acknowledged his presence with the slightest nod of her head.

'Chilly tonight,' remarked Dougal.

She ignored him.

'Haven't seen you around much lately.'

She flung away the butt of her cigarette, grinding it into the pavement with her heel. 'I've been busy,' she said briefly. She half turned, looking away from him down the street, and Dougal felt he was being dismissed.

'Look,' he said, 'I thought you might like to talk, that's all.'

She turned and stared at him. 'Why don't you go and save someone else?'

He was prevented from replying by the sudden eruption of a heavy throbbing that burst onto the night. It was so loud that the air itself seemed to vibrate, not exactly a tune, but a heavy insistent pounding that twisted itself round the gut like some kind of arcane summons. They both stared and then, inching slowly round the corner and down towards them, nosed the long black snout of a car. 'Oh, God,' said Pepper, turning pale as she watched its advance. She turned to him quickly, 'Piss off, will you. It's Carl. He'll kill me if he finds you here.'

'Surely he wouldn't be ...,' began Dougal. But the look of terror on her face silenced him.

'He hates you,' she whispered. 'Just go will you!'

It was too late. The car slid to a stop in front of them and the dark shape of a man uncoiled itself from the front seat. Unconsciously, Dougal braced himself and the man sauntered slowly, almost lazily, towards them. Two feet away he came to a stop, and looked Dougal measuringly up and down. 'I was wonderin' when you were going to turn up again,' he said.

Dougal inclined his head slightly. He discovered he felt rather nervous. 'Well you could have found me any time,' he replied. 'I've been around.'

The man laughed contemptuously. 'Meaning I should have looked?'

He made as if to take a step forward and Pepper said quickly, 'Leave him, Carl. He don't mean no harm.'

Carl hardly even bothered to turn his head. His eyes fixed on Dougal, he snapped, 'Stay out of it, Pepper.' Then, ignoring her, he came up close to Dougal, so that he was standing only inches away, and said softly, 'I'll not tell you again. Stay away from my girls.'

An aggressive spirit he had not known was there reared itself in Dougal's breast. 'And I told you before,' he said evenly, his voice hard. 'They're not your girls. They're individuals, and they *belong* to God.'

Carl laughed. It was not a pleasant sound. 'So He's goin' to fight me for a cut, is He?'

There was something so intensely aggressive about him that Dougal felt unnerved, but he was not about to back down. 'You'd be very ill-advised to fight God, Carl,' he said.

As if he had said something inordinately funny, the black man doubled up in mirth and Dougal looked at him nonplussed. But then, just as suddenly, Carl twisted and reached out, shoving Dougal back hard, and pinning him by the throat to the wall with his huge fist. He brought his face up close and hissed, 'Oh I think I can handle God. If you're one of His boys, I don't think I've got too much to worry about, do you?'

'Leave it out, Carl,' broke in Pepper again. 'He wasn't doing nothing, honest.'

'Oh no?' Fingers tightening round Dougal's throat, Carl rounded on her. 'I'll be the judge of that, woman, not you!'

She glared at him angrily and he raised his other hand as if to hit her. It was all Dougal needed. He twisted violently away, at the same time bringing his own arm up hard, and smashed it into Carl's face. The black man swore and fell back, clutching at his nose, but the next moment he spun back round and launched himself at Dougal, and there was a glint of steel. Dougal was not quite ready for him, and the knife caught him on the arm, slashing through his jacket sleeve. He felt the warm stickiness of blood. Now really angry, he threw himself at Carl, hitting him hard. Years of battering in the scrum paid off. The blow caught the black man squarely on the jaw and he again staggered and fell back. Dougal did not give him the chance to recover. He plunged after him, and again hit him on the side of the head. Carl gave a low moan and sank inelegantly into the gutter. Dougal swooped down and picked up the knife.

'I'll get you for this, priest,' hissed Carl, cradling his now bleeding face in his hand. 'You're goin' to regret you ever messed with me.'

He heaved himself up and staggered to the car while Dougal watched, rigid. His anger had gone now and he was not quite sure what to do. But Carl's anger had apparently intensified, 'You're dead,' he spat, and with that he was gone.

'Oh God,' said Pepper, coming up behind. 'What did you have to do that for?' She sounded appalled. She came forward, joining Dougal on the edge of the pavement, and together they stared after the tail lights of the car. 'He's mad now.'

Dougal shivered. After all the excitement, he discovered he felt rather shaky. 'He seemed pretty mad before.'

Pepper swallowed, and the eyes she turned to him were huge with fear, but the next moment she took in his sleeve. 'Here, you're bleeding,' she exclaimed. 'You're hurt!'

'Am I?' Still slightly stunned, Dougal looked down and discovered a slowly spreading patch of red. 'Good heavens,' he said wonderingly, 'so I am.'

'God,' said Pepper again. She came to a sudden decision. 'Come on.' She made to pull at his other arm.

'Where to?' he asked bewildered. His brain felt slow.

'To your centre,' she flung over her shoulder. 'We ought to have a look at that arm. See if it needs stitching or something.'

She propelled him down the street and into the church hall where Maggie, the woman manning the hall on Regina's rota, looked at them fearfully. 'He's hurt,' said Pepper tersely. 'Have you got a first aid kit or something?'

Maggie paled visibly, but dutifully went to get it. 'I don't like blood,' she announced when she got back. 'It makes me feel ...' She fainted.

Pepper regarded her with disgust, and then turned back to her examination of Dougal's arm. Once the jacket had been removed and the shirtsleeve rolled back, a narrow but quite deep cut, about five inches long, was revealed. 'I don't think it's too bad,' she announced dubiously. 'I don't know really.'

'Just wash it for me, please,' said Dougal wearily. He felt he wanted to go to sleep. 'It'll be all right.'

He sank back and closed his eyes and, after a minute, Pepper went and fetched a bowl of hot water and began, very gingerly, to sponge the wound. She didn't like blood very much either. Halfway through, Maisie arrived. 'Blimey,' she said from the doorway, surveying Maggie, still prone on the floor, and Dougal slumped against the wall. 'What 'appened 'ere then?'

Briefly Pepper told her, and Maisie said, 'Shove over then, I'll do that.'

Dougal, hearing her voice and finally registering who it was, opened his eyes. 'Hello,' he said weakly. 'How nice to see you.'

'You're bleeding,' said Maisie unemotionally. 'This looks pretty bad to me.'

'It'll be alright.'

They all three looked at it, and Pepper said, 'I think I'm going to join her on the floor in a minute.' She looked slightly green.

'Just go,' said Maisie, glancing at her, and evidently deciding she didn't want to have to deal with anyone else. 'I don't mind blood. Get back on the street before Carl misses you.'

'I think he may have other concerns just at the moment,' said Dougal, attempting a weak stab at jocularity.

Maisie ignored him. 'I think you ought to go to the 'ospital with this,' she said. 'It looks quite bad to me.'

But the last thing Dougal wanted was to go to hospital. He could imagine the publicity if that were to come out. 'No,' he said firmly. He shook his head determinedly, and discovered that he really was beginning to feel a bit better. 'I'll be fine soon, honestly. Just bandage it for me and I'll be okay.' He looked across at Pepper and the now reviving Maggie and said, 'And why don't you two go and make us all a cup of coffee or something, and then we can all have a drink.'

They withdrew and Maisie stared at him for a moment longer. She shook her head as if bewailing the folly of mankind, and of Dougal in particular, but then she shrugged and said, 'Okay, if that's what ye want.' She picked up the wad of cotton wool Pepper had discarded, dipped it in the bowl and then began, with long gentle strokes, to finish what her friend had begun. Then she bathed the gash with disinfectant, carefully pressing together the gaping folds of flesh, and finally bandaged it. 'I don't really know what I'm doin' here,' she confided.

He winced. 'You're doing fine ... It's great.'

She wound the bandage tightly round his arm and said absently, 'Carl's really mad, ye know. 'E's got a broken tooth.'

Dougal felt he had gone to some strange other world, where all was peace and love. He felt almost as if he was floating. He surveyed the top of Maisie's head fondly, thinking how nice it was to be fussed over like this. Then he tried to imagine Amanda doing the same for him, and failed dismally. 'Good,' he said dejectedly, brought back down to earth. 'Serves him right.'

Surprised, she looked up, her face only a couple of inches from his, and laughed. ''Ere, you're not supposed to say that,' she admonished. 'Ye're a priest, remember?'

Dougal could not stop himself. That weird, floaty feeling was coming back, and he thought what a rotten day he had had. Then he thought how nice Maisie was to look after him like this. Completely without thinking, he leant forwards and kissed her quickly on the cheek. He intended it as a completely innocent kiss, the sort he would have given to his mother, or to a friend, but Maisie was startled. ''Ere,' she said, jumping back, riveted, 'What was that for?'

Dougal suddenly realised exactly what he had done. It also struck him that, innocent though he had thought his motives were, in fact there was something rather different going on underneath. Horror overwhelmed him as he suddenly realised that he was attracted to Maisie, and he flushed guiltily, remembering Amanda. 'Oh, nothing,' he mumbled, looking down, his ears scarlet. 'I just wanted to say thank you, that's all.'

Maisie stared at him, and the smallest of small smiles suddenly crept onto her face. She finished tying the bandage and then, very carefully, sat down at his side, pressing herself up close. 'Ye can say thank you again, if ye want,' she said.

*

At his flat, over on the other side of Carbery, Nicholas finally managed to dredge up the number of Bingo Drubbins. Bingo had been at prep school with him, and was now an up and coming freelance journalist.

'Bingo!' boomed Nicholas into the mouthpiece of the phone, as soon as there was an answering click from the other end. 'Hi, Nick here. How are things?' He said this as if the two of them had met only a couple of days ago, and totally ignoring the fact they had not laid eyes on each other for at least the last fourteen years.

He was rewarded by complete silence. Then, 'Nick ...? I'm sorry. Nick who?'

This was not quite the response Nicholas would have liked but, undaunted, he tried again. 'Nicholas de Vere. You remember, we were in the same maths set at Beecheys.'

'Beecheys?' said the voice. 'Good God.' Another pause. 'Oh yes, I remember.'

Nicholas gave a forced laugh. He did not think Bingo sounded overly enthusiastic. 'Ha-ah, great times, weren't they.'

'Not really,' said the voice. 'I hated the place.'

Nicholas swallowed. This was going to be harder than he had thought.

'Was there something you wanted?' Bingo enquired.

'No, not really,' said Nicholas hastily. 'It's just been so long, I thought it would be nice to touch base. I wondered if you might be free for lunch some time. I'm in the Church, you know,' he added as an afterthought.

'Really,' remarked Bingo drily. 'Rather an odd choice for you I'd have thought. I still remember the time you chucked my football boots in the swimming pool. I'd have laid odds you'd end up in prison.'

Nicholas laughed uneasily. He never had liked that little swine Drubbins, he reflected. Still, he was the only contact he had. 'Actually,' he said aloud, 'I thought I might be able to put something your way.'

'Like what?' asked Bingo suspiciously.

Nicholas took a deep breath. 'It's to do with that chap Sampratt that there's been all this fuss about in the papers recently.'

From the other end of the line Nicholas heard Bingo yawn. 'Sorry,' he said, 'I don't cover that kind of stuff. I'm not into saints.'

'No, I didn't think you would be,' said Nicholas. 'But would you be interested in the story of what's really going on?'

'What do you mean?'

The voice sounded slightly more alert, and Nicholas smiled. 'Well,' he said nonchalantly, 'our plaster saint would appear to have some flaws.' He began a colourful and highly imaginative outline of Dougal's racy past. 'And some of us are wondering,' he concluded, 'exactly why it is he's decided to start up this venture now.'

'Why are you telling me this?' demanded Bingo.

But Nicholas was ready for this. 'Altruistic concern,' he said, trying to inject sincerity into his voice. 'I knew the line you were in, and some of us, including the Bishop, have been talking over possible repercussions for the Church.' This last, he reflected, was true, although not perhaps with quite the same emphasis he was now giving. 'I just feel this chap shouldn't be allowed to hoodwink people like this. He ought to be exposed before he causes damage.'

'Highly commendable,' said Bingo drily. Nicholas waited while there was another silence. 'Do you really think there's something in this then?'

Nicholas almost hugged himself. 'Absolutely certain,' he said reassuringly. 'I've heard private reports that are most disturbing. I'm sure if you root around you'll find something. It could actually make your name as an investigative journalist, when you think about it … as well as doing a service for us.'

Later, as he lay in the bath, he reflected that nothing distorts a man's clarity of vision so much as the pursuit of self-aggrandisement. Bingo had always wanted his little bit of glory and, driven by the cock and bull story he had just fed him, Nicholas was fairly sure he would find something. Meanwhile, he would do his best to ensure there was substance to the myth.

11

The day for the beginning of the Restore conference dawned fair and bright. For the past week Brian had been growing increasingly distraught, and his consumption of Prozac had doubled, so that he had been walking round with a strange little smile on his face that had had William beside himself with worry. Now it was actually here, however, an odd but quite genuine calm settled over him. The sword of Damocles might well be suspended above his head but it was, he felt, too late now to do anything. He was beyond caring.

Over at St Prosdocimus Dougal was in a very different mood. He packed his holdall with a mixture of apprehension and relief. Apprehension because he was uneasy about what Brian might have said to his brother priests and was worried about the possibility of finding himself a laughing stock; and relief because he had once again ricocheted into an intense hatred for parish life and felt profoundly depressed. More than anything else, he ached for a return to the safe haven of academia.

Sighing, he shoved in his Bible and then stood back, staring distractedly round the room and wondering whether there was anything he had forgotten to pack. He could think of nothing, however, and so he wandered aimlessly through to the study. Hankies, he thought, socks, toothpaste. He continued the list in his mind, coming to a halt in front of the desk and staring dismally at its littered surface. A glossy brochure for Church vestments, a letter asking for help from a newly established mission to Asians, and a whole trayful of mail from people who had read about what he was trying to do at St Prosdocimus and wanted to help. He could summon up the energy to reply to none of them. Almost unconsciously he glanced away, and his gaze came to rest on the phone. With a sickening feeling in the pit of his stomach, he realised suddenly why he had come in.

For the last twenty-four hours he had wanted desperately to talk to Amanda. The intensity of his feelings had actually surprised him, but every time he had tried to speak to her over the last couple of weeks, she had been so strange and distant that he now felt rather apprehensive. Standing there, he wondered if she had fallen out of love with him. Then it occurred to him to wonder whether she had ever actually been in love with him in the first place. And as he explored his feelings and tried to analyse exactly what he felt, he began to wonder what on earth he would do if she said the engagement was off.

His hand reached out, hovering uncertainly. He felt he had to know. But then, just as his fingers were closing over the handset, his nerve failed. There was nothing he could possibly say. Sighing again, he let his hand drop and turned to go.

Just at that moment, however, the phone rang, and Amanda herself said, 'Dougal, hello. It's me.'

Hearing her voice (and suddenly remembering Maisie, about whom he was still feeling guilty), a paralyzing awkwardness overwhelmed him. 'Hello,' he replied.

'Dougal, can we meet?'

She sounded strained, but Dougal was so nervous himself he hardly noticed. 'Yes, of course,' he said, 'but it'll have to be the end of the week. I'm just off to the Restore conference at Walsingham today.'

'Oh,' she replied in a small voice, 'I'd forgotten that. When do you get back?'

'Thursday.'

She digested this. 'Could we meet Friday evening?'

'If you want. Do you want to come here?'

There was the slightest of hesitations. 'Alright,' she agreed. 'I'll come about eight.'

When she rang off five minutes later she was shaking and felt as if she was about to faint. Amanda had done a lot of thinking over the past couple of weeks. She had seen Nicholas twice but, though they had again made love, neither meeting had been very satisfactory and her thoughts had been turning increasingly back towards Dougal. She had told neither man of her pregnancy. Nicholas, because she did not yet wish him to know; Dougal, because she was afraid. Faced with losing him when he discovered what she had been up to she had, quite irrationally, begun to want him back, and a desperate plan had begun to form in her mind.

It was true they had never yet slept together, and so the fact she was having a child would be incontrovertible proof that she had been unfaithful, but it had occurred to Amanda that if she could just get Dougal to fall from his high state of moral rectitude – even if it was only once – she might yet be able to pass off the baby as his. They could still get married. If she failed, then she would tell Nicholas and gauge from his reaction what to do. If he still wanted her, she would marry him. If not, she would have an abortion. The outcome, she felt, was in the hands of God.

Standing there, leaning against the wall and breathing heavily, a part of her felt rather frightened. But whatever other deficiencies Amanda had, she was not lacking in spirit. As soon as she was able, she made herself a cup of herb tea, and then set off for a lingerie shop she had come across in Knightsbridge, determined to buy the most alluring undies she could find. She promised herself that, come Friday night, Dougal was not going to know what had hit him.

The object of her thoughts, in a state of increased confusion following her call, returned to his packing.

Three streets away, in the bedsit where she lived, Maisie swung her legs over the side of her bed and prepared to get up. The hour was somewhat early for her, but she wanted to read her cards. She did not often do this for herself, but she felt she was at a crossroads in her life and wanted guidance. Carefully she shuffled them, and began to lay them out on the table. She discovered a wise man and unexpected love, but there was trouble too and loss. Bemused, Maisie wrinkled her brow and leant forward over the cards, scrutinising them carefully and trying to decipher their inner message. Deep in thought, she reached out a finger and laid it meditatively on the seer. Dougal, she thought, it had got to be him. She knew no one else she could call wise. But what did it mean? Love? And between them? Maisie would have liked to think so. Ever since she had bandaged Dougal's arm for him and he had kissed her, she had been unable to get the priest out of her thoughts. She had been on the streets for the last five years now and saw herself as harbouring no illusions about life. But still a tiny part of her hankered after the romance she read about sometimes in novels and, after the fight with Carl, Dougal appeared to her as something of a romantic hero.

Her finger moved slowly across to the card of upheaval, and a puzzled look settled on her face. Did that relate to the love foretold opposite, she wondered, or was it to the passing of something else? Of a way of life maybe?

Restless, Maisie rose to her feet and went and stared out of the grimy window. There had got to be something better, she reasoned. And every fibre of her being seemed to scream out that there was. There was Dougal. She did not delude herself that he was interested in her as yet, not in the way she wanted. But Maisie was an incurable optimist. Also, and more importantly to her, she was a devotee of the magical arts. She did not know very much, she had only been following them for the last couple of years, but a while ago an older acolyte whom Maisie respected had given her a charm to engender love. It involved mugwort and bulbiferous toothwort, and a funny little rhyme that had to be spoken over something personal to the seeker. The whole package had then surreptitiously to be left with the object of desire. It was a powerful charm, the wise woman had said, and was on no account to be used lightly, but only where there was a sincere desire to awaken genuine love. For the first time in her life, Maisie determined to give it a go.

She dressed quickly and then cast around the room for something suitable to use. She did not have many possessions, but her eyes alighted on the 'Bad Girl' tee shirt she had worn the first night she went round to the rectory. That would do, she thought reflectively. Swiftly she caught it up and sprinkled the entire contents of the matchbox over the front. Then, very solemnly, she recited the rhyme. Nothing happened, but then she was not expecting it to. Not yet. Smiling, she folded the shirt up very carefully, and then stuffed it into her bag. The next thing was to get it to Dougal!

She found him on the point of setting off. He had actually wanted to leave half an hour before, but an urgent call from the rural dean about a faculty for the churchyard had held him up. 'I can't stop, Maisie,' he said hurriedly, as she knocked on the door.

Maisie was undetered. She pushed past him and walked into the front room. 'It's alright, Father,' she said reassuringly. 'I've only come to see how you are.' She looked at him critically. 'Is yer arm alright?'

Dougal nodded, uncomfortably aware that he should already have gone if he was not to miss lunch. 'Fine, Maisie. Honestly,' he said distractedly. 'But you're going to have to forgive me. I've got to be somewhere by lunchtime.'

Her eye fell on his bag. 'Are ye goin' away then?'

Dougal resigned himself to the inevitable. 'Only for a few days. It's a conference.'

As if this was an invitation, Maisie sat down. 'What about?' she enquired.

'Women,' said Dougal without thinking.

Maisie's eyes widened. 'What d'ye mean?' she demanded. 'Yer goin' to a conference to learn about women?' She sounded incredulous.

'No, no,' said Dougal, 'of course not. It's about the role of women in the Church. Whether or not they should be priests.'

'Course they should,' said Maisie.

Dougal looked at her, but at that moment the phone rang. 'Oh no,' he muttered, 'not again. Excuse me, Maisie.'

Distractedly he bustled through into the study and Maisie, left alone, glanced quickly around. Once sure she could not be observed, she rose silently to her feet and crossed over to Dougal's bag. Again glancing round to make sure he was not there, she unzipped the top about six inches, and thrust the tee shirt down as far as she could.

'No, that's fine,' she heard Dougal say from the study. 'But I'm afraid I've really got to go .... Yes ... Quite alright ... Speak to you again soon.'

The phone was replaced and Maisie scuttled back to her seat. 'Dear me,' said Dougal, coming back in, 'I'm beginning to think I'm never going to get away.' He looked at Maisie, 'Look ...'

'It's alright, Father,' she said airily. 'I understand. Ye're busy. 'Ave a good time.' And to Dougal's complete amazement, she left.

'Good Lord,' muttered Dougal after her retreating back. But he was not about to look this particular gift horse in the mouth. Casting one last glance round to make sure everything was turned off, he caught up his bag and prepared to follow in Maisie's wake.

At Walsingham the delegates began to pour in. Beverley met Myra at the entrance. 'We're all set,' she hissed. 'There are going to be fifteen of us altogether.'

'Will that be enough?' asked the Bishop's wife anxiously.

Beverley nodded her head. 'Yes, I'm sure. Any more and they'd have started to get suspicious. This way they won't have an inkling till we actually begin to protest, and the people from the church papers are all here, so we should get really excellent coverage.'

Father Goody, coming into the hall just at that moment, took in the Bishop's wife with a look of affrighted surprise. 'Hello,' he said, 'I didn't realise you were coming. Is the Bishop already inside?'

Myra steeled herself and smiled. 'No,' she said glassily. 'He's not coming. I'm here on my own.'

Father Goody looked even more surprised, but his brain was not functioning terribly quickly following his liquid breakfast and so he merely nodded vaguely, trying to work out what this might mean, and moved on.

Beverley gave a huge sigh of relief. 'Phew,' she said, 'that was close. I thought he was going to ask you why you were here.' She pulled Myra into the shadows at the side of the corridor. 'Look,' she whispered, 'it's probably better if we're not seen talking together in case people start to get ideas, but it's all organised and I've got tee shirts for us all with lots of different slogans on.' She looked slightly worried. 'Some of them don't make a lot of sense on their own, but put together they spell out a protest. So don't worry if you think the one you've got looks a bit odd. I thought we could wear them at the main session tomorrow,' she added, 'when they've got this nutty speaker lined up from Brazil.' The main door again swung open, and another bevy of delegates poured in. 'Anyway, they're in a bag in my room,' she whispered. 'I can't come up with you now. I've got to be around to welcome everyone, but if you just go and help yourself when you take your bag up. And keep it out of sight till tomorrow.'

'Right,' said Myra. A determined look came into her eyes. 'You can rely on me absolutely, my dear.'

Dougal arrived just as Brian and William were carrying the overhead projector through the entrance hall into the main lecture room. 'Whoopsie!' trilled Brian, backing through the door and stumbling over Dougal's foot. He looked over his shoulder and saw who it was. 'Oh, it's you.'

From the expression that came over his face Dougal did not feel this was the most promising of starts. 'Hello, Brian,' he said, with forced heartiness.

Brian sniffed and turned away. 'Honestly, William,' he remarked, 'the people you find in here these days!'

William glared at Dougal, and then together they resumed their rather shaky progress. 'Careful, dear,' floated William's voice, as they disappeared down the corridor, 'we wouldn't like anything nasty to happen to you, would we?'

Dougal stared after them dismayed, but at that particular moment there was nothing he could do. Swallowing uneasily, he took a firmer grip on the handles of his bag and crossed to check the room allocation list pinned up on the wall. More delegates breezed through. They too looked at Dougal, and he thought he saw a couple of them smirk. 'Hello,' he said.

But they merely nodded and, as they disappeared through the double doors that led to the upper common room, Dougal heard a burst of laughter. He felt his ears grow pink. He knew it was ridiculous, but he had the most horrible feeling they were laughing at him.

'Hello,' said a female voice behind him. 'You're Dougal Sampratt aren't you?' Beverley held out her hand as he turned. 'We haven't met yet, but I recognise you from your photograph in the papers.'

Awkwardly Dougal took her extended hand. 'Hello, er ...'

'Beverley Conway,' she supplied.

'Ah.' Dougal surveyed his replacement. 'Yes of course.'

'I'm really pleased you've been able to come,' Beverley went on enthusiastically. 'What you're doing sounds really great. I'd love to hear more.'

Unable to help himself, Dougal inwardly writhed. 'Yes, of course,' he muttered. 'I'll be happy to tell you about it some time ... But if you'll forgive me.'

'Of course,' she said immediately. 'You want to go and find your room. Do you know where you are yet?' She leant across him, staring at the wall and running her finger down the list. 'Here you are,' she said brightly. 'You're over in the ... Oh, that's odd.'

'What is?' asked Dougal.

'Well nothing.' She turned to him, frowning slightly. 'It's just that you're over in the garden annexe.'

'What?' said Dougal. The garden annexe was a rather run-down two-storey prefab on the far side of the college grounds, not normally used for accommodation, but much favoured by the students for its full-size billiard table on the ground floor, and because they could make as much noise as they liked over there without disturbing the main body of college.

'I didn't realise there was anyone over there,' she said.

She scrutinised the list. 'I'm sure there's a mistake. There's no one else over there.'

At that moment Brian, having safely deposited the projector, came back through the hall. 'Oh, Brian,' called Beverley, turning and catching sight of him. 'According to this list, Dougal Sampratt's over in the annexe. Is that right? There doesn't seem to be anyone else over there.'

Brian's face was inscrutable. 'Perfectly right, Beverley,' he said mincingly. She stared at him, and he appeared to feel some sort of explanation was required. 'We just got a bit over-booked, that's all,' he said huffily. 'I realised when I came to go over the booking forms.' He stared at Dougal, eyes hard. 'There were just too many people for main building, that was the problem. And I knew Dougal wouldn't mind.' He smirked slightly. 'After all, he's so macho these days, and he's used to roughing it.'

Beverley looked at him as if he was mad. 'But my corridor ...,' she began.

'Is being held in reserve, dear,' said Brian firmly, and he swept on his way.

'Sorry,' said Beverley, turning back. 'It does seem awfully odd, but Brian's arranged all the rooms, and Tim okayed everything, so I suppose it's right.'

Dougal stood there. 'It's perfectly alright,' he said stiffly. 'I quite understand.' And he did, all too well. It was in his mind simply to turn round and leave, but then he suddenly thought how malicious Brian was being, and how petty. It had never even occurred to him that his one-time friend would do this. And suddenly Dougal felt angry. 'I don't mind at all,' he said firmly. 'In fact I think I might rather like it. The space will give me a chance to reflect.' And with that he turned on his heel and set off after Brian through the double doors.

He was seething, but a hardy little spirit had suddenly reared itself inside him and he thought, 'I'll be damned if I'll let them push me out like this.'

Ten minutes before the first meeting, Father Goody repaired briefly to his study and pulled open the bottom drawer of his desk. He was not anticipating an otherwise very stimulating time, and four bottles now nestled there. He removed the top one, reached for the glass he kept strategically placed behind the picture of his mother, and poured himself a drink. It slid down his throat like a tiny stream of reviving fire. 'Ah, thank you, God,' he whispered, shutting his eyes and savouring the last drop. Then he quickly replaced the bottle, stood up and braced himself to endure the next couple of hours of boredom, which he was convinced the conference promised.

Beverley tapped Dougal on the shoulder just as they were about to begin. 'Dougal,' she whispered, 'look, I've been trying to sort out this room business. Father Goody said it would be okay for you to be in my study.' When Beverley had asked Father Goody about the room arrangements, and Dougal in particular, he had actually snapped, 'If you're so worried, why don't you give him yours.' Beverley had been rather annoyed, but when she thought about it later, it seemed to her an excellent idea. She had not been planning on using her study over the next few days anyway.

'No, it's quite alright,' began Dougal, surprised.

But she insisted. 'No,' she said. 'You'll be much more comfortable, and I've sorted it all out. Look, here's the key.' And before he could say anything more, she had dropped it onto his lap and moved on.

Dougal stared after her back, utterly astonished. It was perfectly true. He would be much more comfortable in Beverley's room. His present accommodation, when he had examined it, had been depressing in the extreme. Clearly no one had slept there in years. The air felt musty, and in places the pea green paint was peeling off the walls. Dougal had never actually been up there before, but he rather suspected that it was normally used for storage. He slipped the key into his pocket, feeling slightly warmed.

Father Goody mounted the dais, a huge beam on his face. 'Brothers in Christ,' he began, 'it gives me great pleasure to welcome you to the Restore conference again this year.' At least, he meant to say that, but it actually came out something along the lines, 'Brushes in Christ, ish gives me great pressure.' He giggled.

'Good God!' said someone on Dougal's left. 'Do you think he's ill?'

There were murmurings from all over the hall as people stared at him in concern, but Father Goody ploughed on as if there was nothing wrong. Swaying slightly, but at least remaining upright, he launched into a long eulogy about the wonderful programme they had planned. After the initial hiccup he actually sounded quite rational, and people began visibly to relax, but every once in a while he would smirk to himself and laugh, especially whenever he mentioned the names of Father Martinez or Father Pascale. The impression he gave was that the whole thing was a joke, and the delegates began to look at each other in concern.

From his seat on the dais Brian looked as if he was about to faint. 'William,' he hissed in horror, under cover of yet another inane laugh from his principal, 'Tim's drunk.'

'I know,' whispered back William. 'What shall we do?'

'Get him off!' said Brian.

But this was easier said than done. When Father Goody mentioned the lecture on the 'Maleness of Rite' by Oswald Pettifence, the vice principal, he seemed to choke, and when it came to 'The Meaning of

Carthusian Liturgy Today' by William, he gave a great bark of what sounded like a laugh and then burst into a cough. William squirmed as the eyes of everyone turned to him. But there was worse to come.

'Finally,' shouted Father Goody, wheezing and taking a firmer grip on the lectern, which was by now his only support. 'Finally, we've got our two visiting speakers from overseas who will be with us tomorrow. The very eminent Father Luigi Pascale, from the English College in Rome, and the totally moronic Father Martinez from Brazil.' He almost doubled up with laughter at this point, and then jerked himself upright and shouted, 'Personally, I put it down to the fact they drink an awful lot of coffee in Brazil! I can't think of any other justification for his loopy ideas, I ...'

'Get him off!' hissed Brian in strangled tones.

As if at a signal he and William rose to their feet and launched themselves at Father Goody. They each clasped an arm. 'Hello,' said Father Goody, surprised. 'What are you doing?'

'Come along, Tim,' said William soothingly.

'What?' repeated Father Goody. 'Where?'

Brian and William began to propel him firmly towards the steps. 'A cup of coffee, Tim,' said Brian. 'Black.'

Father Goody looked bemused. 'But I don't want coffee,' he said loudly. 'I haven't finished yet.'

'Sssh!' said Brian and William together. Then William added urgently, 'Oswald. Take over.'

Almost bodily, they lifted the now protesting Father Goody and heaved him off the stage. At the same time Oswald rose uncertainly to his feet and a couple of cameras flashed from the back of the otherwise paralysed hall.

'It may of course be a minor stroke,' someone said at the coffee break.

Beverley, who had overheard, sniffed. 'Believe that,' she muttered *sotto voce* to one of her co-conspirators, 'and you'll believe anything. He was paralytic.' But the conference decided to take a magnanimous view, and before long everyone was talking about poor Tim, and the strain, and hoping it wouldn't be too long before he recovered.

Dougal felt rather disgusted. He privately thought that Father Goody had definitely looked drunk, and he no longer felt prepared to be quite as magnanimous as he would once have been. As soon as he could he escaped from the crowded lounge, and went to collect his bag and remove it to Beverley's study.

Myra also left the hall. She was in a state of considerable confusion. She had not the slightest idea what was wrong with Father Goody, whether he had been drunk or not. But whatever it was, she felt she did not like the atmosphere. It felt unwholesome. No wonder Beverley was so unhappy at Walsingham, and she determined to speak to dear Hubert as soon as possible and urge him to do something to clean the college up. She went back to her room, made herself a cup of tea, and then spent the next half hour in prayer, trying to still her wildly spinning mind. After that she felt rather calmer, but she realised it was too late to return to the hall. She would have to come in at the side, and everyone would stare. It would have taken a far braver woman than Myra to attempt that particular hurdle. She decided instead to go and collect the tee shirt from Beverley's room, and then have an early night. Maybe she would feel better in the morning.

She slid her feet back into the shoes she had kicked off when she had come in, and then set off down the rambling corridors. The college was quiet now, and Myra had the peculiar sense of walking through a world from which everyone else had disappeared. Halfway there she suddenly paused. She did not know, she realised, whether Beverley had meant her to collect the shirt from her room or her study. The room, she knew, was at the top of the college, in a separate part of the building, but the study was quite close.

Myra stood undecided, trying to establish her bearings and work out exactly what to do. She was not sure, but she rather thought Beverley had specifically mentioned her room. On the other hand the study was far closer, and there was always the possibility that she might have meant that anyway. Myra came to a decision. Rather than trek all the way across college on what might well prove to be a wild goose chase, she would try the study first. Then, if it was locked or empty, she would try Beverley's room.

She quickly turned the corner and walked down the long corridor. Beverley's study was at the end. Slightly nervous in case anyone should be observing her, Myra reached out and tried the door. It opened immediately to her touch and she stepped quickly in, only daring to put on the light once the door was closed. Untidy shelves bursting with books greeted her gaze. Over in the corner stood the desk, with Beverley's computer staring blankly out at the room, as if asleep. In the far corner she was surprised to see that the bed that stood in all the tutors' rooms had been made up, and on top of its wrinkled coverlet stood a bag, the zip top already undone. Myra stared at it, slightly perplexed, but then she thought that maybe Beverley was sleeping there for the duration of the conference in order to make more room. At any rate, there was the bag, and it looked like someone had already been there ahead of her.

Heart pounding, she crossed quickly and thrust her hand deep into the side of the bag. Through the dark square of window she could see below the main hall with the delegates, illumined by the light, staring ahead. A ripple of laughter ran over them and she saw some begin to clap. But Myra was not interested in whatever might be going on below, she had only a terrible fear that someone might suddenly look up and see her. Her heart was beating so loudly that she could hear it thumping in her ears. Petrified, her fingers closed over something soft and she pulled it out, quickly stepping back and away from the revealing square of the window.

Only when she was back in the safety of the middle of the room did she look at what she had withdrawn. It was a pale blue colour, rather a pretty shade she thought, and cotton. It looked right. Quickly she shook it out and held it up, and a scattering of twigs and crushed leaves fell to the floor. Myra wrinkled her nose in distaste. It had been worn. Then she took in the slogan on the front of the shirt and her eyes widened. There, in huge silver letters, were emblazoned the words 'Bad Girl!' How quite extraordinary, Myra thought. But then she remembered that Beverley had said some of the shirts would not seem to make a great deal of sense on their own, and she looked thoughtful. Perhaps the shirts might spell out something like, 'Churchmen try and say you're still a bad girl – but Jesus has redeemed you!' or 'God loves every bad girl and bad boy'. She felt intrigued. But meanwhile, she thought, surveying the shirt critically, she was going to wash it. There was no way she was going to wear a tee shirt that had been worn by someone else. Not even for Beverley.

12

Dougal passed an uneasy night. He was troubled by incoherent dreams but, when he woke in the morning, he could remember none of them, and was left only with a feeling of profound unease. He went down to breakfast promptly, as soon as the bell summoning them had rung, and joined the queue untidily snaking its way round the edge of the dining hall.

'Hello,' remarked the man standing next to him. 'You're that Sampratt chap, aren't you? I've read about you in the papers.'

Those nearest turned with interest. 'Oh,' said another, 'that's you, is it?'

Confronted by a ring of interested faces, Dougal acknowledged that it was.

'If you're going to run a mission,' remarked the first man again, 'I've always thought it would be rather fun to save fallen women.'

He gave what looked unpleasantly like a leer and Dougal looked at him distastefully. 'The queue's moving,' he said stiffly.

'What? Oh yes.' The man turned to look, and they all shuffled ahead three steps. But they had not finished with Dougal yet. 'Don't get me wrong, old boy,' said the man turning back. 'I'm sure what you're doing is absolutely splendid. But I couldn't do it.' He sniggered. 'My wife wouldn't let me for a start.'

'Any chance of saving one for me?' enquired another. 'I could do with a bit of that kind of ministry, for a change. If you know what I mean.'

They continued with ribald comments and innuendo, and Dougal felt his ears burning with anger. He thought of poor Maisie, with her brightness and all her wrong ideas. He thought of Pepper, with her terrible anger and hatred, and he thought of Carl, so violent and cruel, and so casually destroying the lives of the girls he was preying upon. He could contain himself no longer. 'Those girls need help,' he snapped. 'And if you lot were doing your jobs properly, they wouldn't need *saving* in the first place!' Leaning across them, he put a huge dollop of scrambled egg on his plate, grabbed some toast and a cup of coffee, and went and sat by himself on the far side of the room.

A shocked silence greeted this outburst, but Dougal did not care. He felt sickened. He did not want to talk to any of them anymore. 'Bit touchy,' he heard someone remark huffily. 'Pity he can't take a joke.'

By the first session, Father Goody had emerged. He looked pale and slightly fragile, and every time there was a loud noise he winced. 'He's still not very well,' Brian kept going around telling everyone. 'Putting on this conference has been a terrible strain.'

When they started at ten, Father Goody sat on the edge of the platform, and Oswald (who was still smarting from having his own contribution ridiculed) undertook to introduce the speakers. 'We're happy to have with us today,' he announced, looking round the hall with a gimlet eye as if daring anyone to protest, 'the eminent South American theologian, Father Alonso Martinez.' He launched into a description of the good father's pioneering work, especially in the area of Marian spirituality, and from the far end of the stage Father Goody gently, but audibly, began to snore.

After the fiasco of the previous night a clutch of newsmen, both secular and religious, were there in force. How they had picked up on it all no one was quite sure, but it was as if the potential newsworthiness had spread by some kind of subterranean osmosis, and they were all now clustered along the back, looking expectant. Beverley meanwhile had decided to marshall her forces outside the hall, so that they could make a grand entrance all together as Father Martinez began. As well as tee shirts they had placards, and some of them were wearing party hats. Clustering together like so many magpies, Beverley cast a critical eye over them, checking to see they were all there. 'Where's Myra?' she asked.

There was an agitated twittering as they all looked round. 'I haven't seen her since last night,' offered one.

'No, she's up,' said another. 'She's alright. I bumped into her going to the bathroom at six. She said she was going to miss breakfast so that she could pray. Do you want me to go and get her?'

In the hall, Father Martinez rose to his feet to thunderous applause. Beverley came to a decision. 'No,' she said. 'It's alright. I'm sure she'll be along in a while, and we're going to lose impact if we don't go in now.' Her chest swelled and she gripped her placard. 'Ready, everyone?'

There was an answering coo of determined assent, and they all squared their shoulders and hefted the placards above their heads. The tee shirts, Beverley thought, looked rather good. 'Get in line then,' she said commandingly.

Obediently they glanced at each other and then shuffled into ragged order. 'End male oppression now,' they read. 'God the Father and God the Mother'; 'We are co-equal – Christ.' The word 'in' was missing, but that was the tee shirt Myra was destined to wear. 'It's alright,' said Beverley judiciously. 'They'll get the message.' Then she flung open the door and, with her free hand, swung the football rattle she was carrying loudly above her head.

The effect on the hall was electrifying. Father Martinez had just been saying what 'great pleasure' it gave him to be there and he broke off in mid-sentence, going rigid and staring at the doors aghast. Everyone swung round, and here and there men rose to their feet, while the journalists crowded forward, anxious to see what was going on. Beverley and her little phalanx surged forward. 'Father Martinez is a heretic!' they screamed. 'Stop trying to oppress women! Obey the Church!'

There was a blaze of light as the cameras began to click and, at long last, Father Goody stirred and looked blearily around. 'What's going on?' he asked.

Beverley, charging down the centre aisle, headed for the platform at a run, closely followed by her fellow protestors. Two paces from the dais she gave a great leap, entirely ignoring the steps and landing with a resounding bang straight in front of Father Martinez. The shocked priest could only stare at her, but Beverley's unorthodox ascent served to release Brian, who up to that moment had been sitting rigid with shock. He staggered to his feet and made a wild grab at her arm, intending to stave off what he thought might be a physical attack. Unfortunately, however, he misjudged the distance and, as he leant out, he overbalanced and toppled forward, catching the lectern with his left arm. Father Martinez, with a look of horror and anticipating what was going to happen, took a step back and attempted to move aside, but he was too late. The falling lectern jerked up, and banged him sharply on the shins. With a cry of agony he fell back and then collapsed onto the floor, while the notes clutched in his hands shot into the air and then cascaded gently down onto the first two rows of shocked faces.

But the way was left clear for Beverley, and she turned round and shouted triumphantly, 'God is not male. *She* has called us.'

At that moment the door to the hall again swung open, rather timidly this time, and the startled face of Myra appeared just inside the crack. She peered around, trying to see what was going on without herself being noticed. But the attempt was doomed to failure. One of the newsmen, standing alongside the door and catching the movement, wrenched it back, wanting to see who was there and sensing that the spectacle was not yet over. Myra was revealed in her tweed skirt and pearls, grey hair smoothly combed back. 'It's the Bishop's wife, isn't it?' said someone. 'Is he here?'

But the voice died as every eye became fixed on her. Myra had done her best. She had washed and dried the tee shirt, and then tried to pull it into some sort of halfway decent size. But it had defeated her. If on Maisie it had been tight, on Myra's ample frame it was full to bursting, strained and bulging at every conceivable point. She wriggled, uncomfortably aware of the eyes fixed on her, but the movement only made things worse. 'Bad Girl!' proclaimed the tee shirt, the letters stretched across her chest like a rather cruel admonition to lose weight. She took a deep breath and raised a fluttering hand to her face. It was a mistake. The taut threads of the shirt, already strained past endurance, finally admitted defeat. There was a curious thwack, like the low sound of a violin string breaking, and then the next moment a tear appeared at the neck, and began to snake slowly down her front.

On the stage, Beverley's jaw dropped and Father Goody, now fully awake, took off his spectacles, rubbed them and then replaced them on his nose. At the same time Maisie's spell, released into the stratosphere, fluttered enquiringly round the room searching for a suitable target, then aimed itself straight at his heart. '*Is* that the Bishop's wife?' he asked intently, staring at her as if riveted. It occurred to him that he had never before seen such a beautiful creature.

Poor Myra, now thoroughly humiliated, blushed to the tip of her nose and attempted to pull the rapidly disintegrating shirt more closely around her, but it was a losing battle, and the lace topping of her petticoat slowly came into view. Now the photographers went wild, and there was an explosion of lights. 'Oh no!' shrieked Myra, becoming fully aware of them for the first time. She cast an affrighted glance round, clutched at her rapidly vanishing modesty, and fled from the room.

Up on the dais Father Goody half rose to his feet, as if intending to go after her, but the central aisle was still crammed with Beverley's supporters and, looking at them, he seemed to realise the futility of such an attempt. Instead he sank back in his seat, a curious, oddly speculative look on his face. The Bishop's wife, he thought, was magnificent. He could not understand how he had never realised it before.

Over in the corner, Dougal also had a curious look on his face but it was rather different to that illuminating Father Goody's features. Dougal was feeling perplexed. That tee shirt looked familiar. He was sure he had seen it somewhere before. He wrinkled his brow, trying to remember, and then it came to him. Maisie had worn one just like that the evening she had attempted to read his cards. Same colour, everything.

In the main body of the hall, there was another minute's silence and then pandemonium broke out. William helped Brian to his feet, and then led a concerted attempt to eject Beverley from the stage. She was a big girl, and she put up a spirited defence, but after a minute it became clear she was not going to be able to maintain her position, and the next second they had manhandled her down onto the floor. Then it was only a matter of minutes before they hauled her back up to her feet, arms now pinned firmly to her sides, and frogmarched her from the hall. The other insurgents were similarly dealt with, and before long the lectern had been righted, Father Martinez brushed down and some semblance of order restored.

'Just carry on,' hissed Oswald to him. 'We'll deal with this.'

Father Martinez cast him a horrified glance but did not respond. Oswald stared at him then, as encouragement, gave him a violent shove. 'Go on!' he said urgently.

This time Father Martinez nodded. Blinking, and looking as if he was not quite sure where he was, he reached down and took the wad of notes now being held out to him by a helpful gentleman in the first row. But if he had hoped for any help from them, he was doomed to disappointment, because the notes now clutched in his hand were in a complete mess. Swallowing, he tried vainly to sort them into some sort of order, while the delegates watched him with interest. It was a hopeless task and after a second he gave it up. 'Gentlemen,' he began. He cleared his throat and gazed around imploringly. 'Women are gentle creatures.'

13

To his intense surprise, Dougal found on the Thursday that he was actually glad to get back to St Prosdocimus. He drove slowly through the abandoned, litter-filled streets with the feeling that he was coming home, and it struck him that there was something strangely wholesome about the place. It felt honest. By the time he arrived at the rectory a feeling of anticipation had settled on him, and he could not wait to see how things had gone during his absence. He dumped his bag in the study, checked the answerphone for messages, and then set off on a tour of inspection.

Hardly had he gone two steps, however, than he bumped into Regina. The rotund little churchwarden was scuttling down the street clutching a broom, an expression of intense anxiety on her face. 'Dougal!' she exclaimed, 'I'm so glad to see you.'

'Why?' he asked, bewildered.

He thought for a second she was going to burst into tears, but she controlled herself with an immense effort of will and said instead, 'Come an' see.'

With a feeling of dread stealing over him, he followed her quickly down the street towards the church. As they drew near, he thought perhaps something had happened to St Prosdocimus itself, but she led the way past. 'Regina, what is it?' he asked plaintively.

'You'll see,' she retorted grimly.

Then they rounded the corner, and ahead of them Dougal saw the church hall. 'There!' she proclaimed.

Bemused, Dougal stared at it. To him the building did not look any different from usual. 'What?' he asked, his eye raking along and over the walls, and finally up to the roof. But as far as he could see everything looked the same. The grills were still firmly nailed to the windows, the graffitied bricks still proclaimed their usual obscenities, and the barbed wire still curled like an untidy crown around the guttering. 'What's wrong?'

For reply, she stared at him and then said, 'Come in an' see for yo'self.'

He followed in her wake. She pushed open the main doors gingerly, as if apprehensive about what was on the other side and, seeing her reluctance, Dougal pushed past her and went on in. The sight that met his eyes made him pull up short. The interior had been completely trashed. Tables, chairs, cups and saucers had all been broken, and the debris scattered over the floor, topped by powdered coffee and cornflakes. Then the walls had apparently received liberal attention from a spray can, and were now adorned with huge obscene drawings that testified to an imagination and skill that could have been far better employed elsewhere. But far, far worse than any of this was the excrement smeared over everything, and the smell was like nothing Dougal had ever come across before. 'Who on earth has done this?' he asked, aghast.

The churchwarden had come in behind him, and now stood looking miserably around. 'We'd hoped we could get it cleared before you got back,' she announced forlornly.

'But who did this?' Dougal repeated again.

She shrugged. 'Kids. Who knows?'

'Have the police been told?'

Regina cast him a look that spoke volumes. 'No,' she said. 'What de point? Dey not bothered.'

But Dougal was adamant. 'They must at least be informed,' he said. 'We won't be able to get any insurance otherwise.'

Her shoulders slumped. 'What insurance?' she asked.

It was some time before Dougal could extract all the facts. Regina had come over, she said, first thing in the morning to unlock the hall ready for the playgroup. She had found it in its present state. It had been all right the previous night she assured him, and they had even had some of the girls come in at around eleven. They had all thought things were going rather well. When they had locked up it had all been quiet. But in the morning ... this. As for insurance. It was all they could do, Regina informed him, to pay the rates and upkeep. They had not bothered with insurance for the past two years. Dougal was appalled; it had simply never occurred to him that the church buildings might not be adequately covered. Regina was so upset, however, that he hadn't the heart to say anything. 'Well then, we'll just have to try and clean it up as best we can ourselves,' he said determinedly. 'And we'll see what we can salvage from the mess too.'

She brightened slightly. 'I've jus' been to tell Eliston, an' he gettin' together some of the others.'

They worked all day. Dougal took off his coat and rolled up his sleeves, and set to work scrubbing the walls. It was a foul task, and he found himself muttering over and over again, 'I will praise the Lord. In all things I will praise the Lord.' But it brought him no comfort, and he felt a deep and terrible anger. He strongly suspected that whether kids had been responsible or not, the guiding force behind the attack was Carl, and he seethed with impotent rage. This, he knew, had been a warning.

Halfway through the afternoon, Maisie arrived. She had heard about what had happened, and that Dougal was back, from her mates on the streets. Indeed, an inordinate number of people seemed to have heard, and they trailed past, wanting to see for themselves. But Maisie came in. She wanted to check for herself the effects of her charm, and she wanted to help.

'It's not right, is it?' she demanded, pulling up short as she took in the damage and glaring round angrily.

'No, Maisie,' agreed Dougal wearily. He left off scrubbing the wall and sat back on his heels.

'What was that you were mutterin'?' she asked, interested.

Dougal grimaced. 'I was praising the Lord,' he said wryly.

'Why?'

She looked at him as if he was mad and he glanced down at his hands. 'Because,' he said ruefully, 'the Bible tells us that in all circumstances we are to praise the Lord, and to ask blessing for those who wrong us.'

She regarded him a moment longer. 'I think ye mad,' she announced. But then she suddenly banged her bag down onto the nearest table and said, 'What ye want me to do then?'

'Pardon?' He gaped at her.

'I said, what d'ye want me to do?'

'Do you mean you're offering to help?'

She considered the question. 'Yeah.'

Regina, who had been listening, bustled up to her with a bin. 'You can start by puttin all de broken things in here, if you want,' she said.

Maisie thought about this. 'Okay.'

She set to with a will, but all the time she was watching Dougal covertly. She wanted desperately to know whether or not her charm had worked but, from his manner, she could not decide whether there was any change towards her or not.

'Eliston,' called the object of her attention, 'any more cleaning fluid over there?'

Maisie put down the bin and stared at him. The wise woman who had given her the charm had assured her it always worked. Sometimes too strongly, she had warned. But try as she might Maisie could detect not the slightest alteration in Dougal at all. Then it suddenly occurred to her that he was so obviously upset by the damage to the hall, that perhaps his mind was too preoccupied to demonstrate this change. Maisie looked piqued. In her new found romanticism she rather thought love ought to take first place, whatever the circumstances. She decided to help matters along. 'Have you ever thought about getting married, Father?' she asked conversationally.

Dougal, in the act of rinsing a particularly nasty bit from the wall, glanced up preoccupied. 'What, Maisie?' he asked. 'Oh yes, I have actually. I'm engaged.'

Maisie's heart plummeted. 'Ye're what?' she demanded, horrified.

Dougal, totally oblivious of the effect he was having, turned back to the wall and said, 'Her name's Amanda. We've known each other about six years.'

Maisie digested this. 'So when ye gettin' married?' she asked, in a small voice.

Remembering Amanda and the strangeness of her behaviour, Dougal sighed and flung down his cloth onto the floor. 'Heaven only knows,' he said wearily. 'I keep asking that too.'

Over at the Wigspittle and Pole, Carl had just come in and flung himself down at a table in the darkest corner of the room. Danny and his mates, who had been watching for him out on the street, trailed in after him. 'We done it, Carl,' crowed Danny. 'I told you you could rely on us.'

Carl nodded, his eyes narrowed. 'So I hear,' he said. The barman brought over a drink and placed it reverently in front of him, and Carl waved him away. 'Fifty,' he said, turning back to Danny. 'That's what we agreed, isn't it?'

Danny looked crestfallen. 'Sixty ...' he began. Then he caught sight of Carl's face and subsided sulkily. 'Yeah,' he said.

Carl reached into his inside pocket, then brought out the money and laid it on the table. 'Good boy,' he said approvingly.

But when Danny reached out to take it, Carl's hand suddenly flashed out and caught him by the wrist. 'Of course,' he said smoothly, 'you could double, or even ... triple, that.'

Danny, whose standing with the gang had risen considerably over the course of the previous night, glanced up enquiringly at Biff, who nodded eagerly. But Danny, glorying in his new-found prestige, was not prepared to sell himself cheap. He twisted free of Carl and flung himself down opposite, laughing. Carl stared at him for a minute longer and then smiled, a thin smile, and Danny, as if he had been given permission, reached out and took the money. 'Ye mean we could get an investment account or somefink, do ye?' he enquired, once it was safely pocketed.

But Carl was growing tired of games. 'No, I do not mean an investment account,' he hissed. 'But I think you'll find what I'm proposing has interest.' His dark eyes were hooded as he looked down, and Danny noticed that his nose was still slightly swollen from the cut that ran across the bridge. He wondered idly how Carl had come by the injury, but he knew better than to ask. He waited.

In the gloom Carl continued to stare at the table, a cruel expression on his face, then he said softly, 'I want that priest dealt with.'

Danny was so startled he almost fell off his seat. 'But we dun that already,' he protested.

'No!' Carl looked up quickly. 'That was a warning to the girls. But I want that priest put out of the way. Permanently.'

Danny gazed at him appalled, and Carl said sneeringly, 'This one too big for you, little brother?'

Danny became aware of the eyes of Biff and Darren fixed on him. He shook his head violently. ''Course not,' he said loudly. 'I was jus' a bit surprised. That's all. We want five 'undred.'

He had named what sounded to him a huge sum, but Carl barely even glanced at him. He nodded briefly as if the money was almost immaterial and then, in one fluid movement, raised the glass to his lips and downed it in one. 'Lose him for me,' he said, banging the glass back down on the table, 'and you can have six fifty.' He wiped his mouth on the back of his hand and then, for the first time, looked Danny piercingly straight in the eyes. 'Do this fast, and I'll maybe even throw in another fifty. And ...' He broke off, glancing quickly at the young toughs ranged nonchalantly around them. 'And maybe I can use you all some more.' He swung to his feet and headed for the door.

'Blimey!' Biff gave a low whistle as he disappeared. ''E really does 'ate that priest, doesn't 'e?'

'Yeah,' agreed Darren.

The gang was clearly puzzled. 'Why?' said one of them. 'Wot's 'e done?'

They all turned and looked at Danny, as if expecting him to furnish them with an answer, but Danny merely shrugged. 'I s'pose 'e's just gettin' in the way of business, that's all,' he said loftily.

There were crows of derision directed at the absent Dougal. 'We'll show 'im it don't do to get across Carl!' one of them shouted. 'Yeah,' rejoined another, his tone bursting with menace, 'we'll fix 'im good.' But Danny was silent. His brain was in turmoil. Trashing the centre had been one thing, but wasting someone? That was entirely different. Danny, by no means an intellectual giant and not noted for any humanitarian bent, strove to think his way through what had suddenly become the most enormously complicated maze. He could hurt someone, yes, and had indeed wanted to hurt Dougal, although his courage had not quite been up to the mark when it came to it. But to kill someone? Danny was just not sure he could do it. He wasn't sure he wanted to. And, in the same moment, it struck him how much he disliked Carl.

His mates suddenly became aware of his silence. 'Wot's up, Danny?' demanded Biff. 'You ain't scared, are ye?'

Danny pulled himself together. 'Leave it out,' he retorted. 'I was jus' wonderin' the best way to do it.'

'Wh ... ay! Good ol' Danny!' There were shouts and cheers, and then the gang dragged up chairs and flung themselves down around the table. 'Wot we goin' t'do then, Danny?' Darren demanded. 'Tell us the plan.'

Back at the hall Maisie was still trailing round after Dougal, dragging the bin behind her, although she had long since lost any interest in putting anything into it. 'I think,' she said, 'that's there one person meant for all of us, and that we won't be happy with anyone else.'

Dougal, who was finding her persistence rather trying (and still felt guilty anyway), nodded absentmindedly. 'You may well be right, Maisie,' he agreed.

'So d'ye think that's the way it is between you and this Amanda?'

Dougal considered the question. 'I suppose so,' he said doubtfully.

'I mean,' persisted Maisie, 'did ye know the first time ye saw her?'

Dougal's patience finally snapped. He felt he was already up to his elbows in shit, and didn't want any more. 'I don't know,' he said irritably. 'I can't remember.'

Maisie looked at him witheringly. 'Ye would if ye did,' she said. She sat down in front of him, stretching out her long legs, and in that moment Dougal suddenly remembered the tee shirt. He also felt rather bad at having snapped at her.

'Maisie,' he asked repentantly, sitting down by her side and brushing an arm wearily across his eyes, 'do you remember that tee shirt you had? You know, the one with 'Bad Girl' on it? You wore it, I think, the first time you came round to the rectory.'

Maisie's heart skipped a beat. 'Wot about it?' she asked breathlessly.

Dougal screwed up his face. 'Well, you know, it's the oddest thing, but when I was at that conference, someone had a shirt just like it.' He grimaced, remembering Myra's appearance, and then suddenly turned and smiled at Maisie. Dougal had an oddly beguiling smile, when he chose. It was very open and lit up his eyes, and it made him look absurdly young. 'But it didn't look as good on her as it does on you,' he said winningly.

Maisie's heart, already fluttering in a way that had made her wonder if she was about to be struck down by angina, suddenly lurched and fell uncomfortably into the pit of her stomach. 'Didn't it?' she asked breathlessly. She felt torn between confusion as to what could have happened to make Dougal so apparently oblivious to the addition to his luggage, and pleasure that he should have noticed something worn by her on someone else. That he was actually talking about *her* shirt did not enter her mind. She simply assumed that this was coincidence, and that hers was even now tucked away deep down the side of Dougal's bag, maybe even under the lining.

Dougal, anxious to make amends for what he felt to be his rudeness and consciously at his most charming, reached across and squeezed her hand. 'Maisie,' he assured her, being careful to keep his distance, 'I don't think there's anyone could wear that tee shirt as well as you.'

Maisie was on cloud nine. Something *had* happened after all, she thought jubilantly. There was definitely something amorous in Dougal's manner that had been absent before. And Maisie, who had never before known real tenderness from a man, felt a huge explosion of joy. 'Ooh, Father,' she said, 'that's really nice.'

Her eyes seemed to glow like two exploding stars, and Dougal stared at her amazed. Not for the first time, he thought how pretty she was. And then, as he looked at her, he felt a great wave of compassion. Poor Maisie, there could not have been many compliments in her life. Knowing he might live to regret it, he abandoned his arms-length policy and gave her a quick hug. 'Maisie,' he said seriously. 'You're a really beautiful person. And don't let anyone ever tell you different.'

By contrast, at that precise moment, the object of unfortunate comparison was not feeling at all beautiful. Bishop Hubert had just thrust under his wife's nose a copy of one of the more outrageous tabloids and there, splashed unflatteringly across page three, beneath a picture of an equally bosomy, though rather more attractive, beauty, she had discovered herself. By some quixotic trick of fate, the camera seemed to have caught her at the worst possible moment of what she now thought of as a horrendous affair.

'Myra,' said the Bishop in shocked tones, 'is this really you?'

Unable for a moment to answer, Myra shut her eyes and uttered a silent and extremely intense prayer. But when she opened them again he was still staring at her – from which she concluded that one part at least of her petition was not going to be answered. 'Uu ... um, I ... I don't know, dear,' she faltered, playing for time and trying desperately to think of some sort of explanation that would be even halfway adequate. 'Where was it taken? Just a moment and let me get my glasses.'

She fumbled for her reading spectacles and perched them gingerly on her nose. All the while she could feel her husband's eyes fixed on her in righteous disbelief and she swallowed nervously. She hated it when he was in one of those moods. 'Now, dear,' she said, turning and pinning a brave smile on her face.

He waggled the paper angrily in front of her. 'This!' he said again.

Myra winced and, unable to help herself, stared at the paper. Immediately she was caught, like a small rodent mesmerised by a snake. 'Oh dear,' she said. The glasses she realised had been a mistake because now the picture stared back at her in all its harsh awfulness.

'Exactly!' thundered Bishop Hubert, no longer able to contain himself. To the acute surprise of them both, his forbearance suddenly snapped. 'How one earth could you do this to me?'

Myra blinked. 'Do it to you?' she repeated, shocked in spite of herself. 'I didn't do it to you.' Then as an afterthought she added, 'It was a mistake.'

Bishop Hubert looked as if he could hit her – either that, or burst into tears. 'A mistake!!!' he echoed. 'You call this a mistake! What exactly? Going to the conference? Wearing this revolting shirt? Or having the misfortune to be photographed? Have you taken leave of your senses, woman?'

Not in thirty-five years of marriage had Bishop Hubert ever called Myra 'woman'. Never before had he spoken to her like that, and Myra stared at him in shocked amazement. She had felt ashamed before, it was true, and had been wondering how best to tell him ever since she returned home. But never for one moment had it occurred to her that he would explode in this way. She raised her head and peered at him curiously, and the next moment the full enormity of her sin seemed to sweep over her like a great suffocating tide.

'You lied to me!' thundered on Bishop Hubert, in full flight and totally oblivious of the hurt he was causing. 'You told me you were going to your sister's.'

'I'm sorry,' whispered Myra. She cast another glance at the paper and her face contorted in an involuntary spasm of pain. 'I didn't tell you about the conference before because I knew you'd disapprove, but Beverley ...'

Mention of Beverley was a mistake. 'That woman!' snapped the Bishop, rounding on her again. 'I might have known that woman would be at the bottom of this. She incited you to it, didn't she? God in heaven,' he turned away, flinging a hand rather dramatically to his brow, 'I sometimes think the whole world is conspiring against me.'

'But!' began Myra loudly in protest. Then she closed her mouth, unable for a second to think how to proceed. She wanted to say that what had happened was not Beverley's fault, and yet a part of her thought rather bitterly that it was. After all, whose fault was it that she had ended up wearing that dreadful shirt? Beverley had explained to her later that it was not one of the official protest shirts. But that was all well and good, thought Myra. It had still been in her room, and still in the only bag visible. Beverley had said that that was not her bag, and that it must have belonged to Dougal Sampratt. But Myra was not entirely sure she believed this. Why on earth should a respectable and proper clergyman like Dougal Sampratt have a tee shirt with 'Bad Girl' plastered over it crammed into his luggage. If she had stayed till the end of the conference she would have asked him, but she had been so upset by the whole unfortunate episode that she had left. Now she rather regretted that, but meantime, how was she to truthfully answer her enraged husband.

'See?' broke in that worthy, seeing her hesitate, 'You can't deny it, can you?'

'I ... I'm not sure,' faltered Myra, distressingly truthful to the end. 'I'm still not really sure what happened.'

The Bishop looked at her witheringly. 'What you're actually saying is that you have absolutely no excuse for this at all. You shred my reputation by this performance!' He glared at the offending photograph and shuddered. 'And you haven't even the decency to apologise.'

'I'm so sorry,' said poor Myra again in a small voice. She had never before seen him so angry and was at something of a loss how to respond. Her gentle, temperate husband seemed a stranger. And then, as he stood by the window staring out of it, every line of his body rigid with anger, she had a sudden stab of insight. He's worried about his position, she thought. He doesn't feel fully a bishop yet. He's scared what people are going to say. And with this, she thought abruptly of Nicholas and realised, with a dull sense of shock, that the chaplain, always outwardly so attentive, hated him. 'Oh, my poor dear,' she said involuntarily. 'You feel I've let you down, don't you? You feel I've abandoned you?'

He turned on her wounded eyes, brimming with a mixture of rage and pain, and immediately she crossed to his side and flung her arms round him. 'I never realised how difficult you were finding it,' she said.

As if her touch was electric, a convulsive shudder ran through his body, and then he seemed suddenly to crumple. 'They'll use this,' he said heavily, indicating the paper, which he had tossed to the floor. 'All the people that want me out. They'll see this as ammunition.'

But Myra had not led women's groups on spiritual warfare for nothing. 'If God is on our side, who can stand against us?' she said robustly.

'But is He?' asked Bishop Hubert tonelessly. He sounded as if he was not convinced by this any more.

'Of course He is,' said Myra firmly. 'God has brought us to this place. You're experiencing the problems you are precisely *because* He's trying to sort things out. And the enemy doesn't like it!'

The Bishop looked as if he was about to cavil at this, but Myra would have none of it. She was at her most commanding. She felt as if she had suddenly seen a light at the end of a long dark tunnel. She had felt terrible after the fiasco at Walsingham, and the fact that the photos – so disgusting – had made it to the press was dreadful. She had felt a shame that was totally alien to her. But the astonishing onslaught of her husband had been like a bizarre kind of blessing, resurrecting her blasted pride. She was not going to allow a little bit of adverse comment (even ridicule) to overwhelm her, she thought angrily. The battle was far too important for that.

If Myra had been born a couple of centuries before and male, she would have been a war hero or a martyr to some worthy cause. But the battle she fought now was equally vital and her role, she saw very clearly, was to give strength and support to her wounded husband. 'God will not allow the ill-intentioned to prevail,' she said firmly. 'I have acted wrongly, I acknowledge it, but the situation was not at all as it appears from that photograph, and we must stand against this now, Hubert!'

'Is it really misleading, dear?' he asked hopefully. Having vented his wholly uncharacteristic rage, her husband felt totally drained.

'Yes,' said Myra firmly. 'We have enemies here who are trying to undermine us. But we must stand firm. You, Hubert, have to give a lead.'

14

One person at least no longer saw himself as Myra Higgins' enemy. Father Goody was besotted with her. Ever since the conference he had been unable to get her out of his mind. It was most extraordinary, but he felt like a young teenager in love for the first time. He had never in his life felt like this before. He would be sitting at his desk trying to work out the Walsingham budget for the next year and his rogue thoughts would suddenly spin round and away, and yearn towards her. He found himself imagining her in her bath, bubbles foaming around her wonderful, refulgent breasts. Or in bed at night, the sheet drawn up high, veiling her loveliness as she waited in anticipatory longing for ... for whom? For Hubert? Father Goody shuddered at the thought of that loutish clod, that dry stick of a man – the Bishop – defiling the fragile skin of his beloved by his oafish touch.

It could not go on, he told himself. He could not for much longer endure the terrible separation that unkind fate had forced upon them. He had got to liberate her from the prison of her marriage so that they could be united, and so that their love could stand forever like a great shining beacon, alongside all the other great loves of the world. Antony and Cleopatra, Nelson and Lady Hamilton .... Tim and Myra. He ached to demonstrate his love for her. Indeed, he had already done so.

At the conference, after her flight, he had overheard a little knot of priests sniggering together about her appearance, and he had rounded on them mercilessly. Such a creature, he had stormed at them, was as much above them and their sordid little imaginings as an angel from the highest heaven. They had no right to sully her name with their vile imprecations. They had stared at him in astonishment, and he had felt like some kind of medieval lover leaping to the defence of his lady. But the light of his life had not been there to witness this spirited display, and after a while his spirits had sunk back again into gloom. He felt he was never going to see her again, and yet the longing was like an irritant deep in his blood, setting up a wholly unknown fire in his loins.

Now he stared at the phone in his study in an agony of indecision. Should he ring her and tell her how he felt, or not? Father Goody pondered the question, trying to imagine how it might feel from her side. Her tender feelings had been wounded at Walsingham, he could see that all too clearly. He did not now want to add to her pain. Yet on the other hand, surely the declaration of his love would be an unguent. So important was his feeling for her, however, that he felt as if he was treading on eggshells. He had got to get it right. It did not occur to him that this sudden violent feeling for a woman, and a woman he would not previously have thought of as attractive, was at all bizarre. In fact, when he thought about it at all, he simply told himself that it was as if a veil had been withdrawn from his eyes, and that what had been revealed to him in that moment of blinding revelation was something that had existed always, from the beginning of time. Their love was, and ever would be. And now he had realised it.

He reached out a hand and, almost trembling, punched in the number for the Bishop's Palace. A secretary connected him to the chaplain's office. He tried to protest that it was personal and that what he actually wanted was to speak to the Bishop's wife, but she cut him off. 'Hold the line, please,' she said peremptorily, 'we're very busy today. Someone will deal with your call as soon as possible.'

A tinkly version of 'Shine, Jesus, shine' echoed down the telephone line. Father Goody winced. He hated that chorus but, even worse, at that precise moment he felt the last thing he wanted was to be 'dealt with'. He did not want anyone else to know who he was. Against that, however, his longing to hear Myra's voice was so acute that it made him pause. For one heart-stopping moment he hesitated, vacillating between replacing the receiver and trying again later, and trying to brazen it out and win through to her by subterfuge.

While he was still dithering, Nicholas's voice came on the line. 'Bishop's office here,' said the chaplain smoothly. 'How may I help?'

'Er, yes ... hello,' began Father Goody blusteringly. 'I ...'

'Is that Father Goody?' asked Nicholas surprised.

Father Goody cringed. 'Uum, yes, it is actually,' he said, writhing.

Nicholas was instantly all charm. He was fully aware of what the diocesan staff had nicknamed the Walsingham debacle and had felt rather pleased. Not that he personally had anything against Walsingham. If they wanted to carry on the way they did, that was fine. He perfectly understood that some peoples' sexual orientation was different from his own. But he took the view that any trouble in the diocese would very effectively prevent Bishops Hubert's unwelcome intervention elsewhere and was therefore to be fostered. 'How can I help you?' he asked again, oozing friendliness. 'Do you want the Bishop? I'm afraid he's a bit tied up at the moment.' He laughed confidingly. 'He's got this delegation from Uganda with him, don't you know. Between you and me and the gatepost he could be quite a while. They really know how to talk, that lot. And last time I went in they were all praying. Felt to me like they might be at it for the duration. But if you'd like to tell me what it is, I'll get him to phone you back later, as soon as he's free.'

Faced by this bland stream of inane words, Father Goody's brain froze. He simply could not think what to say. Myra rose like a beacon in his mind. He thought there was some reason why he should not mention her, but he could not for the life of him remember what it was. 'Myra,' he brought out in strangled tones, as Nicholas at last paused for breath. 'I want the Bishop's wife.'

Nicholas did not take this for the statement of declaration that it most assuredly was, instead he thought merely that Father Goody had something urgent he wished to discuss. He gave a little 'Oh' of surprise, and then said, 'Is it something about the conference?'

Father Goody clutched at this straw as if suddenly and unexpectedly presented with a life preserver. 'Yes,' he gasped, 'that's right.'

At the other end of the line Nicholas wrinkled his brow, perplexed. He had of course seen all the coverage of the Bishop's wife in the newspapers. Indeed it had been he who had first brought the photographs to the Bishop's attention. But he could not see what it could possibly be that Father Goody wanted so urgently to talk to her about. And why, in any case, should he want to talk to her rather than the Bishop? Nicholas had rather imagined at first, from the agitated way in which Walsingham's principal spoke, that he was ringing in order to try and extricate the college from what was clearly a highly embarrassing situation, but obviously this was not the case. He chewed the tip of his finger reflectively, trying to weigh the respective merits of putting him through, or telling him she was out. 'Was it about anything in particular?' he asked at last.

But Father Goody had had time now to think. 'Not really,' he brought out. 'She just left something at the college, that's all. I thought she might want it back.' That she had left something was perfectly true. She had left the torn tee shirt, flung in angry despair onto the floor of her room. Father Goody had retrieved it, and kept it now safely enshrined in the safe in his office. But that he was offering to restore it to her, which seemed to be the implication, was a lie. Heaven might topple, but there was no way Father Goody would ever part with Myra Higgins' shirt.

Nicholas came to a decision. He still could not work out what Father Goody's call might signify, but he sounded interestingly distraught, and it occurred to the chaplain that if the Bishop's wife was now about to be further embroiled in some seamy Walsingham scandal, then it was all to his good. 'Okay,' he said. 'I'll put you through.'

The ringing tone seemed to go on for an age, and Father Goody chewed his nails in an agony of apprehension. But then, just as he was giving up all hope, the phone was suddenly answered and the rather strident tones of Myra bellowed, 'Hello, Myra Higgins here.'

Her voice was like nectar to the starving wastes of his soul. 'Hello,' breathed Father Goody. It was all he could manage.

'Who is that?' asked Myra. She was beginning to suspect she was the recipient of an obscene call.

'I .. it's me,' brought out Father Goody and then, as he was met with silence. 'Timbo.'

'Timbo who?' demanded Myra suspiciously.

The conversation was not going quite the way Father Goody had planned. He was unskilled at the ways of dalliance, but he dimly realised now that if the situation were not to be hopelessly lost, he had somehow to take command. 'Your sugar plum,' he whispered. 'Tim Goody.'

The effect on Myra was electric. She well remembered Father Goody from his amazing performance on the opening night of the conference, but she could not actually remember ever having spoken to him personally before, beyond the usual exchange of pleasantries. She was the Bishop's wife and he was the principal of Walsingham's rather dubious theological college. There was no need for them to talk. 'Is this some kind of prank?' she demanded icily. It had occurred to her that the Walsingham staff had perhaps decided to play a joke on her.

Father Goody blinked. 'N ... no,' he stammered, wondering why the light of his life was sounding so abrupt. He tried again. 'I simply wanted to talk, that's all. I wanted to hear the sound of your voice.'

Myra became convinced she really was the victim of a rather cruel and puerile joke. She imagined the rest of the Walsingham staff gathered round the phone, tittering behind their hands as they jostled one another to hear. Quite why they should wish to do something like this she did not bother to wonder. Dear Hubert always said there was something rather strange about that lot. Unpleasant even. 'This may appear funny to your perverted little minds,' she said angrily. 'And I don't doubt you've all been having a laugh at my expense after what happened the other day, but I would have thought there were better things with which to occupy your time!'

Father Goody was appalled, and then suddenly understanding came. 'You're trying to tell me there's someone there and you can't talk, aren't you?' he said.

'What?' shrieked Myra. 'Of course I'm not. Good heavens, man, why on earth should it be of the slightest consequence to me whether there's someone here or not?'

'B ... but,' began Father Goody. Then he decided, perhaps wisely, to abandon that line of conversation. 'Look,' he said imploringly, 'you seem to have got hold of the wrong end of the stick, but I only want for us to meet and talk.' He did not add that he then wished to carry her off to some exotic Caribbean island, and to tickle her toes as they lay together on the sand.

Her angry voice exploded into this particular daydream with the finesse of a two-ton truck. 'I think you've taken leave of your senses,' she snapped acidly. 'There can be nothing of any possible interest for us to discuss.'

'But there is,' protested Father Goody. 'When I saw you wearing that glorious shirt the other day ... when I looked at your breasts ...'

A feeling of icy dread suddenly rolled over Myra. There was a hidden agenda here she thought. She was not simply the victim of a joke, this man was after something. And it was not nice. Maybe he was even hoping, through her, to be able to get at Hubert. Perhaps this was some strange form of blackmail, and he was going to try and coerce her in order to ensure the future of the college. She had heard a lot of funny things about Walsingham, and her mind spun dazedly into infinite convolutions of evil possibility, each one more horrendous than the last.

'If we could just hold hands,' Father Goody was burbling on.

Myra came to her senses. 'I feel I should tell you that I am not the slightest bit amenable to pressure from any sordid little scheme your perverted mind may be concocting,' she said angrily. 'Walsingham must face the consequences of its own shortcomings. You cannot bring pressure to bear through me.'

It was Father Goody's turn to be taken aback. What on earth was she talking about? Why did she sound so angry? 'But,' he bleated. It was too late. The light of his life had hung up.

For the next few days his behaviour in college was absolutely extraordinary. Everyone noticed it. By some bizarre process, as the time passed, he convinced himself that Myra too was seething with suppressed longing. There clearly had been someone with her, maybe even Hubert, and her response had been a clever sham, designed to cover both their tracks. What a wonderful woman he thought. Not only beauty, but brains too. He went round the college with an inane little smile on his face, so peculiar that Brian was moved to comment to William that he thought perhaps the events of the conference had unhinged him. That, indeed, was rapidly coming to be the general view of the staff. They could think of no other explanation to account for his strange behaviour. Even Beverley, who had expected to find herself sacked or at the very least on permanent leave, received only a mild rebuke. Within the college Father Goody was reliably reported to have told Father Martinez after the conference that he thought the display of feminine independence to which they had all been treated, rather splendid. The Brazilian priest's response was not recorded, but he had left shortly after, muttering darkly that in his opinion the place ought to be exorcised.

'She really ought to go,' Oswald said angrily to Brian, when they met up with each other over lunch. 'They both ought to go come to that. Walsingham has become a laughing stock.'

Brian, who was doing his best to keep his head down, merely nodded.

'Well, don't you think so?' persisted Oswald. 'We can't have people saying that our principal's mad.'

Willaim, who was just at that moment passing with a tray,

overheard. 'Yes, but Tim's been here an awfully long time,' he interrupted. He heaved himself down opposite and stared up the table. 'Any salt?'

Oswald scowled and in reply pushed over the condiments. 'That's precisely my point,' he said. 'He's been here too long. We need new blood.'

He said the word 'blood' particularly loudly and Brian jumped. 'Better the devil you know,' he protested, dropping his fork. 'Who knows what someone new might do?'

They all looked gloomy. It was perfectly true that Tim seemed to be growing incapable, but none of them relished the prospect of a new broom who might sweep through the college in a terrifying blaze of reform, upsetting everything. 'Perhaps we can persuade him to have treatment,' hazarded William. 'For the drink I mean. After all, I'm sure it's that that's at the root of all this.'

'Do you think so, dear boy?' asked Brian earnestly.

William nodded. 'Bound to be. He gives the impression of being permanently half cut these days.'

They continued to eat for a moment in silence, and then William said suddenly, 'Perhaps we could help him?'

'How do you mean?' Oswald, a forkful of steak pie poised in the air, looked owlish. 'The only thing that I think could help at the moment is if we all got drunk too. We wouldn't notice then.'

'No, no, don't be silly,' said William impatiently. 'I mean that for a start we could try and make sure he doesn't have any further access to booze.'

'How?' asked Brian.

'Well, we all know he keeps it in his study. Maybe one of us ought to creep in some time and clear it out.'

Oswald was appalled. 'Break into Tim's study?'

But William nodded. 'These are desperate times,' he said. 'We either get him on the wagon and dried out, or we're going to find ourselves lumbered with someone new. And we're all agreed we don't particularly want that.'

Oswald looked as if he was about to demur. It was perfectly true he did not want someone new coming in from outside, but he rather fancied himself as principal. Even he, however, was forced to acknowledge that his own appointment, at this present moment in time, was unlikely. Better then to keep Tim for at least a few more months and maybe, during that time, he could build up his own position. 'All right,' he said finally. 'You're on.'

Over at St Prosdocimus Dougal felt shattered. Every muscle in his body seemed to ache. They had finally finished cleaning out the hall at eleven the previous night and by the time he got to bed he felt as if a rhino had charged over him. At least he did not lie awake, as he had been worried he might, but sank into dreamless oblivion the moment his head touched the pillow. When he finally woke at nine the following morning he felt rather groggy and discovered he was so stiff he could not raise his arms above shoulder height. Two cups of coffee later, however, he was beginning to feel slightly more human, and by ten he even felt he could face going back over to the hall.

When he got there, he rather wished he had not bothered. Walking across he had wondered, rather wistfully, if it might look better in the light of day, but this forlorn hope died the minute he stepped across the threshold. The fluorescent lighting, always necessary inside the hall, flickered waspishly beneath his touch, and then lurched on and off three or four times, luridly illuming every pale brown smear and grubby crack. When the lighting finally came fully on, it looked like a bomb had hit it and, unable to help himself, Dougal gave a low groan. There was no way they would be able to re-open it like this. At the very least the place needed repainting, and then there was all the smashed equipment that needed replacing too.

He stared round gloomily, trying to work out what to do, but his brain seemed not to be functioning properly. It simply seized up every time he tried to think of a plan. Whatever they did, he thought desperately, was going to cost money. A lot of money. But St Prosdocimus did not have money. They had not even had enough to pay for insurance, and Dougal knew very well what would happen when that fact came to light with the church authorities. But that was an entirely separate problem; the more pressing need was finding some way to restore the hall. And with no fabric fund in reserve, and no hope of a diocesan loan, how were they to manage?

A little scratching sound over on his left testified to the presence of mice, or even worse. Dougal looked away, shaking his head. He didn't think he could cope with any more problems. His brain churned relentlessly on and he looked around, trying to work out what the barest minimum cost would be if they were to attempt to repaint it themselves. The ceiling at a pinch they could perhaps leave, which left the walls, the woodwork and the floor, which would have to be sanded down and re-stained. Looking at it, he wondered if he could

perhaps take out a personal loan and cover the cost himself. After all, he was always being bombarded with offers of loans from credit companies, who seemed to want to heap on him the most phenomenal amounts of money for a dream holiday or new car. Surely, if they were happy
to lend money for things like that, they could not object to something like this.

He had just decided to spend the day getting estimates from paint companies and then going round the neighbourhood banks and building societies, when he suddenly remembered that Amanda was coming over that evening. He had been so caught up in everything that had happened over the last few days that he had entirely forgotten. 'Oh damn,' he said to himself. It was not that he didn't want to see her. He did. But he just felt as if everything had fallen on him all at once, like a great tidal wave of chaos, and a flood of dread suddenly swept over him as he wondered what it was she wanted to say. He thought perhaps the easiest thing would be if they ate out, but then he remembered that she had been adamant that they eat in and, with a feeling akin almost to despair, he realised he would have to delay his plans for the hall and take time to shop and prepare a meal.

*

Not far away in London, Amanda was also feeling rough. She had been sick already three times that morning. Whoever had said anything about *morning* sickness, she thought, shuddering, must be mad. She seemed to feel sick *all* the time. And as for cravings! The only thing she wanted was to crawl away somewhere and die. She felt as if her body had been invaded by something from another planet. She phoned up work and told them she would not be in because she was ill, and then she went to the bathroom and tried again to be sick. But there was nothing left by now, and she ended up leaning against the wall and clutching her stomach, retching painfully as if her body was trying desperately to find something to expel. She had just decided that she was feeling marginally better when the phone rang. Wearily she shuffled back into the other room and raised it to her ear. 'Yes?' she said miserably. 'What do you want?'

There was a pause at the other end and then Nicholas's surprised voice said, 'Hi, Amanda? Is that you?'

She grunted.

'I just called the gallery,' he said. 'They said you weren't well.'

A horrible pain again gripped Amanda's stomach and she heaved.

'Yes,' she said, recovering. 'I think I must have some sort of stomach bug.' She began to pray that he would be satisfied with that and just ring off.

But he didn't. 'Can I do anything?' he asked, concerned.

'No,' said Amanda ungraciously.

Nicholas felt baffled. He had been so sure everything was going well. He was not used to people behaving like this. He began to wonder whether, despite the fact that her father was a retired bishop, Amanda was such an attractive prospect as a clerical wife after all. 'There's nothing seriously wrong is there?' he asked, beginning to wonder if she was some kind of closet manic depressive.

'No, of course not,' Amanda retorted acidly. 'Don't be so stupid.' And then it occurred to her that this was perhaps a shade rude and that, although she did not want to speak to Nicholas at that precise moment, it might be unwise to antagonise him. 'Sorry,' she mumbled. 'I just feel lousy.'

Shades of the mad woman of Shallot receded slightly and Nicholas said, 'Why don't I come over and see how you are? Have you had the doctor in?'

Amanda felt a flood of panic. 'No ... no,' she said. 'It's all right. I haven't seen the doctor, but I'm sure it's only one of these twenty-four-hour things. I'll be fine. And don't bother to come over. It would be such a fag for you, and you're too busy anyway.'

Nicholas felt relieved. He hated having to try and look after people when they were ill. 'Well, if you're sure,' he said.

'I am,' said Amanda fervently.

Another pause.

'Then I'll ring tomorrow.'

Amanda closed her eyes. 'Do that,' she agreed. 'I'm sure I'll be sorted by then.' She put down the phone.

At the other end of the line Nicholas too replaced the receiver. He stared at it a moment, a speculative look on his face, then reached out, picked it up again, and dialled a number. 'Hello, Stephanie?' he said, when a voice answered at the other end. 'Nicholas here. Nicholas de Vere ... Yes ... Yes, it has been a long time ... I'm fine ... I was wondering if you might like to meet for lunch?'

Bingo arrived at St Prosdocimus later that same afternoon, just as darkness was beginning to fall. He had thought it politic not to park in the immediate area, having done some research over the last few days and discovered the penchant of the local youth for joy riding. He felt he was rather attached to his hubcaps. He parked therefore in a multi-storey car park in the centre of Carbery, and then caught a bus.

As it trundled from the gracious medieval stone centre out to the desolate and crumbling Victorian suburbs, and then lurched its way drunkenly over the speed humps and through to the outermost layers of the faceless council estates that surrounded the city, Bingo felt as if he was passing into some terrible war zone, and his journalistic nose twitched. He had been a bit dubious about the whole thing at first, but maybe Nicholas was right. He felt deep down in his bones that there really might be a story here after all. There was something in the air. Something depressively brooding that almost seemed to strangle the spirit. Bingo's was a sensitive soul.

He got off outside a pub, the Wigspittle and Pole. It looked a dismal sort of a place, and he stared at it with distaste, dismissing there and then any idea that had been taking shape in his mind of starting his enquiries at the local watering hole. Some boys lounging about outside eyed him up and down and, becoming aware of them, he moved off hastily, suddenly worried that they were going to accost him. As he began to walk quickly down the pavement, he heard behind the soft sound of cloth scraping along brick, and then the dull pad of footsteps. Swallowing, he quickened his pace slightly and headed in the direction of the church, which he could see at the opposite end of the square.

In medieval times the Church had always functioned as a place of sanctuary but to Bingo, almost trotting towards St Prosdocimus' barbed wire topped walls, it did not feel very safe at that moment. Behind him he could still hear the footsteps, in what sounded like relentless but unhurried pursuit. And then, just as he was beginning to think something dire was going to happen, the door ahead suddenly opened, and out into the gathering gloom of the afternoon stepped the figure of a woman.

As if she were a gift straight from heaven, Bingo rocketed towards her. 'Hi!' he called, raising a hand. 'I say, please stop!'

Behind him the footsteps halted. Bingo did not bother to look at the woman very closely. He simply wanted the security of her presence. 'I wonder if you could help me,' he panted, rushing up and planting himself in her path.

Maisie looked surprised. 'What d'ye want?' she asked, half turning. Then she too became aware of the small group of boys standing just beyond the circle of light pouring out through the open door. 'What ye doing, Danny?' she demanded. Her eyes narrowed suspiciously, 'Ye not up to ye tricks again, are ye?'

Maisie, having just been in what she regarded as a holy place, felt sanctimonious by association. She had been looking for Dougal, first at the rectory and then at the church. Now she was on her way over to the hall, although since that remained resolutely dark, she had no great hope of success.

Danny, finding himself picked out, shuffled his feet. 'Nuffink,' he retorted.

'Then shove off!' Maisie said sharply. She turned back, smiling sweetly, to Bingo. 'Yes, luv?' she purred. From what she thought of as her close association with Dougal, she felt she was somehow a representative of the church. The rather scared looking man standing before her looked, to her eyes, like he might well be one of her beloved's colleagues. It was her duty therefore to tender what assistance
she could.

As the threat behind him receded, Bingo fully took in Maisie's appearance for the first time. Despite himself, his eyes widened. She had on, for her, a modest outfit. But Maisie's ideas of modesty were rather far removed from those of the wider populace. She had on tight leopardskin leggings, stiletto heels, and a huge sloppy Joe sweater, with a neckline that plunged alarmingly to her waist. Scenting the near proximity of prey, Bingo wriggled slightly and smiled ingratiatingly.

'I was looking for the vicar,' he began. 'But I think you might do just as well.'

Maisie stared at him, trying to decide whether she had before her a potential customer or a seeker after spiritual solace who had somehow mistaken her for a nun. 'How?' she demanded.

Bingo's smile grew. 'Allow me to present my card,' he said, fishing in his pocket. 'Bingo Drubbins. Freelance journalist.'

Maisie stared at the proffered card. 'Oh,' she said, only mildly interested. 'Ye're one of them, are you? I thought you'd all gone now.'

Bingo nodded vigorously. 'So I understand. But I'm working on a slightly different angle. I wanted to do an article on the man behind the myth. You know the sort of thing ... What drives a man like Dougal Sampratt to give up everything? Saint or sinner. The reason why.'

Maisie became more alert. 'Oh, you mean y' want to know about

Dougal!' She said this as if it was revelation indeed and Bingo nodded his head vigorously. Maisie made up her mind. 'Yeah! I can tell you all about 'im,' she said decisively. "E's a saint. Definitely.'

Without more ado she slipped an arm through Bingo's and prepared to lead him away down the street. 'What d'y' want to know then?' she asked.

Bingo could hardly believe his luck. One minute he had thought he was going to be mugged and the next he had discovered Maisie! This was an unexpected find indeed. Her appearance and obvious enthusiasm would, Bingo thought, have aroused alarm in the breast of a saint. 'Well for a start,' he began. 'You could tell me how well you know him. Are you perhaps one of the girls he's trying to help?'

Maisie's beam grew to three hundred kilo-watt brilliance. 'Yeah,' she said proudly. 'I am. 'E's touched me profoundly.'

15

When it came time to get ready to go, Amanda dressed with care. As if in defiance of her pregnancy, she chose a short, tight bottle green shift that had been very expensive, and that showed off every curve and line of her body. Her intention was to look sexy but, when she looked in the mirror, she looked awful. Her skin had a greyish tinge and her hair looked limp. In despair she rubbed on blusher and then, after a moment's reflection, added a smear of scarlet lipstick and an extra coating of mascara. But it did not seem to help very much and, when she glanced at her reflection again, she gave a shudder of distaste. Pregnancy was supposed to make a woman bloom, but it did not seem to be having quite that effect on her. Instead she looked shrivelled and old, and there was that awful acid feeling in her stomach again. She hoped she was not going to be sick.

Moving carefully, she packed a bag of overnight things, reverently folding the expensive nightdress she had bought and placing it carefully in the bottom of the case. Then, for good measure, she added an extra dab of perfume behind her ears, forlornly tried again to puff up her hair, and tottered out to the car. The rest of her life, she felt, would be determined by the outcome of the next few hours.

When she arrived at St Prosdocimus it was dark. She drove straight to the rectory and parked her car outside, carefully fitting on the steering lock and setting the car alarm. She had not ventured into the parish since Dougal's induction and, gazing round as she clambered out, she felt a familiar stab of revulsion. How could Dougal have done this to her? But the next moment she pushed the thought aside. Dougal had done this because he was going to be a name. He *was* a name. She took a firmer grip on her bag and hurried up the path.

Dougal was draining pasta in the kitchen when she rang the bell. He was having a crisis of faith. It had suddenly struck him at around five o'clock. It had been alright during the day while he was rushing round trying to sort things out because he had been too busy to think, but at five o'clock he had decided to have a currant bun and cup of tea and he had sat down in his study ... and begun to think. It had struck him again that, although there was no hope of claiming any insurance, he still ought to inform the police of what had happened, so that they could perhaps keep a closer eye on the hall in the future. Accordingly he had put down his bun and given them a ring. The police officer who had answered the call had sounded bored and then, when he realised it was Dougal he was talking to and that the hall in question belonged to St Prosdocimus, a hint of amusement had crept into his voice. 'It happened last night then, did it, sir?' he enquired.

Dougal grunted assent.

'And you say you've cleared out the hall already?'

Dougal suddenly realised that if he was going to tell the police, they should not have touched it. 'Yes,' he said, slightly nervously. 'But it was such a mess, and we need to get it re-opened as soon as possible.'

'But you're telling me, sir, that whatever evidence there was has now been removed?'

'Well, probably ... I'm sure there's something left somewhere.'

The policeman allowed a pregnant pause. 'And what exactly are you expecting us to do now, sir?'

'Well,' began Dougal again, helplessly. 'I don't know really. I suppose realistically you won't have much hope of catching ...'

But this was apparently the wrong thing to say, because the policeman interrupted frostily, 'And what makes you so sure of that?'

'I don't know. I'd just heard success rates in this type of crime aren't very ...'

'They might be a lot better, sir, if members of the public weren't quite so quick to destroy evidence!'

'Ah,' said Dougal.

'Exactly, sir,' said the police officer, clearly ruffled.

In the end they had arranged that someone would come along later and have a look, just for the record, but when Dougal returned to his chair he discovered that the floodgates had been opened and that the demons, who had been kept under firm restraint during the day, were now clamouring for admittance. In a great wave of misery, he suddenly thought how truly awful St Prosdocimus was. And then it struck him that God was punishing him, although he had not the slightest idea why. It was but a short step from there to a huge outburst of anger, and the Almighty had come in for a great blast of vituperative abuse. Dougal's tea had grown cold, but if he had expected an immediate response from the recipient of his prayers, nothing came, and he had finally leant forward in despair with his head on his hands, internally crying out, 'Why, God? Why?'

When he next looked at the clock he saw, with a jolt, that it was ten past six, and that he had only fifty minutes left before Amanda was due to arrive. The next half an hour had been pure panic, as he dashed round the kitchen and threw things willy-nilly into a casserole. In the normal course of things Dougal enjoyed cooking. His paella was a culinary delight, while his flambéed pork with apricots and brandy was the stuff of dreams. But he was one of those cooks who liked to take a long time, cogitating and tasting, adding a few more herbs here, a dash of freshly ground pepper there ... and a trail of debris in his wake. He was not your daily, meat and two veg sort of a cook. But tonight, because he was in such a rush, he just tossed things in anyhow. Chicken, mushrooms, peppers, a jar of prepared sauce. And then, as he was turning round from the oven, his elbow caught an opened bottle of chocolate and peanut sauce that he had bought earlier to go over ice cream for pudding. In one slow movement, it tottered, and then fell gracefully, head side down, straight into the casserole. A huge heavy dollop of chocolate instantly descended into the middle of the creamy mushroom sauce, and disappeared from view. Dougal gazed at it in horror, wondering what on earth to do. Then he feverishly grabbed a spoon and began to try and ladle it out. But the attempt only made matters worse, because he was in such a hurry that he broke up the chocolate now lying on the bottom of the dish and, in his rush to get it out, swirled it under the chicken. Instantly the sauce turned a delicate variegated brown, and two nuts floated lazily to the top. Behind him, from his study, the clock chimed a quarter to the hour. Dougal stood, in an agony of paralysed indecision. But it was far too late to start again. Uttering a quick prayer to the God he had so comprehensively abused not an hour before, he stuffed the whole lot into the oven. But his depression only deepened, because he suddenly realised, with the most appalling clarity, that *nothing* he did now went right.

Amanda, however, knew none of this and so, when Dougal opened the door, she pinned on her brightest smile, flung her arms round his neck and gave him a big kiss. Unfortunately Dougal was still carrying the saucepan in which he had boiled the pasta, and a large globule of hot, starchy water splashed up and landed on the front of her dress. 'Ouch!' said Amanda. She stared at her front in horror as the huge patch of slimy wet slowly spread out.

'Oh God,' said Dougal. 'Not again.'

'What?' said Amanda.

Dougal recollected himself. 'Sorry,' he said. He put the saucepan down on the small hall table, pulled out his hankie, and began ineffectually to try and dab at her front.

'Don't rub!' shrieked Amanda. 'You're spreading it.'

She snatched it from him and pressed it across her top, trying to blot up the wet. Dougal watched her, crestfallen, and then suddenly remembered that he had put the saucepan onto polished wood. 'Oh no,' he said. He snatched it up again, but it was too late, a pale slimy circle was now firmly imprinted into the top of the table. 'Oh dear,' he said, 'Regina will kill me.'

'Who's Regina?' demanded Amanda, pausing in mid blot.

'The churchwarden,' he muttered. 'You've met her, remember. She cleans for me, and this table belongs to the rectory.'

Amanda looked at it. 'Good job too,' she said sourly. 'It's hideous.'

It was not the most auspicious of starts. Amanda was actually furious about the dress, which she suspected was now ruined, but she fought down her rage and forced herself to smile. Dougal, however, did not seem to respond. She thought he looked listless and he seemed preoccupied. 'What's wrong?' she asked at last, beginning to think that he was angry with her. 'Have I upset you?'

In the act of pouring out a couple of gin and tonics he looked up, surprised. 'No, of course not,' he said. Then he shrugged wearily. 'Sorry, it's just that the church hall got broken into last night, and I've had the most awful day trying to sort it out and I ... I guess I'm just tired.'

The doorbell rang. 'Oh dear,' he said. 'Look, I'm sorry. I won't be a minute.'

He disappeared out into the hall and Amanda heard him say, 'Eliston, hello! Anything wrong?'

There was a muttered response, too low for her to hear, and then she heard Dougal go into the study. 'Look,' he called, 'how would it be if I give you the key?'

Amanda helped herself to another gin. She had a dim idea she ought not to be drinking, but she was so fed up she didn't really care. And besides which, she was afraid it might look odd if she stuck to fruit juice all night. She had just taken a large swig and leant back with her eyes closed when Dougal returned. 'Sorry,' he said again. 'That was Eliston. He wanted to get into the church, but apparently he's lost his key. I've given him mine.' He eyed her drink. 'You alright?'

She nodded. 'Dougal,' she began.

The phone rang. 'Sorry,' said Dougal again. 'I'd better answer it, it might be the police. They said they were going to phone back to fix up a time to come round tomorrow.'

He disappeared for another five minutes, and Amanda finished her drink. 'Not the police,' he announced when he came back. 'A young couple wanting to get married.'

Amanda attempted to look interested, and failed. 'Could I have another one?' she asked, holding out the glass.

Dougal blinked. He was slightly surprised by how much she seemed to be drinking. 'Of course,' he said. He began to mix her another and then said, 'Look, do you want to eat?'

Amanda did not want to eat at all. She could hardly bear to look at food, but she thought that maybe it would be better for her plans if they could get the food out of the way as soon as possible. 'Alright,' she said.

She took another huge swig from the glass Dougal held out to her, and then followed him through to the dining room. Although so pushed for time, Dougal had made an effort. He had placed five candles together in an uneven cluster on the table, and he lit them now and turned off the light. 'That's nice,' said Amanda.

He served up a starter of avocado and bacon, which he knew she loved, and warmed ciabatta bread. Amanda eyed the plate apprehensively, but valiantly took up her fork. 'I've had a terrible week,' said Dougal conversationally. 'Wine?'

'Good heavens,' she said surprised. 'My glass is empty! Yes please.'

A wave of nausea rolled over her, but she choked it down and forced herself to take a mouthful of avocado. 'Uum,' she said. 'Delicious.'

The doorbell rang again. 'It's one of those nights, I'm afraid,' said Dougal ruefully. 'I'm sorry. I won't be a tick.'

As soon as he was out of the door Amanda glanced round for somewhere to put the food. A large potted plant standing on the floor over in the corner caught her eye. Hastily she got up and tiptoed over with the plate. Then, quickly glancing round to make sure she was unobserved, she tipped most of the avocado and all of the bacon down the side of the pot.

'Yes thank you, Eliston,' she heard Dougal say. 'You really shouldn't have bothered ... No, you could just have put them through the door ... That's fine.' She scuttled back and slid into her seat just as Dougal came back through the door. 'Honestly,' he said, 'what a palaver. He'll be over for them again later when they all leave.' Then he saw her plate and checked in surprise. 'Goodness,' he said, 'you ate that fast. You're almost finished.'

'Uu ... um,' said Amanda, delicately dabbing at her lips with her napkin. 'It was delicious.' As if in confirmation, she raised the last forkful of avocado and placed it in her mouth. 'Wonderful!'

'You can have some more if you like,' said Dougal, surprised.

He made to go to the kitchen but Amanda said hastily, 'No that's fine. Honestly. I want to leave some room for the main course.' She reached out for her glass, then changed her mind as another wave of nausea swept over her.

'If you're sure,' said Dougal uncertainly. He resumed his seat and began to eat.

They managed to get through the first course with only one more interruption from the phone and at last, exasperated, Amanda said, 'Please, Dougal, put on the answerphone. This is ridiculous.'

'But I hate doing that when I'm here,' he retorted, 'It seems so rude.'

She looked at him. 'Yes, but we're never going to get to talk at this rate.'

He flicked it on and went through to the kitchen to get the main course. An interesting smell rose into the air when he took the lid off the casserole, and he looked at it dubiously. It was a strange colour, not at all delicate and light as it ought to have been. He pondered what to do and then, in a sudden flash of inspiration, he picked up the second bottle of wine that was standing on the worktop ready to be taken through, and sloshed half of it into the dish. Then he gave the whole thing another stir and floated some cream across the top.

'Hope you're still feeling hungry,' he said heartily, though without much inner conviction, depositing it on the table.

'Oh yes,' said Amanda. She leant forwards, intending to give an appreciative sniff, then recoiled as the aroma hit her full in the face. 'Ye ... es,' she said uncertainly. 'Interesting.'

'Hope so,' said Dougal nervously. 'Thought I'd try a bit of an experiment.' He scuttled back to the kitchen to retrieve the pasta, which he had to put to warm under the grill, and which was now one congealed mass. 'Oh, heavens!' he said, looking at in dismay. There did not seem much more that could go wrong.

'I think I'll just have a small portion, please,' said Amanda, as he sat back down and prepared to dish up.

Dougal swallowed, and ladled a huge spoonful onto her plate. 'It's not as much as it looks,' he said brightly. They both looked at it apprehensively. 'Pasta?'

With difficulty, he hacked off a wedge and placed it beside the stew. 'What exactly is it?' asked Amanda, taking the plate gingerly.

'Chicken, of course,' said Dougal heartily. 'Can't you tell?'

Amanda stared at it. 'No,' she said. 'Not really. It smells ... different.'

'That's the secret ingredient,' said Dougal, a shade too loudly. 'You'll love it.' He finished serving himself and then plunged in his fork. 'Eat up.'

She looked at him a moment longer and then very nervously took her own fork and began to pick at the edge of the food mounded on her plate. The addition of the chocolate had given a curious texture to the dish. It had become thick and slightly stringy, and the mushrooms and peppers seemed to be encased in a kind of sticky cocoon. Even Dougal looked at it slightly apprehensively, but all the great dishes and delicacies of the world, he reminded himself, had come about through experimentation and some of them, like champagne for instance, were even the result of a mistake. He took an experimental taste. And almost choked.

Amanda, seeing him place the fork in his mouth and not wishing to seem rude, bravely took a mouthful herself. In normal circumstances she might have been able to make a show of chewing and then swallowing it, before putting down her fork and saying politely, 'Very interesting ... but a little strong for me I think.' But these were not normal circumstances and the effect of the strange mixture of tastes on her tongue was like a bomb. Her stomach contracted and then heaved, and bile rose in her throat. She gave a strangled cry and half rose to her feet, clutching the napkin to her face. 'Bathroom!' she brought out.

Appalled, Dougal stared at her and then in turn leapt to his feet. 'Upstairs and first on the left,' he said, flinging open the door.

Amanda hurtled past him and dashed for the stairs. A moment later, he heard the sound of her comprehensively throwing up, then there was a pause, then the loo flushed, and there was the sound of a tap being turned on. When she came back a few minutes later she looked pale but composed. 'I'm so sorry,' said Dougal helplessly. He seemed to be doing a lot of apologising. 'Are you alright now? Would you like some more?'

It did not strike him that this was perhaps an insensitive thing to say. He actually had thought the taste rather intriguing, once he had got used to it, and never for one moment did it occur to him that it was the casserole that had made her sick. He simply thought she was a bit off-colour. The look Amanda cast on him in reply made him inwardly shrivel. 'Perhaps not,' he said unhappily.

At that moment, to the relief of them both, the doorbell went again and Dougal fled to the sanctuary of the hall. When he came back he said, 'I really am most awfully sorry. It's the police.'

Amanda shut her eyes. 'What now?' she asked.

Dougal hung his head. 'They want to see the church hall ... Do you mind?'

'No,' said Amanda wearily. 'I don't think we're going to get any peace tonight.'

'You could come over with us.'

The last place Amanda wanted to see was St Prosdocimus' church hall but it occurred to her that, in her present condition, some fresh air might be no bad thing. 'Alright,' she agreed heavily. 'Just let me put on a coat.'

The two plain clothes policemen standing at the door regarded her with interest. 'Evening, Mrs Sampratt,' said one. 'Nice night.'

Amanda did not bother to correct him. 'Yes,' she agreed, 'I'd been hoping so.'

They left the police car parked outside the rectory and walked the short distance to the hall, Dougal leading the way. 'There's not really that much to see now,' he apologised. 'The parishioners have done a wonderful job.'

Amanda stared around gloomily. God, she thought, how perfectly ghastly to have to live in a place like this. They reached the hall and Dougal unlocked the doors. Across the street a little clutch of street girls watched with interest. 'Are ye openin' up, Father?' shouted one.

'No, sorry,' yelled back Dougal, 'not tonight. It's still too much of a mess. We're going to have to paint it I'm afraid.'

The girl made as if to come over. 'We could 'elp you, if you want,' she screamed, advancing a few steps along the pavement.

Amanda winced.

'Not just at the moment thank you, Maisie,' Dougal shouted back. 'I'm just showing the police round.'

'Oh right!'

As if this was an invitation, the girl nodded and strutted across the road. 'Hu ... um,' said one of the policemen with interest, 'it's all true then. You really have set up a centre for the toms.'

Dougal looked at him. A rather sour look, Amanda thought. 'Yes,' he said, 'we're trying to help them.'

'I 'elped clean it up,' said Maisie proudly, joining them.

The policemen appeared to know her. 'Well done,' said one dryly.

Maisie beamed, but her eyes were fixed on Amanda. 'Is this y' fiancée, Father?' she asked.

'Yes,' said Dougal.

'Oh, sorry,' said the policeman, who had addressed Amanda as Mrs Sampratt, 'we thought you were his wife.'

'When's the happy day then?' remarked the other conversationally.

This was the last thing, in her present condition, that Amanda wanted to discuss. 'Can we get on?' she said tartly. 'I think our dinner's getting cold.' She pushed her way through in front of them all and then drew up short as the smell, still lingering unpleasantly, hit her. 'Oh God,' she said. 'It smells like a urinal.'

'Yeah,' agreed Maisie conversationally. 'That's what they used it for.' She placed herself firmly at Amanda's side as Dougal put on the lights and the policemen went in. Dougal glanced at Maisie nervously and opened his mouth as if to say something. But then he changed his mind, and followed after the police. 'It is a bit of a mess, isn't it,' remarked one of those worthies. 'See what you mean about the need for repainting.'

'Ye ... es,' said the other. He was walking round, looking at things carefully, and he suddenly turned and said, 'You know, Dave, I think we will get forensic along after all. I think there's still stuff they could maybe pick up. It could be interesting.'

They began to discuss the merits of trying to discover the identity of the culprits, and Maisie turned to Amanda. ''E's nice, your bloke,' she said conversationally. She was looking at Amanda closely.

'Yes,' agreed Amanda. She was discovering the walk had benefited her and she was feeling a lot better. She turned to Maisie and scrutinised her, and felt a stab of surprise. The other woman was sizing her up with open jealousy. Amanda recognised the look instantly, but the idea that Maisie should have designs on Dougal was so preposterous she almost laughed.

Maisie, in turn correctly divining what was passing through the other woman's mind, bristled. She thought Amanda was a stuck-up cow and, hardly surprisingly, had decided she did not like her. 'Aren't ye worried,' she remarked, 'Leavin' 'im alone the way you do?'

Amanda looked at her coolly, the faintest of smiles just beginning to curl her lips. 'I don't really think there's much competition round here, do you?' she enquired sweetly and then, before Maisie could reply, she turned and walked over to Dougal, slipping a proprietorial hand through his arm.

Maisie looked after her with real hatred. She decided that she had got to redouble her efforts, if it was only to stop the dreadful Amanda from welding her claws permanently into poor innocent Dougal. But looking at Amanda's perfectly groomed hair and so obviously expensive clothes, even Maisie was forced to acknowledge that this might not be so easy and, for the first time since her use of the charm, she felt a twinge of doubt. This was going to be a lot harder than she had thought, maybe impossible – even given the help of the charm. But Maisie was nothing if not a fighter, and an optimistic fighter at that. A determined glint came to her eye and she stuck out her chest. The enemy might have superior forces, but she knew how to fight dirty.

Amanda was at that moment working out her own strategy. She was not the slightest bit disturbed by Maisie's interest. In fact she rather liked it, although Maisie herself she dismissed as wholly beneath contempt. Dougal, she knew, would never be attracted to someone like that. But still, Maisie's so evident admiration had served to remind her that, for all his stuffiness, Dougal was actually a very attractive man. She had rather lost sight of that, distracted as she had been by Nicholas. But now she suddenly felt a stab of real longing. Clinging to Dougal's arm, and first making sure she was not observed by the policemen, she rubbed herself enticingly against his side. He stared down at her in astonishment, wondering what was happening and Maisie, still standing by the door and witness to the little interplay, frowned. Amanda cast a quick, spiteful glance back over her shoulder and then, pinning a huge smile on her face, turned back to Dougal and said enthusiastically, 'Isn't this hall marvellous!' Then she said loudly to the two policemen, 'I think it's tremendous what Dougal's doing here!'

Dougal looked even more surprised and the policemen, who had both rather assumed they were in the doghouse with her, blinked and stared at each other. 'Oh, yes,' they agreed, uncertainly. 'Yes ... it's very good.'

But Amanda did not care about them. One thing she had learned from Nicholas was a bold line of attack. 'Do be quick, darling,' she breathed softly, staring up into Dougal's face. 'I want us to be alone.'

Her meaning was so clear that poor Dougal almost fell over. A great flood of relief swept over him, so intense it was almost physical, and the next moment his body, almost as if it belonged to someone else and had nothing whatsoever to do with him, gave a great shudder of desire. 'Alright,' he murmured back thickly. 'We're almost done here anyway.' Aloud he said, 'Is there anything else you want to see?'

The policemen had by now finished their inspection. 'I think it is worth getting forensic to have a look, sir,' said the senior officer, 'They might not come up with anything after all this cleaning up, but you never know. And we want to be seen to be supporting things on this estate. We'd like if possible to rebuild the residents' confidence.' He turned and was rewarded with a smile from Amanda. 'So we can leave you and your fiancée in peace for the moment I think, sir,' he said. 'We'll send someone round tomorrow.'

Maisie, who had quite cynically stayed to watch the whole spectacle, gave a small cluck of disgust and then turned and walked out.

Dougal could hardly wait to get back. His fingers were almost shaking as he locked up and he felt slightly weak at the knees. After all the knock-backs and rejections of recent months, he was overwhelmed with a desire to clutch at any available crumb, before it too should disappear. He was perfectly aware that what Amanda's body language appeared to be suggesting went against all his deepest convictions – but his relationship with God had suffered a serious pounding since he had left Walsingham, and he no longer felt quite so certain that his moral stance was right. After all, everyone had sex before marriage these days. Many people didn't even bother with marriage, and the latest directives from the bishops seemed to imply that this was fine. And where was his own Puritanism getting him? If God really was against all that kind of thing, why had he not done something to help?

Dougal felt he had been let down. He had stood by God, but God it seemed was not standing by him. So he scuttled back with Amanda, his brain in turmoil.

Amanda, with her newly honed predatory sense, caught some intimation of his confusion. Once inside the front door of the rectory, she leant firmly up against it, and slipped off her shoes. 'Why don't you throw that revolting casserole away?' she said firmly. 'And then we could go through to the lounge and make ourselves comfortable.'

Dougal stared at her nervously and licked his lips. 'If you want,' he said.

Her only response was a low laugh. She looked at him archly, and then turned and walked through to the sitting room. At least, she went through to the sitting room, but Dougal felt her movement could hardly be described as a walk. She seemed to undulate her way through the door, swaying her hips sexily, and his jaw dropped. He had never seen Amanda like this before.

All lingering ideas of morality disappeared. He was like a starving man in a desert. If God didn't like it, fine! Let him do something to help for a change. God owed him! And as he scuttled feverishly through to the dining room, intent on obeying Amanda's every instruction, he was suddenly seized by the conviction that, not only was God otherwise engaged, but he didn't greatly care.

He flung pots and pans into the sink, and scraped the remains from the plates into the bin. Then he rushed back through to the lounge. 'Would you like some coff ...?' he began. Then he dried up, eyes bulging as he took in the sight of Amanda lying on the sofa. She had slipped off her dress and tights and was lying full length in her bra and knickers. They were, Dougal noted with surprise, black lace edged with scarlet ribbon and there was something rather wanton about them. But in contrast Amanda looked like a child. Her long curling lashes fanned her cheeks in a dark smudge and one hand cradled her cheek. She stirred slightly and turned, burrowing deeper into the cushion she had clasped with her other arm to her front. Through her half parted lips came a low snore. Amanda was asleep. She had not meant for this to happen of course, but another side-effect of her pregnancy was extreme fatigue. Dougal had been a long time in the kitchen and, as she had lain there, trying to drape herself attractively, she had simply drifted off.

Dougal stared at her, deflated, feeling like a child who at the last moment has had a particularly desirable present withdrawn. He reached out a tentative hand, wondering whether to wake her. But she looked so deep in sleep and so peaceful, he felt he did not have the right and, bitterly, he let his hand drop back. God had had the last laugh after all. He stared at her a moment longer and then went and got the duvet from his bed. He would use a spare blanket that night. Carefully he placed the duvet over her, and then went and got a coathanger from his wardrobe and hung up her dress, placing her shoes neatly underneath. That done, he gazed at her a moment longer, a puzzled expression on his face, and then turned and went miserably upstairs to bed. He was not sure why, but he had the awful feeling that something momentous had happened.

16

A pale moon glimmered through the darkened window. Oswald swung his torch up and round, taking in the chaos of the study, and then whispered, 'Do you think we could risk putting on the light?'

Brian took two steps forward and fell over a chair. 'Oh blast!' he said. 'That hurt.'

William, still standing over by the closed door, flicked on the light and they all three stared at each other. 'I'm not sure I like this,' said Oswald nervously. 'We could be discovered at any moment. Tim might come in.'

The study had an abandoned feel to it. Untidy bookshelves lined three walls, crammed with books, files, and bulging stacks of curling paper. More books stood in piles across the floor, like the ruins of tumbled ziggurats clinging on in some alien desolation, and around the waste bin next to the desk lay a scattering of screwed up balls of paper. 'Dear me,' said Brian fastidiously, wrinkling his nose. 'What a mess! Tim really has let himself go. At least he used to put things away.'

'Maybe he's writing something,' said William hopefully, surveying the paper. 'Maybe he's started the follow-up to his book on Byzantine ethics at last. What was it? Sumerian morality? He's been talking about it for long enough.'

'Not in longhand, dear,' said Brian judiciously. They all three crossed to the desk and stared at its littered surface curiously. In the small, cleared space in the centre of Father Goody's bulging trays lay another wodge of paper. Across the topmost sheet, in Father Goody's sprawling hand, was written, 'My dearest, darling, most exquisite Honeykins, you fill my thoughts every minute of the waking day, and walk through my dreams like a muse of delight. When I gaze from my window, I see only your loveliness mirrored in the beauty of the trees. Come to me, my darling, say we can meet. Only say the word and put an end to this wretchedness ...' At this point the writing trailed off in a strange spidery curve, as if the author had suddenly lost the thread of what he was saying. Then there was a gap, and then lower down was written, 'Comfort the longing of my loins'. This last, however, was heavily crossed out, and beneath was written, 'Myra, Oh Myra, why will you not talk to me?'

'What on earth is it?' asked William, staring at it in fascination, and speaking for all three of them.

Oswald reached out a hand and picked it up gingerly. 'Well, I don't think it's declining moral standards of the late Sumerians,' he remarked.

'No, of course not,' breathed Brian. 'Don't be silly.' He stared at them owlishly, 'It's a love letter.'

'A love letter!' The other two looked at him as if he were mad.

'This claptrap's not a love letter,' brought out Oswald.

'Yes it is,' insisted Brian. He took it from Oswald's hand and said, 'Look. I think he was writing it to someone, only he didn't have the nerve to send it. At least not this one. I bet all this rubbish over the floor is other attempts too.'

Oswald gazed at him. 'I really cannot imagine Tim caught up on a tide of passion,' he said sneeringly.

But William had swooped down to the floor and scooped up a handful of the discarded balls. 'He's right,' he said wonderingly. 'They're all the same sort of thing, and most of them are addressed to Myra.'

They gazed at each other ominously. This, to all of them, seemed a most disturbing development. Brian swallowed. 'Who do you think Myra is?' he asked nervously.

'Well the only Myra I know,' began Oswald. And then his face froze. 'No,' he said. 'It can't be.'

'It's not a very common name now,' said William.

'And why else would she have come to the conference?' broke in Brian.

But William was looking thoughtful. 'As far as I know she came because Beverley the bearded lady asked her.'

'So what are you saying?' demanded Oswald. There was a kind of suppressed eagerness about him, like a dog that has just caught the whiff of a particularly juicy bone.

William looked uncomfortable. 'Nothing really,' he said. 'It's just that I suspect, from the general tone, that she either doesn't know anything about this, or that she's told him to get lost.'

'Oh dear, poor Tim,' said Brian.

Oswald's nose was twitching. 'No, no, I'm not convinced of that,' he said firmly. 'I think there's something a lot deeper going on here.' It had occurred to him that the post of principal had just come considerably closer, and a scandal involving the Bishop's wife might, he thought, serve his ends very well. If he could somehow bring to the attention of the ecclesiastical hierarchy some terrible scandal, while at the same time presenting himself as a sympathetic character whose sole concern was the good of the Church, he might well be able to put himself on the fast track to preferment. 'I think we must be very careful here,' he said sententiously. 'Obviously Tim's moral collapse has gone a lot farther than we thought but, more worryingly, it might well involve others at the highest level. We don't know, for instance, if the Bishop is aware of this.' He looked at them. 'This, if it came to light, could well threaten the future of the college.'

His words had the desired effect. Brian and William gazed at him, appalled. 'Do you think it will come out?' asked William.

Oswald shrugged. 'Who knows? What if she returns his feelings?' He cast a quick look round about and then said, 'I think we should remove all these papers ... I'll take care of them.'

Obediently Brian and William gathered them all up into a little pile on the desk, while Oswald smoothed them out and lay them one on top of the other. He kept giving a little, 'Tck!' as he read them, shaking his head in shocked disbelief, and William said, 'You know this is really good of you, Oswald. Really caring.'

Once the floor had been cleared and the papers safely deposited in Oswald's inner pocket, Brian said, 'Now I suppose we ought to try and find the booze.'

'Where do you think he keeps it?' asked William.

They looked round gloomily. Father Goody's study, as befitting the principal, was rather large. 'It could be anywhere,' said Brian. 'I've heard alcoholics tend to keep a lot of bottles by them, and that they hide them away.'

Oswald, secure in his new found importance, took command. 'I'll take the desk,' he said (he wanted to have a quick look at Tim's drawers). 'You check the filing cabinets, William. And you have a look behind the books on the bookshelves, Brian.'

Brian looked slightly surprised. 'You've done this before, haven't you,' he remarked.

Oswald did not deign to reply. Indeed he was already pulling open drawers and rifling through the contents. William stared at him a moment longer, a frown knitting his brow, and then shrugged and crossed over to the filing cabinets. 'I think we ought to be quick,' he remarked. 'We've already been here too long.'

Ten minutes later they had amassed a grand total of twelve bottles and five used glasses in the centre of the floor. Brian had taken the opportunity to have a quick tidy of the shelves, and the bookcases now looked considerably neater. Oswald had discovered a rather uncomplimentary, but as yet unfinished, report on himself and that too had gone into one of his pockets. He had decided he would return it later when he had read it through carefully, but it had occurred to him that some judicious editing might be good and might also go unnoticed by Father Goody, given the state he was currently in.

'What shall we do with it all?' asked Brian, as they stood back to survey the fruits of their labours.

'Do you think we've got it all?' asked William dubiously.

Brian sniffed. 'I sincerely hope so, dear.'

They both turned to look at Oswald, who shrugged disdainfully and said, 'I think we just ought to pour it down the sink.'

They took four bottles apiece. Oswald was all for leaving the glasses there, but Brian said they ought to wash them and then put them back. He did not like Tim but, even so, he hated the idea of his being surrounded by so much squalor. 'You can put them back then,' said Oswald unfeelingly.

Half an hour later and the operation was completed. 'I vote we check it through again in three days' time,' said William.

Brian nodded. 'Yes, dear, and then we keep on till Tim's cured.'

They set off down the corridor that led to the main body of the college. 'It's a bit like being a guardian angel, isn't it?' floated William's voice. Behind him Oswald pulled a face. His intentions, he knew full well, were not quite so kindly.

Coming into his study the next morning, Father Goody pulled up short in surprise. He hardly recognised the room for a minute. It looked so neat, and all the piles of paper on the floor had been cleared away. A cold sweat broke out on his brow. Molly, the cleaner, had obviously been round. He would really have to be more careful in the future.

What if she had read his literary compositions? But then he remembered her difficulty with reading in general, and his panic receded as he thought that, even if she had looked at the papers, she would never have been able to decipher them. But, even so, he must not make that mistake again. He crossed over to his bin, and noted with surprise that it was still full. How odd, that she should have cleared the floor but not emptied that. And then he saw the neat row of five freshly washed glasses standing on the filing cabinet and blinked with even greater surprise. In all the years she had been cleaning for the college, he had never yet known Molly to exert herself beyond the defined limits of her job. It was hard enough even to get her to dust, let alone wash up stray cups and saucers. He wondered vaguely if she might have undergone some sort of conversion. But the next moment she had disappeared from his mind completely, as his thoughts reverted yet again to the current obsessive focus of his life. He had got to do something. Matters could not go on like this. He was beginning to feel physically unwell.

He stood by the window, chewing indecisively at his thumb, and then came to a decision. His attempts at writing a letter had proved useless. He had got to go and see her, and tell her face to face how he felt. He would go round to the palace that very morning. He would wait till he was sure the Bishop was safely out of the way and then he would breast the lion's den, like Daniel going to rescue his beloved. But first, just to fortify himself, he would have a little drink.

He crossed over to the nearest bookshelf, pulled out his concordance to the Bible, and thrust his hand deep into the back. Nothing. His fingers closed on empty space and, surprised, he pulled himself up on tiptoe and tried to peer in. But he was still an inch too short and, annoyed, he pulled over the swivel chair from his desk and clambered precariously up onto the leather seat. The gap yawned at him emptily. Puzzled, he reached forward and felt with his fingers either side, wondering if he had somehow managed inadvertently to push the bottle further along the shelf. But his scrabbling fingers found only dust. A wave of unease swept over Father Goody. This was not good. He was clearly beginning to forget things. Obviously he must already have finished this bottle ... but he could not for the life of him remember when.

He abandoned that hiding place and went to search behind the potted palm that stood in the corner of the room. Again, nothing. Licking his lips, a cold sweat breaking out across his brow, he quickly began a systematic search of the room. Everywhere was empty and then, at last, just as he was beginning to fear he was going mad, he found a half empty bottle of Johnny Walker tucked away behind the fire irons that stood at the side of the grate. 'Thank God!' he muttered, distraught. His thirst had been slowly growing with each disappointment, and was now like an unassuagable frenzy raging inside his head. He could hardly even see straight. Not even bothering with a glass, he unscrewed the top and upended the bottle against his lips. The hot liquid coursed down his throat, exploding on his taste buds like a volcanic eruption. Some tiny shred of remaining sanity told him this was not good, but Father Goody did not care. As the liquid slid down, the terrible, consuming longing receded, and Father Goody collapsed exhausted up against the wall. Clouds of cushioning peace billowed around his feet and he glanced at the bottle in his hand. With surprise, he noted that it was empty. Funny, there could not have been much in it after all. Nothing in life seemed to be fixed today. Dully, Father Goody gave up the effort of trying to understand what was going on, and decided he would go and see Myra straight away. Oh ... and on the way he would stop at the off licence.

Back on the St Prosdocimus estate, in the gloomy light of her small room, Pepper stared with misery at her reflection in the cracked mirror. It was no good. The swelling of her stomach was unmistakable now. Carl, with whom she lived, would go mad when he noticed. He had already started to make comments, but he had put down her increased size simply to a gain in weight. At first, when it had been only her breasts, he had looked at her approvingly and said that the punters liked a bit of tit. But more recently, when her stomach had begun to swell, he had started to say that she must diet, and that fat bints did nobody any good.

Miserably, she sank onto the bed, tears welling in her eyes. Pepper wanted this baby, more than anything else she had ever wanted in her entire life. She had no idea who the father was. Carl used condoms like the punters – he said he didn't want to catch anything – but she supposed one of them must have broken. But what would this baby be like? Coloured, like Carl? Or white, like so many of her clients? Once he found out she knew that Carl would not allow the pregnancy to continue, so she was not likely to see. He said kids got in the way. He would be angry with her for having been so careless. But Pepper, after what had happened those years before, could not bear to lose this tiny life that was a part of her body. She imagined it as a child already. A tiny growing soul taking form, flesh of her flesh and so vulnerable. And a fierce protectiveness sprang up inside her. She had lost the first one, but she felt she would kill for this child, for the right to preserve its life. So she began to explore the idea of running away. She knew she could not just leave, because Carl would come after her. She had seen enough of what he had done to other girls who had crossed him, not to know what he would do. And with her, she knew it would be worse, because he always acted like she was some kind of special trophy, the possession of which gave him added distinction. Of all his girls, Carl paraded her. She did not delude herself that he loved her. She rather suspected that any such emotion was entirely unknown to Carl, but he was fiercely possessive of her, and she knew that he would never willingly let her go.

She stood up, laid a hand either side of her stomach and breathed in, staring hard at her body in the mirror. In her womb she felt the tiny fluttering movement of the baby stirring, like an imprisoned butterfly, reminding her it was still there. But Pepper did not need reminding. 'I won't let him hurt you, baby,' she whispered. 'Honest. I'll die first.'

Again she breathed in, turning sideways. But it was useless. No matter what she did the gently rounded swelling of her stomach, jutting beneath her full tingling breasts, stood out like a peculiarly belligerent assertion of life. 'We've got to get away,' she whispered again, her eyes fixed on the bulge in the mirror. 'We've got to go somewhere safe.'

From the other room the outside door banged noisily. 'Pepper!' yelled Carl. 'Where are you? What y' doing?'

He sounded in a bad mood, and involuntarily she sprang back and began to wriggle into her clothes. A short skirt Carl always said he hated, and a huge sloppy Joe. 'I'm in here,' she shouted back. 'I'm gettin' dressed. I'll be out in a mo.'

The door pushed open and Carl stood there, a dark expression on his face. 'That wanker's had the plods round,' he said. 'They're all over the place like a rash. It's playing hell with business.'

She looked at him coldly. 'Then you shouldn't have trashed the hall, should you. They wouldn't be here if it weren't for that.'

He raised a hand as if to hit her, a furious expression on his face, and then suddenly changed his mind and pulled her roughly towards him instead. It took her by surprise and she half stumbled, falling heavily against his chest. His breath, smelling of garlic and spice, came hot on her cheek. 'That's what I like about you,' he said thickly. 'Your big fucking mouth.' Then his lips closed over hers and his tongue rammed itself into her mouth.

Afterwards, when his lust was spent and he was sprawled dozing on the bed, Pepper pulled herself quietly away and retrieved her scattered clothes. She dreaded him waking up before she was dressed. She did not want him to see her. She pulled on her sweater and stared down at his face. Even in sleep, she thought, he looked vicious, his jaw clenched, a frown between his brows. Before they met, she had not known a human being could harbour so much anger. But Carl did. It lay always just below the cracking surface of his mind, like some terrible volcanic magma, perpetually threatening to erupt and destroy whatever lay in its path. But it would not destroy her baby.

Involuntarily her jaw clenched, and at the same moment he opened his eyes. 'What's up?' he said. 'What y' looking at me like that for?'

She forced herself to smile. 'I was just thinking what a big baby you looked.'

He smiled, pleased, and his hand reached out and twined itself round her bare leg. 'I'm just a pussy cat, I am,' he said. 'A great big pussy cat.'

*

Father Goody, driving rather erratically, arrived at the car park of the Bishop's palace at noon and parked his car diagonally across two spaces. The administrative offices for the diocese were in the left hand wing of the building opposite, and the Bishop and his wife lived in a four-bedroomed flat over the synodical chamber that took up the entire lower floor of the right wing.

His head swimming slightly from the combined effects of more drink and the drive, Father Goody got out of his car and headed purposefully for the iron gate, set in the wall over at the side of the building, and marked private. It led directly to the Bishop's quarters and Father Goody knew that, this way, he could entirely bypass diocesan staff.

The Bishop's palace, which had been built in the days when electricity was still unknown, boasted a large iron bell pull for the flat, that ran up the outside of the building and, when tugged, set up a sonorous clanging from somewhere deep inside. Grinning dementedly (he was feeling rather nervous), Father Goody grasped it firmly in both hands and swung on it like a crazed five-year-old. For all his earlier good intentions, he had entirely forgotten to check whether or not the Bishop was there, but somehow that fact no longer seemed important. What mattered was simply that he see Myra and declare to her his undying love. 'Yoohoo! Myra!' he shrieked, reinforcing the summons of the bell, 'It's me!'

The bell reverberated deep inside and Myra, hearing the commotion

below, came to the window and stared out. The sight that met her eyes
made her grow pale. As luck would have it (for Father Goody at least)
the Bishop was away from home for a couple of days and she was there
on her own. She recognised the principal of Walsingham instantly, of
course, and a flood of terror engulfed her. What on earth was he doing?
She skipped back behind the curtain, praying he had not seen her, and
stared down intently.

Father Goody swung on the bell pull again. It had occurred to him
that his lady love was taking rather a long time to answer, but he felt
certain she was there. He knew it in his bones. 'My ... ra, Oh My ... ra!'
he shouted again, his eyes raking the upper windows.

Across the courtyard a window was flung open and a voice called,
'Will you please be quiet! Some of us are trying to work over here!'
Then the speaker registered who it was causing the row, and there was
an embarrassed pause. 'Can I help you, Father Goody?' called the voice,
more temperately.

Surprised, Father Goody checked and looked round. Could that be
Myra, he wondered. He peered shortsightedly in the direction of the
voice, but it was no good. Somewhere between the car and door his
glasses had slipped down his nose, and he could not see. It did not
occur to him to push them back up.

'Myra?' he shouted hopefully.

Secure in the knowledge that his attention was engaged elsewhere,
Myra crept out from behind her curtain and craned forward, trying to
see what he was going to do.

'Ssh!' admonished the voice opposite. Myra recognised her
husband's secretary. 'No it's not Mrs Higgins. I think she's in the flat ...
If you really *have* to speak to her.'

The voice sounded disapproving and Father Goody frowned. 'Of
course I do,' he said admonishingly. 'I've got something very important
to tell her.'

'Well, if you wait,' hissed back the voice, 'I'm sure she'll be down.
But please be quiet!'

The window banged shut and, in the same instant, Father Goody
looked back up at the flat. Myra stood pinned in the living room
window like a frightened rabbit. 'Myra!' exclaimed Father Goody
joyfully.

Myra winced, but it was no good. She had been seen. Unfortunately
for her, the Bishop's wife was incurably polite. She simply did not have
it in her to be rude. It would no more have occurred to her now to

refuse to respond, than it would to have run stark naked across the cathedral close.

Entirely oblivious of the horror sweeping over his beloved, Father Goody relinquished his hold on the bell pull and waved his arms at her over his head. Myra swallowed. She discovered she really felt quite frightened. Shaking slightly, she pushed open the window and called down, 'What do you want?'

This, to Father Goody, seemed ridiculous. 'I want to see you of course!' he bellowed back.

'Ssh!' said Myra involuntarily, echoing the secretary a moment before.

Father Goody looked crestfallen. 'Am I being too loud, darling?' he mouthed up.

Myra surveyed him. 'I do believe you're drunk,' she said tartly, her temperance background asserting itself.

Father Goody considered this. 'Yes,' he agreed equably. 'You may be right.'

Myra took a grip of herself. 'Then go away,' she said. 'You can't possibly come in. Hubert's not here.' She had been going to add, 'He'll be back tomorrow,' but some residual caution made her bite her lip.

'P ... please,' wheedled Father Goody. 'I'll be very good. I promise.'

Myra lent out of the window. 'Go away!' she said more forcefully.

Father Goody's lower lip jutted. 'No,' he said determinedly. 'I won't ... I want to tell you I love you. I'm going to stay here till you open the door!' And with that he turned his back and flung himself down on the step. 'You can't get out,' his voice floated up. 'Not without coming past me.'

Poor Myra was almost in tears. She had not the slightest idea what to do but, very dimly, she felt this whole horrible situation was somehow her fault. Entirely at a loss and in an effort to force herself to be calm, she went and made a cup of coffee. She wondered whether she ought to phone the police, but dismissed that – the scandal, if it ever came out, would be terrible. And Hubert might be affected too. Then, with a flood of horror, she realised that the diocesan staff opposite already knew. Myra had no illusions. She was perfectly aware of both the amusement and the damage that an incident like this could provoke and she now knew, all too well, that Hubert's position was far from secure.

Half an hour ticked slowly past, during which the coffee grew cold. Myra went again to the window and peered out. Father Goody was still there, his ample posterior wedged firmly against the door. That decided her. She again flung open the window and called down, 'If I see you for five minutes, will you promise to go away?'

Father Goody had just been wondering whether he could forsake his post for ten minutes in order to dash back to the car and have a quick drink, but now he looked up joyfully. 'Of course!' he said, springing to his feet and smiling seraphically. 'I give you my word, on my honour as a gentleman.'

Myra glared at him but said nothing. Two minutes later she withdrew the chain from the door and, with a feeling of nausea, pulled it reluctantly back. Father Goody almost bounded through the gap. 'Myra!' he said delightedly. He gripped her by the shoulders and planted a wet sloppy kiss on her mouth.

'Get off!' said Myra revolted. 'You horrible man. Stop that at once.'

She ruffled herself up like an affronted hen and Father Goody stared at her, chastened. 'Sorry,' he muttered. 'It's just that I'm so pleased to see you.'

Hastily Myra shut the door. 'Come upstairs,' she said icily. 'And tell me what it is you want.'

All the way up the stairs she could smell the whisky fumes flowing in great suffocating waves from his breath. 'Exactly how much have you had to drink?' she said over her shoulder.

Father Goody thought. 'Not much. A little drink before I came out ... and then I stopped off on the way.'

'You shouldn't be driving,' she said disapprovingly.

They arrived in the sitting room and Father Goody stared around. 'I can't get you out of my thoughts,' he said.

Any lingering idea that he was making fun of her disappeared, but now that they were face to face, she felt slightly more in control of the situation. 'Don't be silly,' she said briskly.

'I'm not,' said Father Goody. He turned and looked at her and then, in one quick unexpected movement, flung himself at her feet, clasping her knees. 'It's just that I'm overwhelmed with love for you. I've never felt like this before.'

Myra made one feeble attempt to get away and then resigned herself to the inevitable. It crossed her mind how very undignified her position was, but Father Goody's arms were clamped around her legs in a grip of iron. 'Please control yourself,' she said, at her most prim.

Father Goody looked up at her adoringly. 'Only tell me you feel the same,' he pleaded.

Myra considered what to do. 'Yes, I do,' she said. 'But towards my husband. Not you.'

Father Goody looked as if she had struck him. 'But you can't seriously love that dry stick!'

'Why not?' Myra stared at him frigidly. 'I'll have you know we've been married thirty-two years.'

'Exactly,' said Father Goody triumphantly, as if this proved his point. 'You can't know any better. You're in a rut. But I want to teach you about passion!'

Myra gazed down on the chubby upturned moon face of the principal of Walsingham and felt a shudder of repugnance. His glasses, now back where they ought to be, were slightly askew and his clerical collar, stiff and greasily grey, looked as if it should have been changed days ago. 'I don't think you can teach me anything,' she said frostily.

From his position on the floor, Father Goody stared up at her. The chill in her manner and obvious dislike were finally getting through to him. He glared at her with a growing feeling of rage. 'Do you mean you're spurning me?' he asked incredulously.

'If you want to put it in those terms.'

He sprang to his feet and they glowered at each other. He was not a tall man and Myra was rather large, so that she had the advantage of him now by about an inch. 'You can't do this to me,' he said thickly. 'Leading me on the way you've been doing. You can't just throw me aside now.'

'You're drunk,' she repeated.

'Not so drunk I don't know what you've been doing!'

She seemed not to know what to say, and he took advantage of her momentary confusion to grab her again and pull her towards him. He had no very clear idea what he was going to do, but he dimly thought that if he could arouse in her a similar passion to his own, all her resistance would crumple. He still felt absolutely convinced she was repressing her true feelings. He squashed her to him, and his floppy lips once again sought hers. There ensued a brief and undignified struggle.

'Let go,' panted Myra, trying vainly to push herself away.

Crash. They banged into a small table, and a standard lamp went flying across the room. 'You can't mean it,' gasped Father Goody, ignoring it. 'You've led me on.'

'Never!' spluttered Myra, her voice throbbing with repugnance.

They danced backwards and forwards across the room as he struggled to kiss her, and she struggled to resist. But the outcome was never really in doubt. Myra was a strong woman, and Father Goody was already unsteady from too much drink. With a last triumphant shove, she threw him from her and he staggered back across the room, before crashing into the Jacobean sideboard and falling heavily to the floor. 'Now just get out,' spat Myra, panting. 'And don't ever come here again.'

At that moment the old iron bell clanged out again. Myra cast one more disdainful glance on Father Goody and then, smoothing her hair with a still shaking hand and struggling to control her breathing, she turned and marched down the stairs. 'Yes?' she said imperiously, flinging back the heavy oak door. She felt like she had just fought her way through some Promethean struggle for life and she had won, but when she saw who it was she faltered because there, standing in front of her, a carefully schooled look of concern on his face, stood Nicholas.

'Is everything alright?' he asked. 'Barbara said Father Goody was over here, and that he was in something of a state.' His eyes took in her dishevelled appearance and an expression of not entirely friendly amazement crossed his face.

Myra bristled. She distrusted Nicholas. 'Everything's quite alright, thank you, Nicholas,' she said stiffly.

'*Is* Father Goody here?'

Firm-lipped, she nodded. 'Yes,' she said. 'He is, and I'm afraid he's had rather too much to drink, but the situation's perfectly under control. I'm sure he'll be leaving in a minute.'

Nicholas was thinking rapidly. He had not the faintest idea what to make of this development, but it struck him that to have the principal of Walsingham careering around the city drunk was not a good idea. 'I think I'd better come in,' he said firmly. 'I don't think the Bishop would like you to have to sort this out alone.'

It crossed Myra's mind to protest, but a great wave of fatigue suddenly swept over her. She did not like Nicholas, it was true, but for all her apparent confidence she was still rather apprehensive of what Father Goody might do. In that moment she felt that her husband's chaplain could deal with him far better than she. 'Yes, you're right,' she said wearily, standing back. 'Come in.'

Together they went up the stairs, but Father Goody had taken advantage of the intervening few minutes to clamber to his feet and try to restore the room to some semblance of order. When they came in he was standing over by the fireplace, his hand on the mantlepiece for support, but otherwise looking much the same as ever. The shock of all that had happened had had the effect of temporarily restoring him to his senses.

'I thought I'd just pop over and say hello,' said Nicholas smoothly, his eyes flickering quickly around the room. 'Barbara said you were over here.'

'Barbara?'

'The Bishop's secretary.'

The chaplain came farther into the room. He looked wary and Father Goody stiffened. 'Hrumph! Yes, well,' he said. 'That's very kind, but much as I'd like to stay, I have to go.' He shot a venomous glance at Myra. 'So good to talk to you, Mrs Higgins. After the conference last week.'

This last he added with particular meaning and Myra blushed. 'Well, I shall certainly tell Hubert you called,' she said primly.

He nodded and pulled himself up with dignity. 'Of course.' Then without looking at them, he swept past and through the door. 'Don't bother to see me out,' he called back over his shoulder. 'I can find my own way.'

Myra and Nicholas stared at each other. 'I really don't think he ought to drive,' Myra whispered. 'He was incapable a moment ago.'

Nicholas shrugged helplessly. 'I don't see that I can stop him. He seems alright now.'

Father Goody heard the exchange as he went down the stairs, and a cold feeling of murderous rage seemed suddenly to sweep from out of the room and clamp itself onto him. Never once since the conference had it even remotely occurred to him that Myra would not reciprocate his feelings. He had simply assumed that their love was somehow set in the stars. But as he thought of the violence of her reaction and the strength with which she had thrust him away, he felt he hated her. She had humiliated him.

Father Goody knew nothing of the Christian principle of turning the other cheek. As only hours before he had been consumed with love, now he was consumed with an equally strong desire for revenge. He would teach her, he thought, clambering into his car. He would make her sorry she had dared treat him like that.

17

Bingo took up a discreet position outside Dougal's front door. He had a camera with him, and it was his intention to keep a watch on Dougal over the next few weeks and record any comings and goings. Especially if they involved young women.

Inside, Amanda had just finished putting on her makeup. She stared at herself in the dull glass of the mirror and frowned. She had failed. She had woken twenty minutes ago stiff and cold (the duvet had fallen off in the night) and memory had flooded over her. How could she have been so stupid? She had felt certain Dougal was going to respond. She felt her body had betrayed her.

She gave a final flick with the mascara brush and lurched to her feet, the familiar feeling of sickness grinding through her stomach as she became vertical. Then, shivering slightly, she caught up the duvet and wrapped it closely round her shoulders, trying to decide what to do. It was still quite dark in the sitting room without the light on, and she wondered if she could even now creep upstairs and slip into Dougal's bed, but a sound from the kitchen told her that that plan could not succeed. He was already up. She walked carefully to the door, forcing down the rising tide of vomit, and peered blearily through into the kitchen.

'Good morning,' said Dougal cheerfully, turning and seeing her standing there. 'What would you like for breakfast? Toast? Cereal?'

He had lain awake for most of the night, going over and over the unfairness of the situation in which he now found himself. Nothing seemed to have gone right for the last year and, in a deluge of self-pity, he had imagined himself cast adrift on a small boat in the middle of a dark, hostile sea. At around three o'clock he had begun to talk to God, and had told Him what a rat He was, to allow all this to happen when he had been trying so hard to serve Him. If it had struck Dougal at all that perhaps this was an unwise mode of address to the Almighty, it had not seemed to bother him. In the dark watches of the night he had been beyond caring. It was too much. He was sick of it all. He might just as well give up the priesthood and go and earn a lot of money in the city. Amanda would like that ... and why should he flog his guts out in this hole? And then, after he had ranted on like this for perhaps three-quarters of an hour, a thought had suddenly occurred to him. It had seemed to slide into his mind while he wasn't looking, but the effect was so strong it had been like experiencing a sharp shock. In itself it wasn't a very profound thought, as thoughts went, but suddenly it had occurred to him that the only place he could exist was where he was. He might have displeased God somehow, which was all he could come up with to account for his present joyless situation, but in fact he could no more leave than he could take up drug trafficking or pimping, like Carl. For better or worse, following God was all he wanted to do.

After that he had felt like a stray puppy that has attached itself to some passing pedestrian in the hopes of finding a home and then found itself kicked aside. But he knew that wasn't right either; and then he knew, with blinding certainty, that all he could do was wait. And maybe in that waiting it would be possible to trust too. He was still exploring this when he fell asleep, but the result was that in the morning, when he woke, he felt considerably calmer.

Now, in response to his question, Amanda forced herself to smile. 'No, thanks,' she said, shaking her head. 'Just tea please.' She came farther into the kitchen and hoisted herself inelegantly up onto a stool at the small breakfast bar, the duvet slipping down from her shoulders to reveal one softly rounded breast. Remembering his intentions the previous night, Dougal swallowed and looked away and Amanda, catching the look, pulled a wry face. No, she was definitely not going to succeed here. She took the proffered mug of tea and decided that she would call Nicholas.

When she emerged an hour later she was still looking slightly ropy, but she had showered and combed her hair, and at least felt able to face the world. Bingo, hearing the door open, jerked smartly to attention and waited to see who would come out. As Amanda stepped out onto the narrow path, his eyes almost fell out. This was even better than he had hoped. He had rather thought he might catch a few girls going in, but he had never once imagined he might catch someone, who had clearly spent the night there, coming out. He pulled up the camera and began to click furiously. Behind Amanda, Dougal came out carrying a small leopardskin overnight bag. Bingo gave a crow of triumph, and photographed him too. With what Maisie (who was clearly besotted with the handsome young vicar) had already told him, and now this, he could hardly believe his luck. Dougal was clearly a sex maniac of the worst kind, who had managed to come up with a scheme that gave him unrestricted licence to indulge his lust, while maintaining a facade of godliness. Bingo felt he knew the type all too well. He began to frame sentences for the exposé that was taking shape in his mind.

At the gate Dougal glanced around furtively and then gave Amanda a quick peck on the cheek. He hated public displays of emotion. Amanda, rattled by his reticence, pulled him to her and kissed him lingeringly on the mouth. Bingo clicked the camera again. 'See you then,' said Dougal, when he at last managed to extricate himself.

Amanda pouted. 'Give me my keys then,' she said wearily, holding out her hand. 'You took them last night. Remember?'

Dougal looked surprised. 'Did I? Oh yes.' He fished in his pocket, and then slipped them into her outstretched hand.

'Christ!' breathed Bingo. 'I don't believe this, he's paying her.' A look of shock settled on his face.

*

At around the same time, Oswald paid a quick visit to the supermarket and bought three bottles of whisky. He had spent a considerable amount of time over the last few days trying to work out what to do, and it had become increasingly obvious to him that the total but contained discrediting of Father Goody would serve his ends extremely well. The problem, however, was how to accomplish this? The Myra letters in his possession were of course interesting, but he was not absolutely certain who the woman in question was; nor even if she actually existed, or was simply a product of the principal's fevered imagination. There was nothing actually to tie her to the Bishop's wife, apart from the name, and if he were to make an unsubstantiated allegation now, which subsequently proved to be wrong, the effects might be appalling. And it was even conceivable that Oswald might yet find himself a guest at Father Goody's wedding, with everyone saying how sweet it was, and how romantic ... and how unexpected!

Oswald shuddered with repugnance. That eventuality, he told himself, had to be avoided at all costs. But as he toyed with various schemes it occurred to him that the most constructive thing he could do would be to encourage Father Goody's excessive drinking. He therefore bought the largest bottles he could find, and carried them back to his rooms in college in a plain carrier bag. Retrieving one, and having first made sure there was no one about, he tiptoed down Walsingham's deserted corridors to the principal's study. 'Come in!' barked Father Goody in response to his knock.

Oswald slid in through the door, clutching the bottle to his chest. Behind his thick glasses, Father Goody's piggy little eyes gleamed. 'Hello,' he said. 'What's that you've got there?'

Oswald held out the bottle like some sort of sacrificial gift. 'It's for you, Tim,' he said. 'I just wanted to express my appreciation.'

Unable to help himself, Father Goody licked his lips. 'What for?' he asked suspiciously.

Oswald was ready for this. 'I just wanted to say how very much I value all that you're doing for the college and, in particular, how you've been encouraging us all lately to take on more responsibility.'

'Have I?' said Father Goody, genuinely puzzled.

'Of course you have.' Oswald advanced further into the room. 'And I think it's very big of you. The mark of a man of stature.'

'Oh,' said Father Goody. 'I see.'

His eyes were still fixed hungrily on the bottle and, feeling obscurely pleased, Oswald thrust it towards him. 'I know you like a good whisky, Tim. So I thought you might enjoy this.'

Father Goody was already reaching forward to take it. It was entirely true that he had bought another couple of bottles from the off licence on his way to visit Myra, but he had been so upset by all that had happened that they were now almost completely empty. 'Very good of you, I'm sure,' he mumbled. 'Very thoughtful.' Without thinking he began to unscrew the cap, then he suddenly recollected himself. 'Can I offer you a small one, Oswald?'

'No, no, no.' Oswald's face puckered in self-deprecation and he held up a hand. 'I don't, you know. Strictly teetotal.'

'Really?' Father Goody regarded him blearily. 'Don't know what you're missing, if you ask me. But thanks anyway.'

'Don't mention it.' Oswald was already moving towards the door. 'I do hope you enjoy it,' he added, half turning as his hand closed over the knob. He gave an oily smile and disappeared.

Father Goody watched his exit, a puzzled expression on his face. He disliked that slimy little toad, always had done. There was something you couldn't quite trust about the man. Still, it was good of him to bring the whisky. He was quite right. He would enjoy it. Abandoning the conundrum of Oswald's motives, Father Goody poured himself a large tumbler full and then lay back in his chair, savouring the fiery taste as it slid over his tongue. Without moving he allowed the familiar explosion of heat to course through his veins, restoring him to life and then, very deliberately, picked up the phone and dialled the number for the Bishop's flat. It was time to put into operation his plan of revenge.

*

Not far away, Pepper went to see Maisie. 'Can I talk to you?' she asked.

She had gone round to Maisie's small flat which, as ever, looked as if a bomb had hit it. But, for once, she found Maisie trying to clean it up. Maisie had been rather inspired by the transformation to the church hall. It was, however, proving rather harder than she had anticipated and she was glad of a chance to break off. 'Course,' she said, abandoning the task thankfully and flinging herself down on the battered sofa. 'Wot's up? Want a coffee?'

Pepper shook her head. 'No,' she said, 'I don't feel too good.'

Maisie stared at her surprised. For some time now she had been thinking that Pepper was not her usual self. For one thing, the other girl was obviously putting on weight. And a small unwelcome suspicion had begun to form at the back of Maisie's mind. Now she asked bluntly, 'Are ye up the duff, or wot?'

Pepper nodded, her shoulders slumping.

'How long?'

'Three and a half months.'

Maisie regarded her, her face inscrutable. They were an unlikely combination, but they were good friends, and Maisie especially had tried to look out for the younger girl. 'Wot y' goin to do about it then?' she asked at last.

If it were possible Pepper's shoulders drooped even more. 'I don't know,' she said mournfully, sinking down onto the battered armchair opposite. 'It's doin' me 'ead in.'

'Does Carl know?'

'Course not!' The words were out of Pepper's mouth before she could stop herself and her head jerked up in terror. 'Don't tell 'im. He'll kill me when he finds out.'

Maisie did not attempt to argue. She knew that Pepper was right, so instead she rose to her feet and went and put on the kettle. 'Sure you don't want anything?' she asked again, taking a couple of mugs down from the shelf. 'I've got tea.'

Pepper shook her head. 'No,' she said again. 'I can't drink. Not at the moment.'

Maisie accepted this, thoughtfully spooning some coffee into a mug and chewing her lip, an expression of intense concentration on her face. 'Y'd better get rid of it then,' she said finally.

A small sound made her spin round. Pepper had slumped forward in the chair, head on hands, and her shoulders were shaking uncontrollably. 'I can't, Maisie,' she sobbed. 'That's why I've come to see you. I don't want to. I really want this baby.'

Maisie stared at her in complete and utter astonishment. 'Ye're mad,' she said finally. 'Y' can't 'ave it. Y' know that. Wot d'y' want it for anyway?'

As if her words held some kind of terrible power, Pepper stopped and looked up, her eyes haggard and unnaturally large in her pale face. With the red curls tumbling over her shoulders she looked like some kind of bruised angel, fallen out of heaven. 'I want it because it's mine,' she said fiercely. 'It's not anybody else's. It belongs to me.' She paused, and then said more quietly, 'And there's nobody else to care for it.'

Maisie looked back at her, perturbed. She knew that accidents happened. It had happened once to her too. But the St Prosdocimus estate was no place to bring up a baby. Especially if you worked the streets. And especially if you had Carl breathing down your neck. She flicked off the switch for the kettle and went and knelt beside Pepper, taking her hands gently in her own and peering intently up into her face. 'Carl won't let y' have it,' she said. 'Y' know that.'

She was rewarded by a fresh paroxysm of sobs. 'I know,' brought out Pepper. 'But don't you see? That's why I've got to have it ... That's why I've got to get away. This baby's my hope.'

Maisie bit her lip, at a total loss what to do. She knew nothing of Pepper's background. They none of them tended to talk about their past lives, but she had always felt, deep down, that Pepper did not quite belong. None of them belonged, of course. They would not be there if they did, but with Pepper ... Maisie felt it was almost as if she had been exiled. Maisie could not define it more clearly. For herself, she had ended up on the streets because there had been nowhere else to go. Once her mother had been sectioned, it had been either that or starve. And she had not felt particularly bitter about it. There were far worse ways of earning a living. And besides, she fully intended, when she had got some money together, to buy a proper flat somewhere and maybe get some training and make a fresh start. But with Pepper it was different. Somewhere deep inside there was a scarring, and she gave the impression of her eyes always being focussed on something else. Fixed on some distant, nebulous land, that only she could see, but to which she did not want to return. She puzzled Maisie. ''E won't let y' go,' she repeated.

Pepper rose to her feet. 'I know,' she said. She crossed restlessly to the window and stared sightlessly out onto the street below. 'That's why I've come to see you. I want your help.'

A cold feeling of dread stole over Maisie. 'Wot d'y' mean?'

The silence in the room was almost tangible. 'I ... It's just ...' And then Pepper suddenly spun back round, a wild expression of hope on her face. 'Maisie,' she said breathlessly, 'please help me get away. If there's anyone that can do it, it's you.'

Maisie was appalled. Carl was not actually her pimp. In fact, she was almost unique amongst the girls in that she did not have one, but her position was precarious for all that – perhaps even because of that – and she was still scared of him. If she helped Pepper now and Carl found out, her own chances, she knew, would be minimal. He would mark her at the very least, as an object lesson to the others. Almost unconsciously, her thoughts went back to her own last reading of the cards. Trouble and loss, that was what she had seen. And change. Perhaps it was this ... But even so ... Taking a deep breath, she raised her hands and pressed them either side of her face. 'Y'r askin a hell of a lot,' she said.

'Please, Maisie,' pleaded Pepper. 'You're the only hope I've got.'

But Maisie felt she couldn't just commit herself like that. There were so many implications. They might both end up dead. 'Have y' anywhere t' go?'

Her eyes fixed on her, Pepper shook her head. 'Not yet.'

''Ow about family?'

But this was forbidden ground. 'No,' said Pepper harshly. She swung away, staring once more out of the window. 'There's no one.'

Maisie shrugged helplessly. This conversation, she felt, was going nowhere very fast. 'Then wot y' sayin?' she asked plaintively. 'Wot d'y' expect me to do?'

Again Pepper turned. 'Will you help me?' she asked insistently, her voice low.

Maisie knew she was going to live to regret this, but she also felt, obscurely, that she had no choice. Pepper was a friend. 'Yeah,' she said wearily. 'Go on. I'll 'elp.'

The look of relief that burst over Pepper's face was like the sudden eruption of the sun through black banks of massed cloud. 'Really?'

'Yeah.' Maisie nodded. 'I'll do what I can... And pray to God Carl doesn't find out!'

They began to discuss possible means of escape. Pepper rather fancied going to somewhere very remote in Scotland. For the last couple of months, she confided, in fact ever since she had known for certain she was pregnant, she had been salting away as much of her earnings as she could without Carl becoming suspicious. She had increased her charges, she whispered, and then she had placed all the extra in a post office account. It was not a fortune, but she had enough at least to buy herself a train ticket and then to pay for somewhere to live until the baby was born. The big problem, however, was keeping Carl occupied while she actually made her escape and this, she said, was where Maisie came in.

Maisie did not need to be told that Carl watched Pepper like a hawk. He had a whole string of girls but his vigilance, with regard to her, was almost a joke. No one messed with Pepper for fear of what Carl might do, but equally, anyone who saw her go would almost certainly tell him. So her disappearance would have to be sudden and absolutely complete, and there must be no trail left that he could follow.

At this point in the conversation Maisie knit her brows, and then insisted on reading Pepper's cards. 'We need some 'elp 'ere,' she explained when Pepper had tried to protest there was no time.

She began to lay them out carefully. She discovered death by drowning (which, in the circumstances, she didn't feel was particularly helpful) and the turmoil of change. But then, as she turned over the last card, she gave a small squeal of excitement. 'No, it'll be alright,' she said excitedly. 'Look.' She laid a trembling finger on the figure staring up at them. 'It means good fortune, this. It'll come about as a result of unexpected change. You'll be okay. I'm sure.'

Pepper stared at her. 'I'm not sure I believe all this crap, Maisie,' she said hollowly. 'Can't we just forget it and get on? It worries me. I get a bad feeling.'

But Maisie was jubilant. 'That's just Carl, that is,' she said. ''E's enough to give anyone the willies.'

In the end they decided to bide their time till Carl went away on one of his sporadic jaunts. He tended to do this every three or four weeks, and would be absent for a couple of days. He never said when or where he was going, and what he did was a mystery, but when he returned he was usually in a good mood and would then swagger round the streets like some minor potentate who has just made some particularly advantageous treaty. Other times, he would be angry and would lash out blindly at whoever was unfortunate enough to cross his path. But more usually, he seemed pleased.

The last time he had been away on one of these trips had been two weeks ago. If he were to go away again soon, Pepper insisted, it would be ideal. She knew she could not leave it for much longer. If Maisie had guessed her pregnancy, it would not be long before others began to notice too, and then inevitably someone would mention it to Carl. If he did not realise for himself first. But if he were to go away within the next two weeks then, with Maisie's help, she might yet pull it off, and by the time he got back she would be long gone ... and safe.

They arranged for Pepper to start bringing her clothes over to Maisie's, and Maisie agreed to provide a case so that, when the opportunity did arise, Pepper would be all ready to go. Maisie also said that she would throw in a further five hundred quid, which was all her savings so far. 'Don't be daft!' she said, when Pepper attempted to demur. 'Y' can pay me back later. When y've got settled. Who knows? Maybe I could even come and live with y'!'

Trembling, Pepper returned to her own flat and found Carl still sprawled on the bed, but with a six pack beside him now and a vacant expression on his face from too much dope. Carl did not use the crack he supplied but he enjoyed weed. She stared at him with the merest shadow of contempt. Later, when she went out onto the street, she felt a wild hope spring into life. Soon, very soon now, she promised herself, she would be free.

18

Bingo gave Nicholas a ring. 'I say,' he said, 'that tip you gave me was good. That Sampratt chap's got women all over the shop.'

'Has he?' said Nicholas, surprised. His estimation of Dougal rose slightly.

'Yes,' affirmed Bingo. 'I think we're really on to something here. He's knocking women off right, left and centre.'

'Good God,' said Nicholas.

'I'm just gathering more material at the moment,' went on Bingo blithely. 'I want the full picture. But I reckon the tabloids are going to jump at it. We could be talking defrocking here.'

Nicholas was stunned. 'Are you sure you've got the right vicar?'

'Yes, of course,' said Bingo. *The Vicar with the Mission!* It should hit the papers next week.' He rang off.

Nicholas replaced the phone with a feeling of shock. It was entirely true that when he had contacted Bingo he had hoped to cause Dougal some problems. He knew that everyone had skeletons tucked away at the back of their wardrobes. But never, in his wildest imagining, had it seriously occurred to him that Dougal might really be exploiting his position for the purposes of satisfying his unbridled lust. 'Filthy sod!' he muttered disbelievingly. 'Just goes to show, you can't trust anyone these days.'

The thought reminded him that he had not yet broached the subject of Father Goody's extraordinary behaviour to the Bishop. This was becoming a matter of some urgency, as reports were filtering in almost daily of some decidedly odd goings-on at Walsingham. Only that morning he had intercepted an extremely disturbing report from Oswald Pettifence, the vice-principal and liturgy tutor, hinting that for most of the time Father Goody was not only drunk, but incapable. The letter was couched in tones of concern, but Nicholas was seriously alarmed. If it should come before the Bishop, he rather suspected that the latter would simply activate his earlier threat and close down the college out of hand. Nicholas was not himself an Anglo-Catholic, and didn't care tuppence for the maintenance of their traditions, but the removal of the college's influence from the diocese would, he thought, given the inclinations of the Bishop, allow for a total stranglehold by the evangelicals. Steadfastly committed to liberalism and the maintenance of moderate belief, Nicholas thought that this was a very bad idea. It was for this same reason that he had not mentioned to the Bishop Father Goody's bizarre attack upon his wife. He had not actually spoken about it to Myra, but he strongly suspected from her demeanour that hell would have to freeze over before she could be brought to raise the subject. Nicholas was not at all sure what was going on but he rather imagined that he had broken in upon a lovers' quarrel. Better then, possibly, for the Bishop not to know, if the knowledge might destabilise Carbery's precious balance of churchmanship.

The detailed letter from Pettifence, however, was rather more of a problem. If Nicholas withheld it, he would be guilty of actively suppressing damaging information, which, if it were subsequently to come to light, would lead to serious problems for himself. On the other hand, if nothing at all were done, it could well result in a potentially scandalous situation going unchecked. Nicholas frowned. The Bishop had already made it clear that he did not want there to be any fresh scandal arising within the diocese – and heaven only knew what he was going to say when the news about Sampratt broke. In an agony of indecision, the chaplain chewed the tip of his thumb, trying to work out exactly what to do.

At the same instant, the intercom buzzed loudly on his desk and the Bishop's disembodied voice said, 'Nicholas, come in here please. And bring the file on clergy deployment within the diocese.'

Nicholas scowled, but obediently rose to his feet. He made no attempt to get the file, but simply shrugged open the door and pushed his way in. 'It's not here at the moment,' he said flatly. 'The Education Officer's got it.'

Bishop Hubert frowned. 'May I ask why?'

The look Nicholas cast on him seemed to imply that the answer would have been obvious to an intellectually challenged gorilla, and the

Bishop's frown grew. 'Because,' said the chaplain sulkily, 'you said that you wanted a detailed report on areas of clergy expertise.'

'But that was weeks ago,' protested the Bishop.

In response, Nicholas gave a thin smile. Quite, his expression seemed to say, and just look how you're wasting all of our time! 'As you know,' he said aloud, 'these things take time. I believe five secretaries are at the moment attempting to co-ordinate the work areas of industrial chaplains with specified injury units attaching to the medical chaplaincies.'

The Bishop looked puzzled. He opened his mouth as if to say something, and then shut it again, slightly shaking his head. 'Oh, never mind,' he said wearily. 'Just do your best to get it back as soon as possible. We're never going to get anything done at this rate.'

He waved a hand to Nicholas to sit down and the chaplain, as he leant forward, smiled grimly. He agreed. 'Nicholas,' went on the Bishop, 'I want to know the details for my visit to St Prosdocimus. I've got Thursday down here, but no one's briefed me yet.'

Nicholas blinked. He had forgotten the Bishop's visit. 'Ah yes,' he said, clearing his throat. 'I'm afraid there's been a bit of a hiccup on that front. Sampratt phoned a couple of days ago to say that the church hall had been broken into and wrecked. He asked if it would be possible to put off the visit for a week, so I rescheduled it for next Friday.'

The Bishop looked incredulous. 'But why didn't you tell me about this before?' he demanded.

Nicholas winced but, try as he might, he could think of no very good reason at all, apart from his intense dislike of imparting information of any kind to his superior. 'It must have just slipped my mind,' he said lamely.

The Bishop looked at him. 'It seems to me,' he remarked acidly, 'that quite a lot of things seem to be doing that these days.' He laid a sheet of paper in front of Nicholas on the desk. 'Did this slip your mind too?'

Nicholas stared at the paper, and realised he was looking at a copy of heavily amended work rostas for diocesan administrative staff, with remuneration ratings attached. A copy that he had omitted to show the Bishop. 'Ah,' he said carefully. 'I've been meaning to talk to you about that.' He blushed.

Bishop Hubert looked cross. He had begun to realise that everything he did seemed to be blocked. He could not make up his mind whether it was rampant inefficiency on the part of his staff or deliberate malice but, whatever the cause, he was beginning to think that the diocese had a life of its own. His being in charge was a complete illusion. 'I do think I should perhaps have been a party to this,' he said petulantly.

Nicholas swallowed. 'Well, of course, Bishop, if you want to be involved in such detail.' His tone implied that no one in their right mind would want to have to deal with this kind of thing. 'But I'd rather thought you'd be too busy to want to get bogged down in all this administrative stuff.'

'But it's precisely this kind of thing that's essential to the smooth and happy running of the diocese,' complained the Bishop. 'Of course I'm interested.' He fixed Nicholas with a grim stare. 'And if you don't mind my saying, I really do think you're taking far too much upon yourself. Arrangement of staff hours and employment conditions is entirely outside your remit!'

The two men glared at each other and, in face of the Bishop's silence, Nicholas squirmed. 'I'm sorry,' he said at last, stiffly. But his tone did not sound very sorry.

'Is there anything else I should know about?' enquired the Bishop. 'Anything else perhaps that I won't be interested in?'

Nicholas stared down at his shoes. He could think of several things, but none that he was about to share with the Bishop. 'No, of course not,' he said gruffly.

The Bishop stared at him for a moment longer. It was becoming increasingly clear to him that Nicholas was not to be trusted but, short of sacking him, he felt completely baffled as to how to deal with him. He wondered if he ought to go through all the files, but that would be extremely hard to arrange and would arouse comment, and as yet the Bishop was not sure enough of his ground. He sighed. He was beginning to realise it was no easy thing to run a diocese, especially when those under him did not simply fail to support him, but were actively working against him. The Bishop looked at his chaplain with distaste. Unfair as it was, he realised he was going to have to repent over his feelings towards Nicholas. 'Tell me more about what's happened over at St Prosdocimus,' he said heavily.

*

Over at the church in question Regina and Eliston were busily trying to concoct a plan to repair the damage to the church hall. Regina was actually feeling quite inordinately guilty. Ever since she had first confided to Dougal that St Prosdocimus was not insured, she had felt as if all that had happened was somehow her fault. The sight of his worried face and distracted expression, as he had hovered uncertainly while the police conducted their forensic examination, had served only to intensify these feelings. Now, when they had gone and she was once again washing down the woodwork, she found herself wondering if they could redecorate the hall without his knowledge, as a surprise.

'It no good, Eliston,' she declared firmly, slapping a wet cloth onto the door she had been vainly scrubbing. 'Dougal can't be expected to sort all this out by himself. He's our pastor. We got to help him.'

Eliston grunted, but this was enough for Regina to interpret as assent. 'You and I both voted for no insurance after de last vicar left,' she said firmly, sitting back on her heels and staring at him, a martial light in her eye. 'So it our responsibility.'

Eliston made to protest. 'But that was because we didn't have no money.'

'So ... o? I know dat!' Regina's ample bosom swelled. 'But it up to us now to find a way out of dis mess. Poor Dougal. He out of his mind wid worry.'

Eliston looked alarmed. He had grown up with Regina, and been bullied by her for the last sixty years, but he knew better than to try and dissuade her when that light was in her eyes. 'So what you want us to do?' he asked, in turn stopping and sitting back on his heels.

Regina stared at him consideringly. 'We ... ll,' she began. Eliston swallowed. 'Correct me if I'm wrong, but didn't you used to be a painter and decorator?'

Eliston almost collapsed. 'But Regina,' he spluttered, 'that was years ago. I bin retired ten years.' She looked unconvinced and he added plaintively, 'Besides, I had a knee injury. That was why I had to stop work.'

Regina looked down at his knees. 'Dey don't look too bad to me,' she announced.

'I don't use them so much!' Eliston was beginning to feel seriously worried. It was not that he didn't want to help. Neither was he afraid of a bit of hard work. But painting the hall went, he felt, far beyond the order of 'hard work'. It looked as if it would be extremely difficult and what he was trying to point out to Regina was true. He was old, and feeling the full weight of his years. He no longer felt he had it in him to clamber up ladders and along scaffolding, which was what they would need. 'No,' he said. 'I can't!'

The determined light in Regina's eye grew. 'My strength is made perfect in weakness,' she announced. 'Dat what de good book say.

Besides, you ain't so old. You six months younger dan me.'

'Oh Regina!' wailed Eliston.

'Your grandson could help you,' went on Regina reflectively. Eliston felt she had forgotten him. He raised a feeble hand in protest, but he had been right the first time. She was not looking. 'He good boy,' went on Regina. 'He always say he want to help. He could come wid his friends. And then there's Albert and ...'

Eliston cast round in his mind desperately, and then pulled out what he felt certain was a trump card. 'But we ain't got no paint!' he exploded triumphantly. He did not like doing this to Regina, but matters were clearly getting out of hand and something had to be done. 'This all pie in de sky, woman,' he said loftily. 'Ain't no good you making all these plans. We can't paint it wid air.'

But the effect of his words was not quite what Eliston had intended, because Regina obviously took his sudden switch of tack as agreement ... if she could provide the materials. 'Don't you worry 'bout dat,' she said, swallowing determinedly. 'De Lord, He provide. You just get everyone together!'

Eliston had a terrible feeling he was doomed. There was simply no arguing with Regina when she got into one of these moods. He comforted himself with the thought that there was no possible way she could get the paint. But all the same he felt a bit scared and, as she rose to her feet and headed, bristling with purpose, towards the kitchen, he muttered under his breath, 'Lord, you can't really want me to go up ladders. Not at my age!'

Later that afternoon, Regina donned her best coat and hat and set off for The Roxburgh, Carbery's biggest hotel. She had been passing on the bus a couple of days before, and had noticed that they had the decorators in. A large sign up outside had proclaimed, 'Roxburgh Hotels Group. Major refurbishment programme.' Then in smaller letters underneath had been written, 'The management would like to apologise to patrons for any inconvenience, but are sure that the end result will greatly add to the comfort of their stay.'

At the time Regina had snorted contemptuously. She disapproved of squandering the world's precious resources on refurbishing places that quite patently did not need it. But as she stared indignantly at the placard, a still small voice had seemed to whisper to her, 'Go and see them.'

Regina had gone rigid with surprise, and then stared at the sign more closely. 'What? Here, Lord?' she had breathed. There had been no more words, but she had felt the slightest of breezes on her old cheek, like the brush of a hand. 'I can't go in dere, Lord,' she had protested. But as the bus groaned and began to pull away she had found her eyes once more drawn to the sign, and then her gaze had drifted across to the huge entrance. At that moment the uniformed doorman had emerged and bowed deferentially to a man and woman, who had glided elegantly past him down the red carpet that covered the sweeping steps and clambered into a waiting Rolls. She had seen the man slip the doorman a tip as he held open the door, and then the doorman had stood back and just touched the edge of his cap. Looking at this icon of rarified gentility, Regina had felt a flood of pure terror. There was no way this exalted personage would ever let *her* past. She could not give him a tip.

However, the words would not go away and ever since they had been gnawing away at her. It had crossed her mind that she was being unfaithful and that her lack of response demonstrated a want of faith. Then she had begun to wonder if her disobedience might not have lost St Prosdocimus some wonderful opportunity and it was even now too late. That had filled her with dread, and she had got down on her knees and begged the Lord to forgive her her rebellion. But still the words would not go away and so that morning she had determined that, cost her what it would, she would put them to the test. She would brave that terrifying doorman and enter the sumptuous den.

As she arrived The Roxburgh was in something of a state. A fresh consignment of wallpaper, paint and primer had been delivered only half an hour ago. Only it had turned out to be the wrong paint. A noisy argument, that threatened at any moment to degenerate into a fight, had immediately erupted between the suppliers and the firm of decorators carrying out the refurbishment work. It had become so bad that the doorman, who was, as Regina had previously noticed, a large man, had been summoned away from his post to try and deal with it. When Regina arrived, therefore, the coast was clear and she crept up the steps and walked fearfully in, without anyone noticing.

In the foyer she found a scene of complete chaos. The suppliers had dumped all the materials in a heap on a dustsheet in the middle of the floor. The decorators, who had been burning off paint from the long sweep of the curving stairs, had gathered round indignantly and started to remonstrate noisily with the deliverymen. They in turn had begun to fling arms about and shout at whoever could be bothered to listen that they had brought what they had been given, and that it wasn't anything to do with them! Furthermore, if anyone wanted them to take it all away, they'd want paying again. One of the decorators had then angrily flicked the driver in the face with a paintbrush dipped in emulsion and it was at this point that the two had flown at each other. The doorman, who had been dragged in by the frightened receptionist, had then launched himself at the pair, and an unseemly scuffle had erupted.

Regina walked nervously in just as the manager ran down the stairs, gesticulating wildly and shouting for them all to stop 'Immediately!' Waiters appeared, drawn by the commotion and then, as the protagonists were finally pulled apart, Regina sidled fearfully around the imposing mahogany reception desk and took up a position on the far side of the vestibule, against the wall.

'It ain't my fault,' repeated the deliveryman furiously, the paint that was dripping from his face giving him the look of a Red Indian all set for war.

The manager glanced at the drips falling on the carpet, shuddered, and closed his eyes. 'Please stop dripping immediately,' he said.

The deliveryman gave him an aggrieved look, but obediently stepped onto the dust sheet, wiping his face with the back of his arm. 'Look what he's bleedin' done to me!' he protested.

The manager ignored him. 'Antony,' he said frigidly, staring at the decorator who had been involved in the fracas, 'what exactly is the problem?'

Antony pointed indignantly at the paint. 'It's the wrong colour for a start,' he said. 'And they've brought too much. They've even brought emulsion, for heaven's sakes! I don't know what they can be thinking of.'

The driver pulled out his docket. 'It's all down here,' he said furiously, jabbing at the paper with his finger. 'See! Twenty-four tins of apricot emulsion, fifteen of dawn blush, shade, hint of green, and fifty-two tins of quick drying gloss.'

'Quick drying gloss!' exploded the enraged decorator, as if this was adding insult to injury. 'Quick drying! We're not using that stuff in here!'

'Why not?' demanded the driver belligerently, again squaring up to him. 'What's wrong with it?'

The frightened receptionist shrieked and the manager almost danced in between them, planting himself physically in the way. 'Stop this at once!' he bellowed, his voice throbbing with anger. 'Your fighting is hardly going to settle the problem.' He tweaked the docket from the driver's hand and looked at it disdainfully. 'This is not our order,' he said.

'It says it is,' insisted the driver.

This fact was irrefutable, because the sheet had 'The Roxburgh Hotel' stamped in large letters across the top. The manager looked slightly baffled. 'Nevertheless,' he said, 'Antony is quite right. We did not order these things. I signed the forms myself and I remember.'

Regina, standing there at the side of the foyer, felt her eyes widen with surprise. She had always thought the church hall would look rather nice painted apricot, and she thought that a hint of green combined with it would look really good. Without thinking, she stepped forward. 'I know somewhere dat could use dat,' she said.

Her voice was not particularly loud (she was feeling too nervous for that) but, all the same, the effect of her words was electric. Becoming aware of her presence for the first time, they all spun round and looked at her, and the tips of the doorman's ears went pink.

Regina swallowed, and her chin lifted defiantly. 'We could use that paint,' she repeated, 'to redecorate our church hall.'

She was not sure what she expected, but she saw a slight frown cross the manager's face. 'Who are you?' he asked. 'And what's this about a church hall?'

His tone was not unkind, and Regina took courage. 'St Prosdocimus,' she said. 'I'm Regina de Baptista. I'm churchwarden there, and our hall was wrecked by vandals a few days ago. We can't use it no more.'

A look of interest settled over the manager's face. 'St Prosdocimus,' he echoed. 'I've heard of that, haven't I? Do you mean St Prosdocimus the Inferior?'

'It's that place with the drop-in centre for street girls and drug addicts,' mentioned the receptionist helpfully. 'It was on the agenda at the Board meeting last week. They've got that young priest, Dougal Sampratt, down there.'

To Regina, this sounded vaguely encouraging.

The manager stared at her. 'Really?' A puzzled frown crossed his brow. 'You say you could use this paint?'

Regina nodded. 'We not got no insurance, see,' she said, in a rush. 'But the place, it been trashed. We have to close down the centre if we can't do it up.'

To her complete and utter amazement, a slow smile broke out across the face of the man standing in front of her. It was so unexpected that for a second she gaped at him, wondering if he was laughing at her, but then she glanced round at the others and saw that some of them were smiling too, but in slightly mystified encouragement, not mockery. 'That's very, very interesting,' said the manager slowly.

'Why?' asked Regina.

The manager's smile grew. 'Because we were talking at our last board meeting about making a donation next quarter in support of your work down there.' Regina still looked blank and he explained gently, 'We regularly give to charity, and when we read in the press about the conditions over on the estate, and what your vicar was trying to do, we felt he ought to be helped. The directors all voted for the St Prosdocimus centre to be included on our list.'

Regina swallowed. She could hardly believe her ears. If what this intimidating looking man was saying was true, then their immediate financial problems might well be solved. 'Hallelujah!' she breathed, an answering beam breaking out across her own face. 'De Lord be praised.' She almost felt a loud chorus coming on, but she restrained herself. Something told her that this might be going a bit too far and the last thing she wanted to do was alienate any possible benefactors. So instead she took her courage in both hands and said, 'If yo goin' to give us some money anyways, why not give us de paint too?'

The manager stared at her a second longer and then burst out laughing. 'Tell me,' he said, when he had recovered himself, 'what on earth made you come to us today?'

Regina shrugged helplessly. 'I saw yo' sign a few days ago,' she said. 'An' de Lord, He tell me to come and ask you. So I did.'

She was aware of the naked curiosity now on the faces of those standing around. Even Antony and the deliveryman appeared temporarily to have forgotten their differences. But the manager merely nodded. 'Well then,' he said, 'if the Lord told you to come, perhaps we'd better see what we can do.'

In an amazingly short space of time, and following a series of phone calls to the suppliers, the managing director and the hotel's accountant, Regina found herself the proud possessor of all the wrongly delivered paint. What's more, the driver had agreed to re-load it and take it over to St Prosdocimus. Then the manager said, 'How are you going to do it? It's one thing to have all the paint, but church halls tend to be very big and quite difficult if you're not used to it. Have you got enough manpower?'

Regina was about to say, 'Of course!' but then honesty suddenly re-asserted itself and she hung her head. 'I'm not sure,' she confessed.

The manager stared at her. 'Are you trying to tell me you could use some more help?'

She looked at him.

'Uum, I see.' He looked round. 'Antony!' The decorator came over, blow torch in hand. 'Do you think we might be able to spare any help for this lady?'

Antony looked dubious. He thought it a splendid thing for The Roxburgh to support charity, but he was not too keen on being asked to shoulder some of the burden himself. 'Oh, I'm not sure,' he began, shaking his head. 'It would be a big job, and I daren't get behind with the schedule here.'

The manager turned back to Regina. 'Do you have any help at all?' he asked.

Regina nodded vigorously. 'Eliston, de other churchwarden, he was a decorator before he retired, an' he say he help. An' den dere's his grandson, and one or two others ...'

At that point one of Antony's subordinates, who was still busily scraping away at the stairs, looked up and called, 'I don't mind helping, guv. I'd like to.'

'You'd have to do it on your own time then,' said Antony huffily. 'This contract can't afford for you just to take off.'

The young man rose to his feet. 'I don't mind,' he said cheerily. 'I'm sure it wouldn't take that long. I'll bet Pete over there, and Andy, wouldn't mind giving a hand too. We could do it in a weekend.'

The manager turned back to Regina, smiling broadly. 'There you are then,' he said, 'it looks like you've got some help after all.' And then he took the young man aside and said, 'Tell you what, Dave, you and the others do this and I'll give you sixty quid between you. It's not much I know, for a weekend's work, but it's something.'

Antony looked even crosser, but Dave's face split in a huge grin. 'Great,' he said. 'Thanks, but there's no need. We've been talking about that place, and we think it's great too.'

'Then I'll give the money to you,' said the manager, turning back to Regina. 'Look on it as another donation to the work.'

19

Darkness was just beginning to fall as Amanda rang the doorbell to Nicholas's flat. She had left work early, secure in the knowledge that her boss was tied up at an art sale in Hertforshire and could not possibly be back before seven. So she took the unprecedented step of closing the gallery at lunchtime, and then crawled her way down to Carbery in the early rush hour traffic.

She arrived at five. As she stood in the darkened overhang of the porch, she felt rather nervous. The denuded branches of the trees in the small front garden had a desolate feel and it suddenly occurred to her, What if he were not there? Or didn't want to speak to her?

She shivered apprehensively. What had seemed so easy in London, now seemed fraught with undisclosed risk. She had not seen Nicholas at all in the last two weeks, and his phone calls had become less frequent. She had even begun to wonder on the way down whether he might not have found someone new, and as she sped down the motorway, tears of self-pity had begun to course down her cheeks. Why on earth did Dougal have to be so obtuse?

At that moment footsteps sounded from inside the hall and a light was switched on. Then the door was pulled back, and Nicholas's face appeared. 'Hello,' he said, startled. 'I wasn't expecting you.'

Amanda's tear-stained face gazed back at him. 'Can I come in?' she said imploringly. 'I want to talk.'

He led the way into his tiny sitting room and poured them both a drink. 'I've only just got back,' he said apologetically, 'so you'll have to excuse the mess. I've been touring the outer reaches of the diocese with the Bishop.' He made it sound like they had been on a trip to Siberia.

'The old boy's in a bit of a strop. Raising Cain at the moment, as a matter of fact. I'm having to keep on my toes.'

Amanda accepted the proffered drink and looked round distractedly. She had not actually been to Nicholas's flat before and, in normal circumstances, would have felt curious. Vaguely she noted that it did not look messy, simply unlived in, as if he had been away for a few days. But these were not normal circumstances and she lacked the energy to wonder about this. 'I had to talk to you,' she said haltingly.

He settled himself in a chair opposite and looked at her enquiringly. 'Is anything wrong?'

But now it came to it, she suddenly discovered she did not know what to say. She had been over and over this conversation in her mind on the way down but now, sitting opposite him in the rather unwelcoming room, her mind went blank. She swallowed painfully. 'It's just that ... ,' she began, and then she dried up.

Nicholas waited. He had been feeling rather aggrieved with Amanda since their last conversation. He could not understand why she should have become so apparently offhand. Also, although he would die rather than admit it, he was still feeling extremely jealous of Dougal. There was a lurking suspicion at the back of his mind that, deep down, Amanda might actually prefer his rival and that he, Nicholas, had been merely a bit on the side. That anyone should be favoured in preference to himself, Nicholas considered intolerable. In these circumstances, Stephanie had been a welcome relief.

Amanda looked at him helplessly, wondering why his expression was so stony. Then, 'I'm pregnant,' she blurted out.

Nicholas's jaw dropped in astonishment. 'What?' he said. 'Pregnant? – who's the father?'

Amanda looked as if she could have hit him. 'Who do you think?' she snapped back.

Nicholas was so eaten up with jealousy that he said the first thing that came into his head. 'Dougal?'

Amanda leapt to her feet, furious. 'I've already told you, Dougal and I don't do that!'

Nicholas also stood up. 'Are you saying it's me?' he asked incredulously.

This was too much. Amanda burst into a fresh flood of tears. 'Of course I am,' she hiccuped. 'How many men do you think I've slept with recently?'

It was on the tip of Nicholas's tongue to say he did not know but, perhaps wisely, he restrained himself. He stared at her in deep shock, and then it occurred to him that perhaps he ought to phone Stephanie and tell her he couldn't make it tonight after all. 'Excuse me,' he muttered. 'I've just got to make a phone call.'

He left the room abruptly and Amanda broke off crying to stare after him in astonishment. She could not believe her eyes. How could he simply walk out of the room like that? When he came back five minutes later, she had resumed her seat and was staring woodenly at the blank television screen. 'I'm sorry,' he said lamely, realising from the set of her shoulders that she was annoyed. 'I just remembered something.'

'It was obviously very important.'

'Yes,' he agreed. He felt slightly flustered. It had never actually occurred to him that Amanda might become pregnant after what they had done. For his part, he had looked on the encounter simply as an assertion of territory, while the fact that she had not yet slept with Dougal had given him a sense of glorious one-up-manship. He felt he had made a fool of his staider rival. That she was now pregnant, however, gave a wholly new dimension to the affair. 'Are you sure?' he asked, pouring himself another stiff drink, and playing for time as he tried to work out what to do.

'Of course I am,' she snapped. 'I bought a kit.'

'I see.' He took a deep gulp and almost choked.

'I don't know what to do,' said Amanda furiously.

He finished coughing and leant up against the sideboard, wheezing gently. He was so shocked by her news, he was unable to think straight. The first thing that crossed his mind was that she should get rid of it, and as fast as possible. But then it suddenly struck him that if it got out, or worse still, if she refused and went ahead and had the baby – and then told someone it was his, and that he'd tried to make her have an abortion – then his name, in church circles at least, would be mud. He'd be finished. So maybe he ought to marry her. And then, as he thought about it some more and his initial horror receded, he realised that his was what he'd actually wanted in the first place anyway, so perhaps her pregnancy was no bad thing.

He looked at her speculatively, trying to weigh up the pros and cons. When she had grown so cold after he had forced the pace in the woods, he had rather thought that he had over-played his hand, and had been resigning himself to defeat. That, indeed, had been why his hatred for Dougal had been growing so intense. But now his plan was on the point of succeeding after all. If he offered to marry Amanda and she kept the baby, then inevitably people would say they had been a bit precipitate, but no one minded about that sort of thing these days. With a bit of skilful handling, everyone would just say that it was a love match. That they had followed passion in the face of all the odds. And then, thought Nicholas, Amanda's father would inevitably exercise his influence on their behalf. He would not want his daughter's husband to remain a mere chaplain to the horrible Hubert!

He stared at her, a look of dawning wonder on his face, and Amanda blinked hopefully. 'My baby, you say?' he asked numbly.

She nodded. 'I'm sorry. It's been a bit of a shock, hasn't it?'

'No.' He shook his head violently, and then nodded. 'Yes, it has rather.' Then, as she continued to look at him, he added, 'I thought you'd gone off me.'

She hung her head. 'I've been so worried, I didn't know what to do. And I've felt so awful too.' She looked up at him pleadingly, 'I'm sorry I've been so off. I was just scared.'

He had been standing as if frozen but now, almost as if her words released him, he put down the drink and crossed swiftly to her side. She stood up questioningly, and he took her in his arms. 'Oh, my darling,' he murmured, pulling her roughly to him. 'I'm so sorry. I do understand.' He buried his face in her hair and said quickly, 'Don't worry. It'll be alright. I'm really pleased ... it was all just a bit of a shock, that's all ... We'll get married.'

A wild explosion of joy burst in the pit of Amanda's stomach. 'Do you really mean it?' she asked, pushing herself away so as to be able to look into his face.

Nicholas had a brief vision of prison doors slamming shut, and uniformed warders with large keys, but he reminded himself again that this was what he really wanted. 'Of course I mean it,' he said firmly. 'It's wonderful.'

*

Five days later, in the middle of the evening, Father Goody took up his position in the Bishop's back garden. It was beginning to rain. He had actually arrived a couple of hours beforehand, and had watched the Bishop leave for a confirmation service out in one of the villages. Then he had seen Myra come to the windows of the lounge and draw the curtains, and a fiendish glee had seized him. He had no very clear idea what he was going to do, but on one thing he was determined. Somehow he was going to break his way into the Higgins' flat, take some of Myra's underwear (he thought this would frighten her) and then leave before his presence could be detected. It was not that he enjoyed the prospect of terrifying defenceless women, but over the last couple of weeks a rather horrifying change, one that he felt entirely powerless to resist, had stolen over him. It was as if, once he had begun to slide gently down the slope of alcoholic self-obsession, the whole cliff face had suddenly given way, and he was slithering willy-nilly into some terrible vortex of chaos.

There was an obstacle to his plan, however, in the form of the six-foot high brick wall, topped with broken glass, which surrounded the episcopal garden. Father Goody was not an agile man. Neither was he particularly fit. Forty minutes and three failed attempts later, he had cut hands and a gaping tear in his right trouser leg. The injuries, however, served only to fuel his resolve. Panting, and casting aside all last remnants of caution, he flung his coat over the jagged top, heaved across a dustbin that he had found round the corner, and then once again launched himself recklessly into an attack on the summit.

The noise of the bin scraping across the tarmac surface of the car park was horrendous, and Myra came to the window and peered out into the dark, trying vainly to see. The inky darkness welled up before her, so thick she felt she could reach out and touch it. But beyond the ragged form of the ash tree at the bottom of the garden, she could make out nothing. Then, in the quiet, she heard again the low agitated panting that had caught her attention just before the terrible dragging sound, followed by a rattle and a low curse. Seriously alarmed, and deciding that this could not after all be the rampaging hedgehog that she had first imagined, she went and turned off the lights, and then again came back and peered out into the night. This time, as the darkness settled around her and then cleared slightly, she made out below the small patch of velvety lawn, edged by the beds in which, only earlier that day, she had planted tulip and anemone bulbs in readiness for next spring. She let her gaze travel slowly over the herbs, with the heavy wisteria behind and then her eyes wandered up and beyond to the darker line of the wall. She was totally unprepared for what happened next. As she stared down, momentarily diverted and thinking how pretty the garden looked in the moonlight, the darkened form of a man suddenly heaved itself up, fingers scrabbling for a hold along the top. The next instant his body seemed to pop up from out of the darkness beyond and land with a kind of sickening lurch onto what should have been the jagged line of glass. Only she saw now that he had covered it with some kind of material, a blanket maybe or a coat. As she stared out, paralysed with horror, she saw him steady himself and then slowly pull the top half of his body upright, so that a leg straddled either side of the wall.

Myra gazed down, the terrible pounding of her heart thundering in her ears. For a second she thought she was going to faint. She had not the slightest idea who the man was, but it was clear he was attempting to break in. Shutting her eyes and swallowing, she forced herself to be calm. She could hear the faint scraping of his shoes brushing against the rough stone of the wall. Somewhere far away, in a quiet corner of her brain, she thought, 'The police. I must phone the police.'

Hardly daring to breathe, she stepped quietly back, absolutely terrified that he would at any moment look up and see her staring down. Then, once she was sure she was beyond the line of his vision, she turned and almost ran towards the phone. But in the darkness she misjudged the distance, and banged up hard, first against the coffee table, and then against the edge of the sofa. Almost crying with frustration, she pushed herself round, feeling in front with her hands. She longed to turn on the light but was too scared. The next second her fingers closed over the phone lying on the sideboard and she pulled it up to her face. But it was no good, in the darkness she could not make out the numbers to dial. She would *have* to put on the light.

Whimpering slightly now, she staggered through into the hall and flicked on the light there, at the same time keeping the door to the lounge open behind her. She could not see what was happening down below of course, but quite irrationally she felt safer in the knowledge that with just a few steps she could get back to the window. The hall light seemed to have a strange, ominous tinge but she did not care. Hands shaking, she punched in 999 and then half collapsed against the wall, the phone wedged to her ear.

The phone seemed to ring and ring. It seemed to go on for ever. From down below she imagined she heard a little cry of triumph, and closed her eyes with dread. 'Please, God,' she whispered. 'Please ... let someone answer.' It crossed her mind that in the time it took for the emergency services to respond she could have been killed or even worse. She imagined all the switchboard operators sitting round enjoying a cup of tea, while behind them the unheeded phones rang and rang. 'Oh answer the phone!' she cried.

As if in reply, there was a little click and a disembodied voice said, 'Emergency. Which service do you require?'

'Police!' broke out Myra. 'I want the police. There's an intruder trying to get in. He's in the back garden!'

She was becoming hysterical and the voice, maddeningly, said, 'Please be calm, madam, while I put you through.'

'I am calm,' spat Myra. 'I need help.' All thoughts of how a bishop's wife ought to sound had gone, blasted away by terror.

Another eternity. She strained her ears, trying to hear, and then another voice said, 'Police. How can we help?'

Somehow, she never quite knew how, she gave her name and address and told them what she had seen. The voice at the other end was reassuring. 'Don't worry, madam. We'll have a car with you within the next ten minutes.'

There was a sound of breaking glass below. 'That's too long,' shrieked Myra. 'I can hear him breaking in!'

'Alright, madam,' went on the voice, 'now just ...'

But Myra was not listening any more. With a little sob she threw down the phone, and then dashed back into the lounge and took down from the wall the knobkerrie Hubert had brought back from a trip to Africa. She had never liked it very much. It had always looked to her to be rather vicious. But she thought it was perfect now. Gripping it in both hands, and holding it menacingly before her, she stole down the stairs and towards the kitchen, from where she had heard the breaking glass. Pushing open the door as soundlessly as she could and hardly daring to breathe, she relaxed her grip just enough to reach inside and turn on the light. Two seconds passed, and then the fluorescent lights whirred and flickered on and off, and then at last gave a little 'Twuck!' and came fully on. In the garishly flickering light, Father Goody's hand and arm was revealed, poking through the broken pane of glass. He had been trying to find the catch to the window, in order to open it and clamber in.

As the light went on, it was his turn to freeze.

Myra took one look at the arm, gave a blood curdling shriek that echoed and re-echoed through the night, and then brought down the club on the offending appendage with all the force she could muster. By nature she was a pacifist, but all thoughts of the evils of violence and the fear of hurting another human being disappeared beneath the flood of terror and absolute desire for self-preservation that overwhelmed her.

'A ... argh!' shouted Father Goody in agony, as if in reply.

'Take that!' yelled Myra, bringing down the club again. Through the distortion of the glass she made out a horrible face, leering at her terribly; the eyes, to her, a mask of hate.

Outside, Father Goody danced up and down frenziedly, clutching at his fingers. It felt as if they were going to explode. He skipped agitatedly in a circle, one minute thrusting his hotly throbbing hand under his arm, the next waving it in the air, as if performing the intricate steps of some demented dance.

'I'll teach you to frighten poor defenceless women!' shouted Myra, taking courage from the commotion now going on in the garden and heading for the kitchen door. But at that moment the front doorbell rang and she paused indecisively and looked round.

Father Goody heard it too, and he broke off his dance to listen, a cold sweat breaking out across his brow.

Myra cast one more glance out into the inky blackness of the garden and then spun on her heel and ran into the hall. 'Quick! He's in the garden,' she panted, flinging open the door and pointing to the kitchen. 'I caught him trying to get in through the window.'

The two burly policemen outside gave her one startled look, and then rushed through the door past her. 'He's there, Mike!' she heard one shout. She heard them unlock the outer kitchen door and pound across the patio and out into the garden. It was all too much. Giving a little 'mew' of exhaustion, she collapsed feebly onto the floor, the knobkerrie falling from her hand.

Outside, Father Goody cast one frightened glance at the policemen as they thundered through the kitchen and then took to his heels. All thoughts of the pain in his hand went as he hurtled back towards the garden wall. The grass under his feet felt soft, and then a small pond suddenly loomed up in front of him. Too late. He splashed straight through the middle and on. Then, three paces from the wall, he gathered himself up and launched himself in an almighty leap, straight at the top.

The policemen pounding across the grass behind him, pulled up short, staring in astonishment as the fleeing figure before them suddenly threw itself onto the wall.

'A ... ah!' shouted Father Goody again, as his hands closed over the glass.

'Grab him, Pete!' yelled a voice, as the policemen again resumed their chase.

Father Goody felt a hand close over his foot. It was all the encouragement he needed. Giving one last almighty kick behind, he heaved himself up and onto the top, a leg straddling either side. Behind he heard a muttered exclamation, and then felt his left shoe torn off. Cold air whistled up his trouser leg, but Father Goody ignored it. He was free. Heedless of the pain from the glass, he swung his shoeless foot up and over and then dropped to the other side.

Before him the palace car park stretched empty and dark. The only car now there, apart from his own, was the white Astra belonging to the police. Father Goody did not pause. Fumbling in his trouser pocket for the keys and almost beside himself with terror, he ran blindly across the short space to his car, wrenched open the door, and tumbled in. As he turned the key in the ignition, he rammed his foot down hard against the floor and was rewarded by a loud roar of power. Then he pulled sharply on the wheel and swung away, the tyres screaming in protest. Behind, he heard a shout but it was too late. As he hurtled through the palace gates he saw, in the mirror, first one and then another figure run out from the house, arms waving. Without a pause, he changed gear and accelerated away, and at the same moment a triumphant burst of exhilaration seemed to explode inside of him. He had done it! He had got away! He was so relieved and it was so intense that, almost unconsciously, he broke into a loud rendition of the Alleluia chorus.

Half an hour later Bishop Hubert received a phone call. 'Sergeant Davies of the Carbery Police here, sir,' said the unknown voice. 'There's been an incident. I wonder if we could ask you to come home.'

'Pardon?' said the Bishop.

'Nothing to worry about, sir,' reassured the voice. 'Your wife's quite alright, but she needs someone with her and she's asking for you.'

'My wife?' echoed the Bishop incredulously. Then, 'What's happened?'

There was a small silence, then the voice said, 'I'm afraid there's been an intruder, sir. But I must repeat, your wife is quite alright. Just a little distressed.'

The Bishop rushed straight home, and found a WPC sitting upstairs with his wife, while down below a scene of crimes officer, on his knees, assembled a little pile of what looked to the Bishop to be rubbish on the kitchen floor. 'What on earth's going on?' he asked, shocked.

The policeman regarded him owlishly. 'From what we can make out, sir, and from all your wife has told us, it appears you may have a stalker.'

The Bishop stared at him disbelievingly. He felt as if the world had suddenly dissolved into chaos. Everything had been perfectly normal when he had left home earlier. 'What do you mean?' he asked, blinking hard behind his glasses.

'Well, sir,' the policeman rose heavily to his feet, at the same time delicately retrieving a small scrap of cloth. 'Your wife tells us that you have received a number of phone calls over the last couple of weeks, where the caller has either hung up immediately, or engaged in heavy breathing. And on two occasions,' he looked hard at the Bishop, 'she says there have been threats.'

Unable to help himself, the Bishop sat down heavily on the nearest chair. 'But surely they were mistakes,' he said plaintively. 'Or pranks even. You know what young people can be like.'

The policeman stared at him curiously. He had just spent the last half an hour talking to the Bishop's wife and had the distinct impression that there was something he was not being told. 'We feel it might be rather more serious than that, sir,' he said levelly. 'And we've got evidence. Rather a lot as a matter of fact.' He indicated the pile. 'We've got a shoe, a coat ... these fibres ... and quite a large amount of blood.'

'Blood?'

'Yes, sir. From the glass on top of the wall. The intruder would appear to have cut himself quite badly.'

'Oh, my God,' said the Bishop. A feeling of numbness seemed to slide over his brain, temporarily paralyzing his capacity to think. He fought against it, struggling hard to understand. It seemed totally bizarre, but it suddenly struck him that the general opposition he had been experiencing within the diocese was assuming a tangible and infinitely more frightening form. He wondered vaguely who on earth could be behind it - some disaffected opponent of women priests? Satanists ... ? Nicholas?

'Would you like to see your wife, sir?' asked the policeman gently. He thought the old boy looked as if he was taking it rather hard.

The Bishop blinked again, and looked up. 'My wife?' he repeated, dazed. 'Oh ... Oh yes, of course.' Trembling slightly, he rose to his feet and followed the policeman haltingly up the stairs.

Father Goody was equally a prey to confusion. His mood of euphoria lasted all of ten minutes and then the huge wrought iron gates of Walsingham loomed in front of him. As he turned into the rather ugly entrance, it suddenly struck him what he had done. Realisation that was almost physically painful flooded over him as he scrunched to a noisy halt on the gravel, and he looked down at his bleeding hands in disbelief. Surely that could not all have just happened? It must be a dream – a nightmare rather – or some terrible mental aberration. But his hands and tattered clothes said otherwise.

A feeling of absolute horror swept over him as a large globule of thickening blood gathered slowly on his thumb, and then dripped heavily onto his knee. He must have been mad. He felt as if he had been caught by some crazed delusion that had blasted him away from all touch with reality. But now, in the full awfulness of temporarily restored vision, he realised what a complete idiot he had been. Myra Higgins had never been in love with him! It was more than he could bear. Almost reeling under the weight, he staggered from the car and began to push his way blindly towards the college. He had got to have a drink.

But just as he was about to push open the door, it swung back and Oswald stepped out.

The meeting was entirely fortuitous. Oswald had been working late on an article for the journal *Liturgical Practices and the Modern Man*, and he had suddenly had an overwhelming craving for a bar of nut chocolate. It was too late for the college bar, so he had decided to walk down to the late night garage on the corner and buy one there. He heard the car screech to a halt just as he came into the hall, and immediately assumed it was a group of boisterous ordinands returning late. As his hand closed over the huge iron ring on the door, he felt a small glow of sanctimonious pleasure; he would enjoy reprimanding them. 'What is the ... ?' he began, and then pulled up short as he saw who it was.

Father Goody presented a strange sight. His tie was askew and his grey V-necked sweater was torn at the cuffs, while his trousers looked as if they had had a close encounter with a lawnmower. Oswald's eyes travelled slowly down, taking in the cuts and bruises, and Father Goody's loss of one shoe. 'Are you alright, Tim?' he asked uncertainly.

It was a stupid question. 'Drink,' gasped Father Goody, which was by now all he could manage. 'I must have a drink ... Feel awful.' He pushed past Oswald and then seemed to recollect himself slightly. 'A ... accident,' he stuttered over his shoulder. 'Must have something to steady myself.'

'Oh dear,' said Oswald. He peered out into the car park, wondering what sort of state the car was in. But as far as he could see, it seemed fine. This was actually a minor miracle, because as he drove back Father Goody had narrowly missed two lamp posts and a parked van, but Oswald of course knew none of this. The liturgy tutor stepped back into the college and stared after the principal's back, a small frown knitting his brow and then he made up his mind to follow.

Father Goody ignored him. The last thing he wanted was Oswald's company, but he lacked the energy to tell him to go away. As he drew nearer to his rooms his pace quickened, so that he took the last few steps at an ungainly run. Oswald followed hard on his heels. 'Let me help you, Tim,' he panted.

'No,' spluttered Father Goody. 'It's quite alright, really. I'll be fine just as soon as I've had a drink.'

He found his key, flung open the door and rushed in, heading for the full bottle that he knew was in the second drawer of the filing cabinet. Unfortunately, however, Brian and William had that evening conducted another of their searches. They were becoming used to all Tim's little hiding places and, as ever, had been thorough. Father Goody rushed from cabinet to bookcase to desk, giving strangled little cries as he went, but it was no good. The room would have done justice to a temperance campaigner. There was absolutely nothing there.

Oswald observed all this narrowly. Although he had not on this occasion helped, he knew immediately what had happened. 'Can I help? Can I get you something, Tim?' he asked.

Father Goody turned on him haggard eyes. 'A drink!' he said hoarsely. 'I must have a drink.'

Oswald did not feel it appropriate to offer to make him a cup of cocoa. 'Just a moment,' he said tersely. 'I think I may have something in my room.'

He turned and sprinted out and Father Goody slumped exhausted into a chair. 'Good man,' he muttered, closing his eyes.

Oswald was back within seconds and banged down a bottle of scotch on the desk. It was becoming rather expensive, he reflected, funding Father Goody's little habit. Still, from the state of him it looked like it might be beginning to pay off. Father Goody did not move. Oswald smiled expectantly and cleared his throat and, roused, the principal opened a bleary eye and stared at the bottle uncomprehendingly.

'A drink?' prompted Oswald, rather piqued by his lack of response.

Father Goody blinked. He was actually deeply shocked by all that had happened and, under the strain, had fallen asleep. Jerked awake in this fashion, therefore, he was for a second unsure where he was.

'What?'

Oswald felt annoyed. 'I've brought you the drink you wanted,' he said loudly.

'Oh?' Dazed, Father Goody struggled forward. He felt there was something terribly important that he had to remember, but for the life of him could not recall what it was. But his hands and legs hurt so much ... It felt as if he had been battered. As if from a great distance, he saw Oswald standing in front of him, arms akimbo, a sour expression on his face. He took in the whisky on the desk, and a great feeling of weariness again flooded over him. There was something so important ... he knew there was ... He reached out a hand, gave a small 'Ugh!' and passed out.

Oswald stared at him in disgust. He might have known, the man was paralytic again. He glared at him distastefully, wondering what to do. Father Goody really was in a terrible state. Oswald's disapproving soul was revolted, but he supposed he ought to do something. He couldn't just leave him there all night. Gingerly he reached down and inserted an arm under Father Goody's back. Then, bracing himself, he heaved the principal's inert body to its feet. It was harder than he anticipated and for a second, taking the strain of Father Goody's weight, he almost collapsed. But Oswald was not about to let himself be defeated by a drunk. Regaining his feet, he shoved Father Goody roughly in the back, wedged him against the desk, and then jerked him onto his feet. With a low moan of protest, Father Goody stood up.

At the best of times Father Goody, with his portly frame, was not the most graceful of individuals but now, totally inert, he abruptly floundered forward and across Oswald like an untidy and extremely heavy sack. Oswald began to pant slightly and a cold sweat broke out across his brow as he struggled to drag Father Goody over to the bedroom. Halfway there, the principal returned briefly to consciousness and made an effort to go back to the desk. 'No!' shrieked Oswald, seeing all his effort about to be wasted and struggling to pull him back.

'Wanna drink,' said Father Goody, suddenly remembering his earlier thirst.

'I'll bring you the bottle in a minute,' promised Oswald, his breath coming in rapid gasps.

Father Goody floated back into unconsciousness.

Somehow Oswald managed to get the principal to his bed, and flung him down on top of it. Then he heaved his legs up onto the covers, at the same time dragging his pyjamas out from under the pillow. Father Goody snored gently, and Oswald began to wonder whether it was really worth all the effort. He looked down at the principal curiously, wondering what had happened to get him into such a state. Both his arms and legs were covered in cuts, and some of them looked deep, almost as if he had been slashed. Oswald frowned, and then went and got a flannel and towel from the bathroom. He supposed he ought to clean him up. With a feeling of the deepest revulsion he began to remove Father Goody's clothes and bathe his wounds. Half an hour later he had finished, and Father Goody was in his pyjamas and safely tucked up in bed, snoring gently.

Oswald looked down at the filthy, tattered clothes he had removed and came to a decision. The only thing these rags were good for was the bin; but the thought came to him that that might be a waste. He was intensely curious as to what might have happened and it occurred to him that they might constitute evidence of some kind. Not that he suspected anything criminal, he simply thought that they would testify to the principal's immoderate behaviour and therefore provide justification for his removal.

Gnawing reflectively at his lip, he folded them carefully, then bundled them all together and took them to his room.

20

Regina's decorators started work on the church hall. The first Dougal knew about it was when two large vans pulled up and parked outside the scruffy doors, just as he was going into church. He hurried over, surprised, and discovered Regina standing in the doorway, a huge beam pinned on her face.

'De Lord has given us paint,' she announced proudly.

'Where's it all come from?' asked Dougal, stunned. The banks had all refused the loan he had been after, and the painful subject of the cost of redecoration had been the main focus of his prayers for the last three days. He was not quite prepared for the idea that the petitions he had been hurling at heaven might have been answered.

'The Roxburgh,' said Regina, as if this was the most natural thing in the world.

'Where d'you want this then, luv?' demanded Dave, just at that moment striding past with three huge tins of paint balanced precariously in his arms.

'Do you mean the hotel?' spluttered Dougal.

'Of course.' Regina smiled seraphically and then turned to the painter. 'You come with me,' she said. 'I show you.'

She bustled off like a launch guiding a liner into port, and Dougal stood staring after her in astonishment. 'But who's going to pay?' he bleated plaintively. He had not the slightest idea how Regina might have contrived this and it occurred to him, after the fiasco with the insurance, that she might have landed them in further debt.

'You no worry,' Regina called back over her shoulder. 'It taken care of. You jus' need faith!'

That, to Dougal, sounded ominous.

Two more young men followed after Dave, similarly laden. 'Morning, vicar,' said one, pushing past. 'Nice day for it!'

'Yes,' said Dougal. Not an inspired reply but, in the circumstances, it was all he could come up with.

He watched open-mouthed as the decorators spread dust sheets over the floors and heaved up scaffolding. They were clearly professionals and seemed to know exactly what to do, unlike Dougal himself, who felt like a spare part. Ten minutes later Eliston arrived. He was wearing overalls too. 'Mornin', Dougal,' he said cheerily. 'You come to help as well?'

Dougal leapt on him. 'Eliston,' he hissed, 'what on earth's going on here? Regina says she got the paint from The Roxburgh.'

Eliston nodded. 'She did. She asked them, and they gave it her.'

'But why?' asked Dougal, even more bewildered by the blandness of this reply. 'And who are these painters? Are they from The Roxburgh too?'

Eliston shrugged. 'I dunno,' he said laconically. 'But I'm glad they're here. My old bones ain't what they used to be!'

Across the road Danny and his cronies also observed these developments. 'They're goin' t' do it up then,' said Biff perceptively.

'Yeah,' agreed Darren. 'We'll let them finish, then we'll go an' trash it again.' He laughed unpleasantly.

'Shut up!' said Danny, rounding on him.

The others all looked at him. 'Why?' demanded Biff, growing aggressive in turn. 'What's up?'

Danny stared unseeingly across the road. 'You're jus stupid, you are,' he said, ignoring Biff. 'Ye don't think, any of you. Carl didn't say nuffink about trashin' the place again.'

They digested this slowly, Biff obviously trying to work out whether there was some subtlety he had missed. 'You sayin' we got t' do for this priest bloke first instead?' he brought out at last.

Darren looked as if he had been struck with divine illumination. 'Oh yeah, right,' he said. 'Good thinkin'.'

But that was not what Danny was thinking at all. Ever since Carl's commission he had found himself caught on the horns of a dilemma from which he could not break free. He could not understand it. He hated Dougal with an intensity that stunned him. He simply could not forgive the priest for having made such a laughing stock of him in front of his friends. And yet ever since they had trashed the hall, he had been dogged by a feeling of intense shame. It was an entirely new sensation for Danny and he could not at first identify it, but in the days following he found that he could not get what had happened out of his mind. It was almost, he thought, trying vainly to make sense of it, as if the figure of the priest was haunting his thoughts. Somehow, in ways that remained totally inexplicable to him, it was as if breaking into the hall had opened a door that gave unrestricted access to Danny's soul. The effect was not pleasant.

'You got a plan then?' demanded Darren.

Danny shook his head. 'No,' he said. 'Not yet.' The rest of the gang waited perplexed, and at last he brought out, 'I'm not sure about all this anyway.'

'Why not?' Biff stared at him incredulously. 'You 'eard wot Carl said. 'E'll give us almost a grand.'

Danny spun round, eyes blazing. 'You're mad,' he spat. 'Ye're talking about killing someone here. 'Ave you any idea what that means?'

There was a minute's stunned silence. The others looked at each other uncomprehendingly, and then Darren said, 'You gone yellow or something?'

The spectre receded a little from Danny's mind. But he felt as if it was watching him and he was suddenly angry. 'No, course not!' he snapped back. 'I jus' don't want to make a balls up of it, okay?'

He turned and flung angrily away, and the others stared after him, unsure what to do. 'If you ask me,' said Biff judiciously, and ignoring the fact that nobody had, 'Danny wants to do this by 'imself. 'E fancies 'imself in the big time. I reckon 'e thinks if 'e does this alone, Carl'll take 'im on as one of 'is boys.'

They looked at each other stunned, and then Darren breathed, 'Cunning bastard! I'd never 'ave thought of that!' As if at a signal, they all turned and stared after Danny's retreating back, a new respect in their eyes.

*

When Father Goody woke the morning after his debacle at the palace, he was a changed man. His obsession with Myra was at an end, overwhelmed by a terror of arrest. He also had an excruciating pain in his head, but that was entirely separate to the feeling of horror that swept over him as he opened his eyes. He could remember with appalling clarity all that had happened right up till the moment when he had tumbled into his car and headed for home. He supposed he had got back all right, but what had taken place subsequently was a total blank. He had the vaguest recollection of hands fumbling with the top of his trousers, but the memory was so hazy he thought he might have imagined it.

Heaving himself to his feet, he lurched unsteadily through to the study, pain exploding through his head. I need a drink he thought, peering round groggily. Almost as if in answer, his eyes alighted on the bottle standing waiting on the desk. 'Good grief!' he said, pulling up short and staring at it in surprise. It struck him that he must have been in a really bad way the previous night, to have left a bottle out like that. Molly, or even Chantelle his secretary, might have seen it.

Gingerly he crossed over and noted dully that both women had indeed already been in. His morning post and the newspaper were stacked in a neat pile beside the phone and beside them was a note, reminding him that he had two interviews with prospective ordinands later in the day, and that he had agreed to act as spiritual director to a Father Reginald Cuthbertson from one of the villages just outside Carbery. 'Father Cuthbertson wanted to know if he could drop by early this afternoon,' Chantelle had written, 'I said you were free at three.'

'Oh, God!' said Father Goody, sinking down into his swivel chair and reaching for a glass. He sloshed in a good three inches of scotch and took a long pull, then slumped forward with his head on his hands. He felt terrible. A tiny little voice at the back of his head told him this ought to stop. With practised ease, Father Goody ignored it. He waited for the hammering in his brain to subside, and then opened one eye and stared at the post. He did not think he could face that quite yet. Dimly he wondered if anyone might have noticed his return last night, and then dismissed the idea. No sense worrying before there was need, and he had enough to contend with emotionally with his flight from the police. He took another swig and then dragged across the paper, pulling it open on the desk in front of him. The headline leapt out. 'HALO SLIPS FOR RANDY REV.'

A feeling of absolute horror swept over him, so intense it felt like the bones in his knees had turned to jelly. He gave a low inarticulate moan, fingers scrabbling wildly at the desk, and then pulled the paper towards him. Staring at it feverishly, beneath the headline he made out the photo of a man, head turned slightly aside, kissing a woman on the cheek. It was indistinct, but the light just caught the collar, clearly showing what he was. Father Goody stared at it uncomprehendingly, and a feeling of disbelief swept over him. Kissing a woman! How had they taken a photograph of him doing that? What on earth had he been doing last night? And then, as he stared at the picture more carefully, his feeling of unreality increased. The man was undeniably a priest but, equally clearly, it was not him. For one thing, the figure in the photograph was obviously much younger, and he looked tall and slim. Also, although the head was turned aside, obscuring the face, this served only to emphasise the thick, dark hair that fell just below the collar. Father Goody did not have very much of this commodity, and what he did have was grey.

His eyes grew round and he took a long, lingering breath that was pure relief, sensation slowly returning to his frozen limbs. Whoever this man was, it was not him. All the same ... He stared at the picture again. There *was* something about the figure that was familiar, and he felt as if he knew the woman too.

He let his eyes travel slowly down the page, scanning the first few lines of the article and then he went rigid with shock. 'Self-styled saint Dougal Sampratt,' he read, 'was exposed last week as a sex-crazed lecher, whose centre, ostensibly to help prostitutes and drug addicts, is no more than a front for vice and sex. In an undercover operation carried on over the course of a week,' the article went on, 'freelance reporter, Bingo Drubbins, witnessed over a dozen assignations kept by the randy rev with "his girls". One even spent the night and ...'

Father Goody read no more. The paper dropped from his nerveless fingers back onto the desk, and he stared with unseeing eyes out of the window. Down below the grounds of Walsingham stretched bleak and empty, a scattering of dead leaves just covering the grass, but he registered them hardly at all. Dougal! Always so apparently upright and disapproving. Who would have thought it?

Never for one moment did Father Goody doubt the veracity of the article. It was on the front page. It had to be true. Besides which, he had always thought there was something a bit odd about Sampratt. He looked at the picture again more closely and suddenly realised who the woman was. Of course. It was Amanda, his fiancée, and from the photograph and report, she had quite clearly spent the night with him. Quite unconsciously Father Goody gave a long, low whistle, remembering all too clearly the long and boring talks Sampratt had insisted on giving to local sixth-formers on the virtues of pre-marital chastity.

He supposed the fact that Sampratt was engaged to Amanda made the situation marginally better, at least in the eyes of the world, but it could not help disguise what a hypocrite he was! And it certainly could not explain all these other women he was apparently involved with.

After all the upset he had experienced over the last twenty-four hours, Father Goody felt a sudden and most unchristian spurt of glee. He had always loathed Dougal's air of moral superiority and rectitude. His exposure would serve him right. But then, just as he was hugging himself at the prospect, another thought struck him, and it was so terrible that, for a second, it again made him freeze. If the papers had got on to Sampratt's peccadillos like this, how long before they discovered and revealed his?

He was instantly catapulted straight back into the horror of the previous night. For the first time that morning he looked properly at his hands, registering, with a dull sense of shock, the deep cuts and bruises that now covered them on both sides. How long before they healed? He had not the slightest idea, but it would not be overnight, and meanwhile others could not help but notice. He shuddered, staring at the dried blood, and suddenly realised that his hands and lower arms were far cleaner than they should have been. If, that is, he had just tumbled straight into bed as he had assumed. A look of puzzlement spread over his face as he thought again of the hands struggling to undo his trousers. There had been someone there, he was sure ... but who? Almost as if his mind was coated with marshmallow, he struggled to remember, but it was no good. He could not get beyond dark, probing fingers and the shadowy presence of a man ... and a bottle that had seemed to materialize out of nowhere.

Father Goody felt he was skating on very thin ice. Dimly he remembered that he had left his coat behind on the Bishop's back wall, while he seemed to recollect a policeman grabbing hold of his shoe. It could not be long, surely, before they traced these items back to him, and when they did ... He gave an involuntary shudder, his eyes jerking back to the picture of Dougal emblazoned across the front page. It suddenly struck him that he had got to do something. That he had got to get away before he himself was discovered and unmasked in this revolting way. He chewed at his lower lip distractedly, trying to think what to do and, almost as if it been waiting there, a memory floated into his mind. It was of a holiday long ago to the Greek islands. He had gone one day on an all-male tour to a monastery on one of the remoter islands, from which women were excluded. At the time it had struck him as a rather bleak existence but now, sitting there all alone in his study, it had a hitherto unsuspected charm. He could go there, even if only for a short time, and sort himself out in absolute safety. Then, hopefully, by the time he got back, the episode would have blown over. The police, he knew, were very busy. Surely, if they did not make an immediate arrest, they would not waste time on something as trivial as this. And even if they did question him, if a long enough time had elapsed, he could simply say that he had been away and could not remember.

He breathed a quick and insincere prayer of thanks for divine inspiration and then, with trembling fingers, retrieved from the bookshelf his worldwide directory of monasteries, convents, and retreat centres. He could not remember the exact name of the place, but the listings were all followed by a brief description, along with a star rating for excellence. Five minutes later and he had found it. It had three stars for comfort, a warning about accessibility, and an exclamation mark for discipline. Father Goody checked slightly at this last, but it would have to do. Moving quietly, as if frightened of being overheard, he tiptoed back over to the desk, lifted the phone, and dialled the number on the page. A singsong male voice answered in Greek. Taking a deep breath, and trying to dredge up the last remnants of his New Testament scholarship, Father Goody said, 'Hast thou an upper room?'

There was a moment's stunned silence, and then the voice said in flawless English, 'Do I take it you wish to come and stay?' Father Goody booked an immediate retreat.

While Father Goody was thus engaged, the same newspaper found its way to the Bishop's office. Nicholas intercepted it as one of the secretaries was walking through, carrying an assorted pile of broadsheets and tabloids for the Bishop's perusal. 'Hey ho,' he said blithely, 'and what are the headlines today?' Then his face froze. Unlike Father Goody, he knew instantly who the woman staring up at him was.

'Yes,' said the secretary, misinterpreting his look and sighing. 'The Bishop's not going to be too pleased. Looks like we're about to be hit by another scandal.'

She walked on past, and Nicholas collapsed stunned onto the nearest chair. He was truly, deeply shocked. Only three days before, he and Amanda had announced their engagement and he had gone with her to be introduced to her parents. It had transpired, during the course of conversation over dinner, that she had not yet broken the news to Dougal. 'Dear, dear, Amanda,' her mother had chided, 'I don't particularly like the fellow, but you really ought to have told him before agreeing to marry Nicholas here.' She had looked at Nicholas approvingly and smiled, and for his part Nicholas had felt smug. Later on in the evening, Amanda's father had taken him aside and asked if he might be interested in moving to a little parish with a vacancy that he knew of, just round the corner from Sloane Square. Nicholas was delighted, and it had suddenly hit him that he was very much in love. But now, from his brief glimpse at Bingo's article, it struck him that Amanda was being rather less than honest. Not just with Dougal, but with him too!

Nicholas felt numb, and his shock gave way to rage. Amanda had sworn to him faithfully that she had never slept with Dougal, and yet the article stated categorically that she was leaving the rectory after having just spent the night there. In which case, she was clearly lying. And if that was so, how could he be sure this baby she was carrying really was his?

He was jerked to his feet by a loud shout from the inner office. 'Nicholas!' bellowed the Bishop, in a tone of the greatest astonishment. 'Come in here at once!'

Nicholas scrambled to his feet and somehow managed to lurch his way across the room. He had gone very white and there was a thin blue line along his upper lip, and the Bishop looked up as he staggered in and said, 'You've seen it then?'

Nicholas nodded.

'I can't believe it.'

Bishop Hubert was sitting at his desk, a distraught expression on his face. Now he too rose to his feet and crossed distractedly to the window. 'I would never have thought this of Dougal,' he brought out.

Nicholas laughed bitterly. 'You ought to know, Bishop, you can't trust anyone.'

The Bishop spun back round and looked at him more closely. 'My dear boy,' he said, in tones of concern, 'whatever's wrong?'

For answer Nicholas raised a hand to his face, and then flung himself down on the nearest chair. He felt he could not stand any longer. 'It's Amanda,' he said brokenly.

A puzzled frown crossed the Bishop's face. 'Amanda?' he repeated. He came back slowly to the desk and picked up the paper. Then he looked back up at Nicholas, startled. 'You don't mean ...?'

'Yes,' said Nicholas. 'The same. She's agreed to marry *me*. She said it was all over between them. She said she'd never slept with him.'

The Bishop stared at him in consternation. 'I see,' he said. He felt he ought to say more, but he had never been very good in one-to-one pastoral situations. 'Well ... Perhaps it's not what it seems.'

Nicholas looked as if he could have hit him. 'She says she's having my baby.'

It was the Bishop's turn to sit down. 'Do you mean you've slept with her too?'

Nicholas hung his head. 'I got carried away,' he mumbled. 'That's all.'

'Dear me,' said the Bishop. 'Are all my clergy carrying on like this?'

For answer Nicholas sniffed and looked away. He was so angry with Amanda, he had not the heart to try and be charming any more. The Bishop stared at him for a long moment and then sighed. 'Maybe they are,' he said. He came to a sudden decision. 'Nicholas, I can see what a shock this has been for you. It may perhaps serve as a reminder to you about the benefits of chastity. Still,' he went on hastily, catching the look Nicholas threw him, 'this is not perhaps the moment to go into all of that. You're clearly upset, and quite obviously there are things now that you are going to have to sort out. Equally obviously, you are not going to be much use to me in this state, so I suggest you take the rest of the day off and go and try and find Amanda and have a talk. But, dear boy,' he added, as Nicholas sprang impetuously to his feet, 'remember that our Lord tells us to forgive. Whatever Amanda may or may not have done, let love temper your ... ' He found himself addressing empty air. Nicholas had gone.

Totally bowled over by this double blow, Hubert tailed off, turning to stare again in dismay at the newspaper still on the desk. He felt unsure what to do. If there were one priest in the diocese whose integrity he would have staked his life on, it was Dougal, and yet here he was being exposed as a sex-crazed maniac who preyed upon the vulnerable and weak. The Bishop felt as if nothing was certain any more. When he had shouted for Nicholas, he had had in mind for the chaplain to phone Dougal and tell him to come over to the palace straight away. Then he himself had been going to contact the diocesan solicitor to ask what he ought to do. Only now it appeared that Nicholas was also involved. Feeling dazed, the Bishop reached across for his diocesan directory, found Dougal's number, and then picked up the phone. He was answered immediately. 'St Prosdocimus' vicarage. Dougal Sampratt here. Hello.'

'Dougal,' said the Bishop. 'Bishop Hubert here.'

'Hello,' said Dougal again, surprised. He was feeling, for him, extraordinarily cheerful. The work on the church hall was going well, and Dave the decorator had said that two more evenings and another weekend would finish it. Dougal could hardly believe the way things were turning out. Regina had explained to him all about the paint and then, almost as if in confirmation, he had had a visit from Terence Elliot, the manager of The Roxburgh, who had explained that he wanted to come and see for himself the work that was going on. Not over at the church hall, he insisted, when Dougal had said hang on a second while he just got the keys, but at what Dougal himself was doing out on the streets. Dougal had been stunned and it had begun to sink in that something amazing really was happening at St Prosdocimus. So now he said enthusiastically, 'I'm really pleased you've phoned. I've been wanting to have a word.'

'Yes,' said the Bishop heavily. 'I rather thought you might.'

Something in his tone sounded slightly odd and Dougal paused. 'I'm sorry,' he said uncertainly, 'were you ringing about anything special?'

The Bishop swallowed and said, 'Yes. I feel we should meet to discuss these reports in the paper.'

Back in his study Dougal looked blank. 'What reports?'

'The reports exposing what you've allegedly been up to.'

'What I've been up to?' repeated Dougal.

'Don't try and act as if you don't know what I'm talking about. It won't help.'

'But I don't,' protested Dougal. 'Honestly. I haven't the faintest idea what you're talking about.'

The Bishop passed a tired hand before his eyes. 'Do you mean you haven't seen the papers yet?'

Dougal had the terrible feeling that the ground had just upended. 'No,' he said apprehensively. 'What do you mean? What's in them?'

With a sensation of acute misery, the Bishop realised Dougal knew absolutely nothing of the allegations that had been made. He did not want to do this, in fact he hated it, but he knew he had to. 'You are,' he said heavily.

Dougal had a curious singing in his ears. He was still totally at a loss but, from the expression in the Bishop's voice, he almost had a premonition of what the latter was about to say. 'Go on,' he said, his voice strained.

'There are photographs, Dougal,' said the Bishop. 'It's no use denying it. These are very serious allegations that are being made and, in the circumstances ...' He had been about to say 'I want you to come in and discuss it', but he changed his mind. He was never entirely certain afterwards why but, whatever the reason, he heard himself say, 'I wish to come over and see for myself what's happening.'

'Of course,' said Dougal. He swallowed. 'When?'

The Bishop bit his lip, trying to remember his schedule for the next few days, then abandoned the attempt. Whatever he had down, this was far more important. 'I'll come tomorrow evening,' he said dryly. 'Don't try and lay on anything special. I want to come out with you round the parish and see exactly what's going on.'

After that he put down the phone, but he felt he could not face work any more. He needed a break. He decided to go back over to the flat and ask his wife to make him a cup of coffee. If the truth were told, he was rather worried about Myra. Ever since the appalling conference at Walsingham, she had seemed edgy and preoccupied. The Bishop had never known her like this before and that, in turn, had made him feel disturbed, while his own personal sense of acute hurt had done little to ease the situation. He had tried talking to her about it, once their initial row had blown over but, having taken her stand under the flag of righteousness, she had refused point blank to discuss the matter and he had subsided, baffled. He had even gone so far as to make a short trip over to Carbery's Christian bookshop and had purchased a book on trauma counselling for the middle-aged and elderly, but it went on and on about the psychology of stress, and psychiatric intervention combined with spiritual regeneration. He could make neither head nor tail of it and so after a while he had abandoned it.

Now, as he pushed open the heavy front door and began to climb the stairs, he heard voices from the sitting room above. 'There's no mistake, madam,' said a man's deep tones. 'The outfitters have identified it.'

'But that's … impossible,' came Myra's tearful voice.

Seriously worried, the Bishop leapt the last three remaining stairs and rushed into the sitting room. Myra was sitting in an armchair looking strained and across from her, on the sofa, sat two of the policemen who had come round after the attempted break-in the previous night. One was holding a rather tattered coat. Hubert recognised it immediately as the one the scene of crimes officer had been poring over on the kitchen floor. The other held a man's badly scuffed brown shoe. They all looked up as he came in and Myra rose to her feet, an expression of such acute misery on her face that he was, for a moment, stunned. 'Whatever is it, dear?' he asked, unable to help himself.

'Oh Hubert,' she wailed. She looked for a moment as if she was going to run to him, but she took one pace forward and then halted, starting back and raising a hand to her face instead. 'It's just so ghastly,' she said, biting her knuckle distractedly.

The policemen also rose. 'Ah, good morning, my lord,' said one. 'We're glad you've been able to come over. We just brought these things for your wife to have a look at again. We think that we may possibly have identified the owner.'

'Good heavens!' said the Bishop, turning and staring at them amazed. 'Have you really? My word, that was quick.' Then his wife's low sob made him spin back round. 'What's wrong?' he asked again.

The policemen looked at Myra, and she looked down at the floor. The silence grew. 'They think they might belong to ... someone from Walsingham,' she brought out at last in a tremulous voice.

The Bishop thought he must have misheard her. 'What?' he asked, cupping a hand behind his ear.

'Yes, my Lord,' said the same policeman who had spoken before, only this time speaking more loudly, as though he thought the Bishop's hearing might be impaired. 'Father Timothy Goody, the principal, is one of our suspects. And two of the tutors.'

Myra winced and the Bishop felt his jaw drop. 'Surely not?' he said. 'There must be some mistake.'

The policeman came forward. 'We don't think so, my Lord.' He pushed the coat with its tattered label facing up, towards the Bishop. 'These are, I believe, a well known firm of clerical outfitters, and they have positively identified this coat as one of three sold at Walsingham on their last annual visit to the college. According to their records,' he consulted the notebook in his other hand, 'one was bought by the Canon Timothy Goody, one by the Reverend Oswald Pettifence, and the last by a Reverend Brian Mulligan.' He raised an interrogative eyebrow. 'I take it you would, of course, know all three gentlemen?'

The Bishop nodded. He felt stunned. He had absolutely no idea how to respond. The idea of a senior clergyman clambering over the back wall and then trying to break into the palace via the kitchen was so preposterous it almost made him laugh. And then he suddenly remembered the terrible fiasco at Walsingham and Myra's strangeness ever since, and a shadow seemed to fall across him. He opened his mouth to say something and looked across at his wife, and found her eyes fixed on him in an expression of what looked to be terror. 'Myra?' he said.

She shook her head, and his sense of unreality grew. 'But I don't understand,' he brought out. 'There must be some mistake.'

'We've already thought of that, my lord,' said the policeman.

The Bishop winced. He did wish the man would stop addressing him as 'my lord' all the time. 'Please,' he said, 'you don't have to keep calling me 'my lord'. Could we just stick to 'sir'?'

The policeman blinked. 'Yes of course, sir. If that's what you really want.' His tone implied that this was a social levelling of which he strongly disapproved. 'The thing is,' he resumed, 'if a coat belonging to Canon Goody, or indeed one of these other two gentlemen, should indeed prove to have been stolen, and should then just happen to have turned up here ... it would be rather a strong coincidence don't you think, ... sir?'

'Well, I ... I don't know,' faltered the Bishop helplessly. He looked again at his wife, but she had averted her eyes and was now looking resolutely out of the window.

'It's not really a problem, sir,' broke in the other policeman. 'As we said last night, we've got a quantity of blood and we can run DNA tests too. If the coat was stolen, these will exonerate all three of these gentlemen completely.' He let the alternative hang in the air, and then said, 'We simply wanted you to know the line of enquiry we're pursuing.'

They left. The Bishop showed them to the door, then clambered heavily back up the stairs to Myra. She was still standing where he had left her, the same stricken look of disbelief fixed on her face as she stared out of the window. 'Myra?' He said tentatively.

She flicked a dry tongue across her lips and then turned and looked at him. Her face was ashen and she seemed somehow to have turned in on herself. The Bishop was reminded of a very small deer at bay. For the first time the tiniest seed of suspicion began to unfurl in his mind. 'Is there something I should know?' he asked.

21

The Roxburgh phoned up and withdrew the paint. 'We find we need it after all,' said an unknown voice.

'Is it because of the article in the papers?' asked Dougal, swallowing. 'Because I can assure you, there's absolutely no foundation ...'

They were not interested. 'No, no, nothing to do with that,' they said crisply. 'We're not influenced by newspaper articles. As I said, we just find we need it after all. Someone will be along to collect it later today.'

Dougal did not believe it, but there was quite patently nothing he could do. He phoned up the central office of the newspaper that had run the article and spoke to the editor, who was smarmily polite but unresponsive. 'Can't help you I'm afraid,' he said. 'I don't like this sort of thing any more than you, but it's not our policy to reveal the names of sources, and you must understand that we have a public duty to expose this kind of thing.'

'But it's not true,' protested Dougal.

'That's what they all say.'

Dougal thought rapidly. 'At least give me the chance to put my side,' he said desperately.

'No,' replied the editor. He hung up.

Dougal went to see Regina to tell her what had happened. 'I already seen it,' she said flatly.

Dougal began to wish that the earth would open up and swallow him. 'It's not true,' he tried again. 'None of it.'

Regina picked up the paper and looked at the photograph of Amanda. 'This looks pretty true to me,' she remarked.

'But it's Amanda!'

She turned reproachful eyes on him. 'Does that make it any better, reverend?' He noticed the Dougal had gone. 'It says here she spent the night.'

Dougal closed his eyes. In that moment he felt totally alone. The absolute futility of trying to explain to anyone what had really happened swept over him. Nobody would believe him. 'She did,' he agreed, shrugging helplessly. 'But not the way it looks there. She wasn't well.'

Regina looked at him suspiciously and he went on, 'Would I lie to you?'

She shrugged. 'Everyone seems to lie dese days.'

This was too much. 'But not me!' he burst out. 'I'm telling you the truth. Why are you so ready to believe this filth instead of me?'

She stared at him for a second longer, eyes narrowed, and then said, 'Is dat really de truth you tellin' me now?'

He nodded.

'Why dey print dis stuff den?'

'I don't know.' He ran a weary hand across his forehead. 'I guess there's so much corruption about these days that people just see it everywhere, even where it's not. It's as if nobody wants there to be any goodness anymore.'

She digested this and, glancing at her, Dougal noticed for the first time the deep care lines running down the side of her face. She was old, he realised, and very, very tired. 'Honestly, Regina,' he said more gently, 'this is all lies.'

She came to a sudden decision. 'I believe you ... I tink,' she announced. She took a deep breath, pondering hard. 'I don't believe de Lord would have given us all dis paint, if you dun what de paper says.'

'Ah,' said Dougal. 'That's what I was coming to talk to you about actually.'

If Dougal was knocked for six by all that had happened, Regina was absolutely shattered. Despite what she said, deep down she didn't know what to believe any more. She had grown to like Dougal and, even more important, to respect him. When he said the article was untrue, then of course that was right, and yet ... And yet, at the back of her mind there still persisted this tiny seed of doubt. What if he really had done what the paper alleged? Regina felt old. She had lived so long and seen so much, and she grieved deeply for the way society had gone. No one seemed to have any values any more. She had prayed and prayed to the Lord to send them someone, and when Dougal came she really believed that the prayers had been answered. But men were men, she told herself. They had these needs. What if Dougal had simply been powerless to resist? She did not believe he was a bad man. Nothing would ever make her believe that. But she began to wonder if in fact he had feet of clay.

She was so upset that, as soon as he left her, she bustled straight round to Eliston, and poured out all her fears to him. In reply Eliston grunted, stared at the paper, then at her, and then said emphatically, 'Don't be so stupid, woman!'

'What?' exclaimed Regina.

'I said, don't be so stupid!' he repeated. He pointed an enraged finger at the picture. 'Dougal's not the way they make him out to be here. He's a good man. Think, woman! Think of all that's happened ... Think of that evil (he said a word Regina thought was unrepeatable and she shut her eyes in horror) Carl!' If Dougal done what this paper say, none of all this would have happened.' He peered at Regina judiciously. 'You know what going on here,' he announced. 'Dougal being attacked by the forces of darkness! We got to help him, woman.'

Eliston had never before called Regina 'woman' so many times and all at once, and she looked at him with respect. 'You tink I been listening to de devil?'

He nodded. 'Stop up your ears and tell him to go away, woman. And let us support Dougal. He needs our help!'

They called a prayer meeting.

Maisie saw the article too, and she also thought it was a pack of lies. But in her case that was because she knew where some of the information had come from. She recognised some of the phrases she had used, wildly distorted it was true, but hers nonetheless. When she saw the picture of Amanda, she felt enflamed with jealous rage, but then she noted how Dougal's face was turned away, as if in repugnance, and she began to wonder about that too.

Pepper came round, carrying two large carrier bags stuffed with clothes. She dumped them unceremoniously on Maisie's floor and then flopped down exhausted on the sofa. 'It's bleedin' 'ard this,' she announced. 'I'm sure Carl's beginning to suspect something. He's watching me like an 'awk.'

Maisie looked at her apprehensively. 'Y' don't really think he's suspicious, do y'?'

Pepper shrugged. 'I dunno. He's always a bit strange.' But the tiny cloud at the back of her eyes did not go away.

Maisie, however, was too preoccupied to notice. She accepted Pepper's remark as simply that, a throwaway comment anyone might make. 'Have y' seen this?' she demanded, thrusting the paper into Pepper's hands.

Pepper glanced at it and grunted. 'Yeah,' she said. 'Load of bollocks isn't it. He's so untouchable, I think 'e's a eunuch!'

'A wot?'

'One of those blokes who's 'ad 'is balls cut off.'

A reflective look came over Maisie's face. 'Oh no, I don't think 'e's 'ad that done.'

Momentarily distracted, Pepper looked up. 'You fancy him, don't you?' she demanded.

'Might do.'

Pepper gave a small explosion of laughter. 'Maisie, the vicar's wife!'

'It's not that funny,' retorted Maisie, offended.

Pepper laughed till the tears came to her eyes, but then she sobered suddenly. 'No,' she agreed. 'It's not funny at all.' She pulled herself upright and said seriously, 'Maisie, don't start to think like this about that priest bloke. It just won't happen. Not with a bloke like that.

Something in her tone percolated through to Maisie. Something hard. For days she had been building ever more elaborate castles in the air. She had seen herself in tweeds, with a sensible haircut, dispensing tea at the women's institute, and everyone being nice to her. She had seen herself with Dougal, with four small children (three boys for him, and a girl for her). And she had seen herself living somewhere so nice. The country maybe, but somewhere so far removed from St Prosdocimus as to make her present reality no more than a bad dream. But Pepper's words and her earnestness suddenly pricked the bubble, and the fantasy exploded. 'I don't see why 'e shouldn't marry us,' she said in a small voice.

Pepper looked at her. 'People like you and me, Maisie, don't marry,' she said bitterly. 'We just get used. Give 'im a chance, and he'll use you too.'

Later, when she went back to her own flat, she found that Carl had been in and gone. There was milk splashed all over the kitchen table and, when she went through to the tiny bedroom, she found clothes scattered all over the floor. Glancing across to the opened chest of drawers a small bubble of ever-present fear burst in the pit of her stomach, making the baby kick as if in response and then turn. She crossed over quickly, and looked down at the contents now scattered across the floor. Had he realised, she wondered. Was he checking her clothes? She reached down nervously, and picked up a string of beads. She was trying to be so careful, moving only little bits at a time, but inevitably the contents were growing low. She went through to the bathroom, and saw that the cistern top had been removed from the loo, while a little trail of water led from it across the floor. An hysterical laugh rose to her lips. Carl always kept his supply of crack in the loo. Maybe he'd just been after his stash, that was all.

She turned back to the bedroom, beginning to pick up the clothes from the floor and shove them back anyhow into the drawers. Then abruptly she sat down on the bed, hugging her knees to her chest and shivering violently. She had got to get away.

*

Strangely enough, in all the turmoil, there was one person who had not yet read the newspaper report. Amanda, blissfully ignorant of the very large sword at that moment suspended Damocles-like over her head, had been busy booking the crypt of Westminster Abbey for the biggest society wedding she could contrive at such short notice the following week, and had then sent out three hundred invitations. She was in heaven. If there were seven parts to it, she was at about stage nine. Dougal would never have agreed to so much ostentation, but Nicholas had actually suggested it. Daddy was to marry them, and Mummy had said 'Let's go to Jasper Conran for a dress.' Now her greatest fear was that in the intervening days her stomach might suddenly balloon, spoiling the classical line she craved, and she had gone on a strict, but healthy, diet in which avocado and orange juice figured prominently. She was beginning seriously to wonder how she could ever have imagined herself to be in love with Dougal in the first place. Nicholas was so much more fun.

Once released by the Bishop, the present object of her adoration sprang into his car and headed down the motorway for London. He was so angry he felt he could burst. As it was he thrust his foot down hard against the floor, and vented his frustration on every passing motorist unwise enough to get in his way. He arrived at Hampstead in one hour and twenty minutes but then it was another forty minutes before he could find somewhere to park. When he did it was on the opposite side of the Heath to Amanda's and so he had to rush across the hill without his coat in the thin drizzle; cursing the London traffic, permit parking, dog mess on the paths ... and above all, Amanda.

Arriving at her door, he rung the bell furiously, then pulled back into the shallow overhang of the porch in an effort to get out of the rain, which was now falling in earnest. A pale light was flicked on from somewhere up above, and then her happy footsteps clattered down the stairs. Nicholas scowled.

'Nicholas!' shrieked Amanda, flinging back the door. 'How wonderful! What are you doing here?' She flung her arms in delight round his neck and planted a huge kiss on his mouth. 'Ugh!' she said, pulling back. 'You're all wet.'

Nicholas's frown grew. 'I've got to talk to you,' he said, through clenched teeth.

Startled, Amanda looked at him, for the first time taking in his rather dishevelled appearance. 'Of course,' she said, rather less certainly. 'Come in.'

She stood back to allow him in, and immediately he pushed past her and up the stairs. On the way down he had thought that once they were face to face his anger might abate, and they would be able to discuss the matter rationally and come to some sort of arrangement, but now he discovered that her happy radiance served only to intensify his wrath. He felt she had made a fool of him.

'Why didn't you tell me?' he shouted, rounding on her as soon as they got up to her flat and she had closed the door.

In the narrow hall, Amanda faltered. 'Tell you what?'

Almost shaking with rage, Nicholas tore the rolled and rather soggy newspaper from out of his pocket and flung it at her feet. 'This!' he spat. 'Your precious Dougal!'

Amanda went white. 'What do you mean? He's not my precious anything.' She attempted a stab at jocularity, 'You are.'

'Oh God!' said Nicholas. He flung away in disgust and now, seriously worried, Amanda stooped down and retrieved the paper. The photograph on the front page stared up at her. It would be true to say that it had not been improved by its mode of transportation, but it was clearly recognisable for all that. Quickly she read the article underneath, and a great singing blackness suddenly engulfed her. When she came to a couple of minutes later, she found herself sitting on the sofa, and Nicholas was sloshing brandy into her mouth. 'Don't give me that!' she shrieked, as the fiery liquid burned across her tongue. 'I'm pregnant!'

'Don't remind me,' said Nicholas harshly. Seeing she was recovered, he rose to his feet and demanded, 'Whose baby is it?'

Shaken, Amanda stared back at him. She opened and shut her mouth uselessly and then said, 'It's not true.'

'What's not true?'

'None of it.'

'You mean you didn't spend the night with him?'

'No ...' Amanda went pink. 'Well, yes. But not the way this article makes out.'

Nicholas was relentless. 'How do you mean then?' he said sarcastically. 'That it was actually an overnight meeting of the women's temperance league against vice, and that there were four hundred other women there too?'

'No,' she said distinctly. She looked annoyed. 'I mean we never slept together.' A frown gathered on her face and she said, 'How on earth did they get this story anyway? Who wrote it?'

It was Nicholas's turn to blush. 'Oh, I don't know,' he said vaguely. 'Just some reporter I guess.' Then he added, 'You know what they're like.' But then it suddenly occurred to him that she was changing the subject, and he said furiously, 'It says you *did* sleep with him.'

With immense dignity Amanda tottered to her feet. 'Who are you going to believe?' she said chillingly. 'This disgusting piece of smut? Or me?'

When Nicholas left half an hour later, they were still at loggerheads. To his intense rage Amanda kept denying it but he found it difficult to believe, after his chat with Bingo, that she might be telling the truth. 'We can't get married,' he said vehemently at last. 'Not till I'm sure that it really is my baby.' Then it occurred to him that he would look even more of a fool if they waited for the birth, and then went through all the paraphernalia of blood tests. 'We can't get married at all!'

Amanda had gone very white. 'You're just saying you don't trust me, aren't you?' she demanded.

He glared at her. 'Well, how would you feel if you suddenly discovered I'd been sleeping with people right, left and centre?' Stephanie had conveniently slipped from his mind.

A picture suddenly floated into Amanda's mind of Westminster Abbey, vol au vents, and the wedding dress she had ordered. 'The invitations have already been sent out,' she said, in a small voice.

'They'll just have to be cancelled,' said Nicholas harshly. And then he relented slightly, 'Unless, that is, you can prove to me absolutely categorically that this did not happen.'

Amanda tore back to Carbery to see Dougal. She found him in a state of near siege in the rectory, and a bevy of delighted photographers wildly clicked her picture as she went in. 'I'm most awfully sorry about all this,' said Dougal penitently, as she flung off her coat. 'It's not true, any of it. I'm not sure where it's all come from.'

Amanda ignored him. 'You've got to tell Nicholas,' she burbled feverishly.

'Tell him what?' Dougal asked. He had been worrying about Amanda's reaction all morning, thinking she might be annoyed by the allegations that he was a lecher and pervert, and dreading the fact that she might believe it. Several times he had tried to phone her, but on each occasion he had only got through to the answering machine, and that had left him with the horrible feeling that she was trying to avoid him. Her appearance on the doorstep had filled him with wild joy. She had obviously rushed down to give him her support, only now he was not so sure.

Amanda flicked her head impatiently. 'Tell him we never slept together.'

Dougal's brow darkened. 'What's it got to do with him?' he demanded.

Amanda could take no more. She felt she was having the most awful day, and now on top of everything else, she felt sick. She burst into tears. 'We're getting married,' she hiccuped.

Dougal was even more puzzled. 'I know we are,' he said. 'But I still don't see what that's got to do with him.'

'Not you and me!' shouted Amanda, exasperated. 'Me and him!'

Dougal went rigid with shock.

'I'm pregnant,' she screamed, even more incensed by his reaction.

'Pregnant?' he repeated, stunned. 'But how? When?'

Amanda started crying again. 'How do you think? The normal way. Only now he says he won't marry me because he thinks you might be the father.'

Dougal sat down hastily on the nearest chair. He was finding it very hard to comprehend what was going on. The whole world seemed to have gone mad. 'I ... I don't understand,' he stuttered.

'Oh Dougal, don't be so bloody dim!' shouted Amanda. 'It's obvious, isn't it? I've fallen in love with Nicholas, and now I'm having his baby.'

The look he turned on her was so full of pain that for a moment even she faltered. 'I see,' he said quietly. He passed a hand before his eyes. 'I'm sorry. I never realised.'

Amanda was suddenly angry. 'That's just your problem,' she said bitterly. 'You never do realise.'

He sat there staring at the carpet, a great tide of despair lapping at his feet. 'When's it due?' he asked at last.

Baulked of the row she had been anticipating, Amanda sat down. 'May,' she said hollowly.

He nodded. 'I've always wanted children,' he said vaguely.

Amanda pulled a face but said nothing.

'How long's it been going on?'

She shrugged. 'Three or four months. I don't know. I'm not sure.'

He looked up at her then. 'You mean, all that time, when you've been engaged to me, you've been sleeping with him?'

She flushed uncomfortably. 'Not all that time. Only some of it.'

He sat for a long moment in silence, and then said quietly, 'I think you ought to go.'

'But what about Nicholas? You've got to tell him. If you don't he won't marry me, and I'll have to get rid of it!'

She sounded outraged rather than upset and he stared at her, appalled, wondering for a moment if he had misheard. But the expression on her face belied that and he realised, with a sense of shock, that she didn't really care. Not about the baby. Not about him. And Dougal, who sincerely believed that all life was sacred, felt himself shrivel. 'I don't know,' he said brokenly. 'Please. I just can't think at the moment. I can't take any of this in.'

She left, and he continued to sit in the chair, a blank expression on his face, as if all sensation had been temporarily blotted away. He felt totally adrift. None of the certainties that he had held on to in life seemed to make sense any more. He was despised, ridiculed, and everyone he loved seemed to have abandoned him. What was the point of anything?

He sat there for a long time until finally, in the gathering gloom of the afternoon, he rose heavily to his feet, put on the light and drew the curtains, and went and made himself a cup of tea. He was numb. He had tried very hard, but somehow he could not get his mind round this latest blow. He thought dispassionately about the baby Amanda said she was carrying. He wondered how big it was, and if it had fingers and toes? He wondered if it knew. And then suddenly, as he stared down at the sugar bowl, he began to cry.

22

———

'Bingo,' came the oily voice of the editor of *The Daily Comet*, 'any chance of a follow-up to this randy rev story?'

'Urgh,' said Bingo. He had been out celebrating making the front pages the previous night and had a hangover.

'Yes, well,' said the editor, not unsympathetically, 'what I had in mind was something more along the lines of the girls' perspective. You know the kind of thing. Where and how does he find them in the first place? How do they feel about being used like this ... and does he pay them like a normal punter, or is there something else going on?'

Groggily, Bingo attempted to drag his disordered thoughts together. 'I'm supposed to be investigating some sort of housing scandal today,' he brought out, 'over in Kilburn.'

'Forget it,' said the editor. 'Whatever they were going to pay you, I'll treble it. This story's got mileage in it. I want to run with this one for a while. By the way,' he added, 'I had the randy rev himself on the phone yesterday. Tried to tell me it was all lies – but sounded as guilty as hell.'

Bingo grunted. 'Well he would tell you that, wouldn't he?' he said. 'That kind always lies.'

The editor laughed. 'Get me something really juicy,' he said. 'I don't care what it takes.' He hung up.

Back in Carbery two plain clothes police officers were at Walsingham. They found it rather an odd place. At eight fifteen they pushed their way through the oak double doors of the front entrance, and found themselves in a small, deserted entrance foyer. There was a crucifix on the wall and a vase of dispirited looking honesty on a small table underneath. They went through the next set of doors into a semicircular hall cum reception area, with pigeon holes on one side and a large poster advising them that God was good on the other. It too was empty. Beyond stretched the dining room, around which lurked a smell of cabbage but no signs of life. and beyond that lay the Walsingham gardens, bleak now in the greyness of a damp autumnal morning.

'So what do we do now, guv?' enquired the younger of the two officers. 'Where do we go?'

His superior frowned. 'How the hell should I know? I've never been here before.'

He pushed open a door at the side and they both peered down the long corridor beyond. It was very quiet. 'Do you think they're all praying or something?' whispered the younger. He seemed rather intimidated.

Unconsciously tiptoeing, they made their way down the hushed corridor. They saw a number of signs: Library; Principal's Oratory (open for private meditation between 6 – 9. Please observe silence); Lecture Theatre 1; Chapel. 'Where's the principal's office then?' hissed the constable.

The inspector looked at him. 'If I knew that, Matthew, I wouldn't be wandering down this corridor now, would I?'

They turned a corner, and almost fell through some heavy velvet curtains into the space beyond. Sixty-two pairs of eyes turned and stared at them. The inspector pulled up short. 'Oh, I'm sorry, gentlemen,' he began loudly. At the same moment he became aware of two things. First, that the crowd before him were all on their knees, and second, that three of the men were women. Beverley, seated at the back in one of the staff stalls nearest to him, glowered, and he said hastily, 'Madam!' Then he became acutely uncomfortable, feeling he should not have spoken at all.

A young man on the left rose silently to his feet and went and got them both books. Still silent, he motioned with his hand for them to sit down and, in the absence of any better idea, they complied. Both now realised that they had stumbled in on the morning office. About five minutes elapsed, which the inspector occupied by looking at the books they had been given. One was a copy of the office and the psalms and the other was a hymn book. He brightened slightly at this. He was not a religious man, but he did enjoy a good sing, and some of the old hymns he thought were rather good.

At the end of the five minutes, as if at a signal, all sixty-two rose silently to their feet and a robed figure, whom they hadn't noticed before, glided forward to a position just in front of the altar. Brian, that morning, was wearing his very best lace cotta, the one that had been specially designed for him by his friend Mark. There was no special reason for this finery. He had just been feeling rather low, that was all, and had thought that a little religious ostentation might lift his spirits. 'Christ have mercy,' he sang. 'Lord have mercy,' sang back the congregation. At least it should, the inspector felt, have been singing, but he had never heard anything like it before. It sounded all light and ethereal. 'A ... amen,' chanted Brian.

Hymn books were opened, and a hushed voice said, '114.'

The inspector found the appropriate hymn with interest, and was pleased to note it was one of his favourites; one they used to sing at school. From somewhere above an organ began to play the familiar opening notes. The inspector cleared his throat, smiling to himself, and then, as the music began, launched into a deep-throated bass. After about four words he became aware of a shocked silence all around and, looking up, found Brian's eyes fixed on him disapprovingly. He stopped and, with an almost audible sigh of relief, sixty-two mouths opened, and a sound that was incredibly sweet and pure tiptoed into the air. After that, the inspector did not dare try again. He felt he had been rebuked. Next to him, the constable glanced sideways and suppressed a snigger, and then they both stood stiffly waiting for the end.

At the close, Brian processed slowly out and then the whole chapel turned and began to file silently out in order, till the two policemen found themselves left alone with a rather frosty looking individual, who stepped forward and said quietly, 'May I help you, gentlemen?'

The inspector fished in his pocket for his card and said, 'Yes, Inspector Bateman of Carbery Police. We wanted to have a word with the principal, Canon Goody.' He raised an eyebrow. 'Would that be you, sir?'

Oswald, for this was who it was, examined them closely and his thin nose twitched. 'No, I'm sorry,' he said deliberately. 'I'm afraid Father Goody's not here at the moment. He went away late last night.'

'Indeed, sir?' The inspector's tone was harsh. He was getting rather fed up with this Walsingham place. 'May I ask where he's gone?'

Oswald turned and began to lead the way out of the chapel. 'Greece, I believe,' he said over his shoulder. 'He's gone into extended retreat in a monastery over there.'

The two policemen skipped after him, 'That's a little unusual, isn't it, sir? In the middle of term.'

'Not at all.' Once beyond the curtain, Oswald paused, turned slightly, and said, 'We are a religious institution you must understand, retreat is quite normal.'

The inspector's eyes bored into him. 'And had he been planning this for some time?' he asked.

'I really couldn't say.' Oswald smiled thinly. 'Perhaps you'd better wait till he comes back and ask him yourself.'

The inspector decided there was something smug about this individual that he did not quite like. 'And who might you be then, sir?' he asked.

Oswald had suspected the identity of the two visitors from the moment they first blundered in. Along with the rest of the college, he had at first been rather surprised at Father Goody's sudden removal, but Brian and William had immediately begun to whisper to everyone that Timbo had gone to get himself sorted out and be spiritually renewed and that, in the circumstances, it was a jolly good thing, because poor Timbo really had been overdoing things a bit lately. They had given the impression that they were somehow a party to this decision, and the entire college had accepted this interpretation without further comment. But now, finding himself in the presence of two plain-clothes police officers, Oswald began to wonder if there was perhaps more to it than met the eye. However, he did not want the police poking their noses around the college, and so now he became effusively obstructive.

'There's something a bit funny about that bloke, sir,' opined Matthew as soon as they were outside. 'I think he's hiding something.'

The inspector looked reflective. 'You felt that too, did you?' he asked.

The sergeant nodded.

'Well then, I think perhaps we ought to take a closer look at the place. Matthew,' he looked up. 'We've got the grounds. Get me a search warrant, specifically naming the rooms of the three gentlemen who bought coats last spring.'

Bishop Hubert was also contemplating a search of Walsingham, though not of the judicial kind. The more he thought about it, the more uneasy he had become. Never before, throughout their long years of marriage, had he ever once suspected Myra of infidelity but now, as he began to try and piece things together, it was the only explanation his brain could supply. Why else should Myra have been behaving so strangely? And what on earth could have made her go to that wretched conference at Walsingham in the first place, if it wasn't to keep an assignation with someone? The Bishop no longer believed it was about making a protest. It was plainly absurd. Beverley, he knew, would delight in such disruptive activity, but Myra? Never!

And then, as he thought about it some more, he began to remember the admiring glances Father Goody had cast upon his wife. Then he remembered a phone call that he had intercepted one night. The caller had been male. He had said 'hello darling', and then, when the Bishop replied, he had hung up. The Bishop had had an odd sense at the time that it was Father Goody, and he had begun to wonder about the rumours circulating the diocese about the principal's drinking habits. He had wondered if he ought to arrange for some counselling for the poor man. Now, however, he began to wonder if the principal's excesses were not simply a manifestation of some greater wrong, namely the illicit passion he felt for another's wife! The Bishop could quite imagine that if he were ever in that position, he too might be driven to drink, by guilt as much as by anything else. And so his thoughts churned round and round, growing ever more fanciful, until he had consigned his wife to an irredeemable state of sin, and a green-eyed monster seemed to have wound unshakeable tentacles around his throat. He determined that, for her own salvation, he had got to have it out with her.

He found his wife in the kitchen, chopping beans for supper. 'Myra,' he began, flinging back the door and striking a pose, 'we have got to sort this out!'

She jumped, startled, and dropped the knife. 'Wh ... what do you mean?'

He advanced farther into the room. 'I mean I know what's been going on.'

Myra went deathly white, and then sat down heavily. It was all the confirmation the Bishop needed. He looked at her gravely. 'How long has it been going on?'

Myra began to cry, from relief as much as anything else. 'I'm not sure. Looking back, I think it all really began at that awful conference at Walsingham.'

The Bishop closed his eyes. So that was it! He had been rather hoping that, when it came to it, she would deny it. And yet here she was, making not even a show of protest. 'Why didn't you tell me?' he asked heavily.

'I was frightened what you might do.'

Moving very carefully, he came round the table and sat down opposite her. Behind, he could see the dried flowers and herbs hung from the overhead airer, their soft, delicate scent filling the air. Still snivelling into her handkerchief, Myra said brokenly, 'And I was so worried about you too. I was scared what people might say if it all came out.'

'That was good of you,' he said dryly. He stared at her bent head, and a deep feeling of repugnance swept over him. Not just for Myra, but for everyone. For life. He had trusted this woman absolutely, and she had betrayed him, there was no other word for it. He had been made a cuckold, and her distress seemed to be merely over the fact she had been found out. He tried vainly to think what to do. He thought of the prophet Hosea, told by God to marry an adulterous wife, and shuddered. He was not sure he could manage that. But divorce? His career as a bishop would be at an end. But worse than all of that, was the prospect of the long lonely years stretching endlessly before him. His face grew hard as a wave of terror rolled over him, and he sat staring fixedly ahead. At that moment he might have been carved out of granite.

Myra blew her nose loudly, and at last summoned the courage to look up. The last few days had been an absolute nightmare for her. She had wanted desperately to share with Hubert the details of all she had been going through; of how Father Goody had been pursuing her so relentlessly for so long; of the phone calls; of his insane declaration of love. A couple of times she had tried to steel herself to tell him, but it had been no good, she had been petrified; first, of the hurt he might feel and, second, because he might think she had done something to encourage the man. Now, however, the truth was apparently out. How he should have discovered it she had no idea. Maybe Nicholas had told him. But whatever the source, Myra felt the most enormous flood of relief. She was not by nature secretive, and she had felt as if she was being duplicitous. Now it was out of her hands. The truth was terrible, but they were reunited in its searing light and, whatever the future held, they would face it together.

All this was passing through her mind as she looked up, but the expression on her husband's face made her recoil. He looked so bleak and angry. 'Hubert?' she said, seriously alarmed and stretching out a tentative hand.

He flinched and jerked away. 'Don't touch me, woman!'

Myra recoiled as if she had been hit. 'But why?' she began, bewildered.

The Bishop could stand no more. 'Leave me alone,' he gasped, staggering to his feet. 'I've got to get away. I've got to think.' He stumbled towards the door, his breath coming in great painful gasps, and thrust his way down the stairs.

'Hubert,' called Myra again.

Down below there was a loud slam from the front door, so violent it made the house shake. Trembling, Myra rose to her feet, not at all sure what had just happened. With a feeling of unreality, she crossed to the door and stared forlornly out into the darkened hall. But it was no use. He had gone.

23

The police got their search warrant and went back to Walsingham. The request had caused some consternation amongst the senior ranks down at headquarters. No one had ever heard of a theological college being searched before. 'You'd better have got it right,' the chief superintendent said worriedly, calling the inspector into his office. 'There'll be hell to pay if they complain that we're conducting a search without sufficient grounds.'

'It's alright, sir,' said the inspector. 'Trust me. I've got a gut feeling about this one. They're hiding something.'

They arrived at midday. Ten uniformed policemen, three plain clothes officers and a dog. 'You never know,' the handler said hopefully, 'there might be drugs too.'

Brian was just finishing his weekly seminar on the ethics of genetic engineering when he looked up through the window and (as he related afterwards with rolling eyes) saw a dozen cars pulling noisily into the car park. In fact there were only four, and one of those was the dog van, but Brian always was rather given to exaggeration.

'I think it must the ecclesiastical police,' remarked one of the ordinands helpfully.

Brian cast a look on him designed to strike terror into his heart, and rather stiffly dismissed them all. Then he gathered together his books and scuttled off in search of William. He was rather flustered by the police interest of the last couple of days. His conscience, he told himself, was clear, but he was not entirely sure that he could vouch for that of other members of staff. For instance, he had noted some rather suspicious brown parcels being delivered to Beverley of late. Running up the stairs and along the corridor to William's rooms, Brian felt a flood of terror. Any fresh scandal, he knew, and that would be the end of Walsingham. Then what would he do? Dimly, in the outer reaches of his consciousness, Brian saw the spectre of a parish.

Downstairs, with much shuffling of shoulders and clumping of boots, the police were just coming en masse through the front doors. Chantelle, Father Goody's secretary (at something of a loss in her boss's absence), saw them from her office above and ran down to intercept them in the inner hall. 'Yes?' she said tartly. 'May I help?' She was a rather austere woman in her mid fifties, iron-grey hair caught back in a tight little bun at the nape of her neck, no makeup and a disapproving expression. Her tone implied that, whatever it was she was offering, it was certainly not help and, in spite of himself, the inspector faltered.

'We have here a warrant to search these premises,' he said pompously, at the same time drawing the warrant out of his inner pocket and waving it straight in her face. He had not intended to be rude, but he felt rather intimidated by her.

Chantelle was not impressed. She sniffed. 'Why?'

'Pardon?'

'I mean why should you want to search the college?'

The inspector reflected that members of the public were not supposed to speak to him like this. They were supposed to be properly subservient and awed, but she sounded like a disapproving housemistress who had just discovered a small child being naughty behind the bicycle sheds and he squirmed, suddenly catapulted back to the age of nine. 'We have reason to suspect there is vital evidence here relating to the attempted break-in at the Bishop's palace three nights ago,' he said stiffly.

Chantelle, who was deeply religious, sniffed again. 'Members of the college wishing to contact the Bishop usually do so by telephone,' she informed him coldly. 'I'm sure you won't find anyone here who has been involved in attempted robbery.'

'Did I say robbery?' The inspector glared at her, and behind he heard one of the policemen give a muffled snigger. 'Please take me to your acting principal,' he snapped, infuriated.

Chantelle looked at him for a long second and then shrugged. 'Alright,' she agreed. 'Follow me.'

She led the way down the long corridor, past the chapel and up the twisting stairs at the far end. Oswald's study was on the third floor of the east wing. 'What do you mean you're going to search the place?'

he asked, shocked.

'Not the whole college, sir, at this juncture. We want to start with the rooms of the three priests who bought coats last spring from the clerical outfitters who visited this establishment.'

Oswald went white. 'I bought one of those coats,' he said hollowly. 'They were on special offer. I remember.'

'So I understand, sir,' agreed the inspector. 'You, Canon Timothy Goody and the Reverend Brian Mulligan.

Oswald digested this. 'Where would you like to start?'

The inspector ran a finger reflectively down his nose. He had discussed this on the way over with Matthew, and they had decided that the best thing would be to search the rooms of all three men simultaneously. 'After all, we don't really know which one of them it might be, sir,' Matthew had advised. 'And if we pick the wrong one first, that could give the one who was guilty a chance to get rid of the stuff.' Quite what 'the stuff' might be that they were hoping to find, they were neither of them very sure, but they both felt absolutely positive that there was something there. 'We'll search all three at the same time, sir,' said the inspector crisply. 'I understand from his secretary that Canon Goody is still away.'

'*Father* Goody,' said Oswald absently.

The inspector blinked. 'What?'

'The form of address,' replied Oswald vaguely, not even bothering to glance up. He was trying to work out what all this might mean and whether it would be in his interests to inform on Father Goody or not. 'It's 'Father', not 'Canon'. That's our title.'

The inspector breathed heavily. He was growing more than a little tired of all these poncey forms of ecclesiastical address. It seemed that each time he opened his mouth, he got it wrong. 'Father Goody,' he repeated, with emphasis, 'is away. But if you and ... Father Mulligan?' Oswald nodded. 'If you would both like to accompany a couple of my officers, we'll make a start.'

In the event they could not start the searches straight away, because it took them a good half an hour to find Brian. When he was finally unearthed, closeted with William, he looked positively terrified. 'But why me?' he protested. 'What's going on?'

Briefly Matthew told him about the attempted break-in at the palace and Brian looked appalled. For the first time he really did begin seriously to suspect that 'my darling hunneykins' was the Bishop's wife after all. He opened his mouth to say something, but realised that that would serve only to land Father Goody in extremely hot water, so he shut it again immediately. 'It wasn't me,' he said, in a small voice. 'Honestly.'

All his protests, however, were to no avail and by the time he went up to his rooms with Matthew, they found that the uniformed officers had already made a start. 'Hey, Jim,' came a loud voice as they turned down the corridor, 'you sure we're in the right room? There's a load of women's stuff here!'

'That's nothing, mate. You should see the makeup I've got over here!'

Brian shut his eyes and mentally wept. 'Honestly,' he told William later, 'I felt violated. Raped.' His torment, however, did not end there. The policemen went through everything and piled all his carefully hoarded finery in a giant heap on the bed. 'Nothing actually to tie him to the break-in,' said Matthew crossly at the end. 'Though I think he bloody well ought to be charged for this lot. It's disgusting!'

The officers searching Father Goody's rooms similarly had little success. 'Clean as a whistle, guv,' reported back the officiating officer. 'All we've found are books, Bibles and icons. Oh, and we think that maybe he likes writing poetry too, but nothing else. He seems alright,' he added reflectively. 'Sort of what you expect a priest to be.' Brian and William, on their last foray, had done an extremely efficient job.

Oswald, when it came to his turn, felt not the slightest concern at all. He knew he was innocent. He stood at the side of the room with a sour look on his face, as the policemen rifled through his drawers and cupboards. 'You see,' he was saying sanctimoniously, 'there's absolutely nothing ...' Just at that moment, from the bedroom, he was interrupted by a loud shout.

'Guv,' came the excited voice of the young constable who had been given the unsavoury task of investigating Oswald's underwear, 'I think you ought to come and see this. There's something here.'

They all crowded through into the bedroom, Oswald, in spite of himself, going pale. Staring over the shoulders of the policemen in front of him, he felt a wave of horror. The young constable was waving in the air, like some kind of olympic trophy, Father Goody's tattered, blood-stained trousers, while on the floor at his feet lay the principal's similarly bloodied sweater and shirt. Oswald cursed the malicious spirit that had suggested to him that he ought retrieve the wretched things and bring them back to his room. Then an officer, on his knees in front of the wardrobe, pulled out a shoe. 'I think this may be of interest too, guv,' he announced.

After that, Oswald hardly knew what was happening. In a very short space of time he found himself being cautioned and then placed under arrest. And then, under the astonished gaze of the students and staff, they led him downstairs. 'I'm innocent,' he kept burbling. 'They're not mine. They belong to Father Goody.'

'Yeah, yeah,' said one of the policemen unsympathetically. 'The prisons are full of innocent blokes. We only lock up the ones who haven't done anything. Save it for the station, mate.'

The Bishop was informed by phone later the same day. 'We've got our man,' said the inspector tersely. 'He's denying it all of course at this point, but then again they always do. It won't help him. We've got the rest of his clothes.'

The Bishop swallowed. 'Father Goody, I suppose?' he said hollowly.

'No.' The inspector sounded surprised. 'Father Oswald Pettifence actually.'

'Father Oswald?' repeated the Bishop. 'You're joking surely?' He sounded stunned.

'No, sir,' said Bateman with some acerbity. 'I can assure you I do not joke about people under arrest. We have found the rest of the clothes Father Pettifence was wearing when he attempted to break in, along with the second shoe.'

Bishop Hubert replaced the receiver, his brain in turmoil. He felt he had no sooner got things straight, than they had all been upended again. He had utterly convinced himself that Myra was involved in a torrid affair with Tim Goody. She had even admitted as much, he thought incredulously, and yet here were the police saying they had arrested Oswald Pettifence! It made no kind of sense. Was she involved with both of them? And then, as he thought about the scene they had had, it occurred to him that Myra had never actually admitted to an affair with the principal at all. So far as he could recollect, they had neither of them mentioned names. So had he then been wrong? Was it after all Pettifence who had made such a fool of him?

In a sudden spasm of anguish, the Bishop writhed. This was intolerable. He had got to know. Hardly knowing what he did, he rose to his feet and began to move towards the door. At the same moment it opened, and Barbara poked her head in. 'Bishop,' she said brightly, 'I've had the Mothers' Union on the phone. They want to know if you'll talk about marriage when you go to them next month. I know Nicholas usually deals with all this kind of thing, but he's not here at the moment, so I wondered what you wanted to do?'

She laughed, to the Bishop's ears an oddly brittle sound, and he stared at her bemusedly. 'Oh, I don't know,' he said vaguely. 'Anything. Whatever they want.' Then he stumbled roughly past her, leaving her staring after him, open-mouthed.

'But ... ,' she began.

He waved a hand. 'Not now, Barbara!'

It was not till he was halfway across to the flat that it suddenly struck him what he had just agreed to talk about, and he pulled up short, horrified. Him, talk about marriage? To the Mothers' Union? He gave a loud bark of rather manic laughter and a wild look came into his eye. Oh yes, he could tell them about marriage! He could tell them about the cruel perfidy of women and the non-existence of the marriage bond! He'd tell them how stupid it was to trust!

By the time he reached the flat and was clambering heavily up the stairs he was rather hysterical, and he tried vainly to calm himself. He was only partly successful. With almost murderous rage, he pushed open the heavy living room door, and found Myra seated at her little Jacobean desk over in the corner writing a letter.

'I suppose you're writing to him,' he spat through clenched teeth.

Startled, Myra looked up, and then stared at him as if he were mad. 'Him?' she repeated. 'Who? What are you talking about?'

The Bishop advanced farther into the room, his hands at his sides clenched into two hard fists. 'Well, I'm not exactly sure,' he said icily. 'Would it be Goody, or Pettifence? You tell me.'

'Goody or Pettifence?' Myra repeated again. 'Have you gone insane?' She rose to her feet, an expression of complete amazement on her face.

This was too much. 'Don't try and act as if you don't know what I'm talking about!' shouted the Bishop, the fragile hold he had been keeping on his temper finally snapping. 'Your lover, woman! Which one is it?'

Myra was so shocked that she took a step back, causing her to fall into the chair just behind. 'I ... I haven't the slightest idea what you're talking about,' she said plaintively.

'I know it's one of them,' spluttered the Bishop, almost dancing up and down in front of her with rage. He found it almost unbearable that she should attempt to deny it all now. With a dull sense of shock, he realised he was no longer particularly interested in anything she might have to say. All the pressure and strain of the last few months suddenly erupted in one massive explosion that rocked him to the core, and all the bitterness and resentment that he had kept bottled up, spewed out, like lava gushing from a fault line. Normally so quiet and reserved, so peaceful, he found he could no longer hold anything back. And as his wife sat there, a hand pressed over her heart, her face absolutely drained of colour, he ranted and raged around the room, accusing her of every vile sin under the sun, and delineating for her in minute detail the terrible conspiracy that he felt was being perpetrated against him in the diocese.

Throughout it all, Myra sat there mute and helpless, after a first initial protest too stunned to react. Finally, when he had wrenched every last drop out of his system and could dredge up nothing more, he said brokenly, 'Have you nothing to say?'

In the sudden quiet that fell, Myra blinked, then opened and shut her mouth uselessly. 'I don't think there's much left after all of that,' she said at last, feebly. She shook her head dazedly, as if trying to clear her thoughts, and the Bishop felt suddenly ashamed.

'I'm sorry,' he mumbled. 'I just feel so upset. I couldn't take any more.'

She looked at him closely. 'Perhaps now you're calmer, you could tell me exactly what's happened.'

As if she had prodded an exposed nerve, his head jerked up and the wild look came back into his eye. But just as suddenly as it had flared up, it died. 'The police have arrested Oswald Pettifence,' he said heavily. Then, seeing her look of complete bewilderment, he added, 'You know, the vice-principal of Walsingham. You *must* remember him.'

She shook her head. 'I'm not sure ... Oh, wait a minute, yes ... I do know. I met him at that party for Dougal Sampratt, didn't I? And I think he gave one of the addresses at the conference too.' A puzzled look came into her eyes. 'But why have they arrested him?'

The Bishop peered at her, then after a second fished in his pocket for his spectacles and placed them on the end of his nose, as if he could not quite believe his eyes. 'You mean you really don't know him?' he asked incredulously.

Myra shook her head. 'Not really. Well, to say hello to, I suppose, but nothing more.'

It was his turn to sit down. 'But I thought ...,' he began.

Her eyes narrowed. 'Yes?' she said. 'Exactly what *did* you think?'

It was borne in upon the Bishop that he might, just possibly, have made the most awful mistake. 'You ... and him,' he said in a small voice.

Myra's eyes narrowed even more. 'Yes?' she prompted again.

The Bishop squirmed. 'You,' he repeated. Then he swallowed.

'Me?'

'An affair ...'

A look of such anger came over Myra's face that the Bishop flinched. 'Well, you did admit it,' he said defensively.

Myra rose to her feet. Whereas a moment before her cheeks had been deathly white, now they flamed scarlet with indignation. She drew herself up to her full height and took a deep breath, so that her chest swelled. She looked magnificent, like some avenging Valkyrie sweeping in on the horns of the wind, and poor Hubert felt himself shrink. 'You stupid man!' she cried imperiously. 'I admit to an affair? When?'

She seemed to be expecting some kind of an answer, and after a second he said falteringly, 'This ... this morning, dear.'

She glared at him. 'Sometimes, Hubert,' she said witheringly, 'I think you're the most stupid man alive. I never admitted to anything of the sort!'

The Bishop digested this. 'Then what did you admit to, dear?' he asked timidly.

Myra ruffled like an enraged hen. 'I do not actually recollect admitting to anything. If memory serves aright, it was you who said you knew it all.'

The Bishop began to wonder if he was experiencing a particularly unpleasant nightmare. It was perfectly true of course, what Myra was saying, but he had assumed from her manner earlier that that was in itself an admission. Now she appeared to be saying that was not the case after all. The Bishop shook his head bemusedly. He thought women were very strange. He decided to try again. 'The police say Oswald Pettifence was the intruder, and that they have the evidence.'

Diverted by this fresh intelligence, Myra frowned. 'Goodness me,' she said in disgust, 'are all men incapable of getting anything right?'

The Bishop wondered if he might risk asking what she meant, and then decided against it. He discovered he was rather frightened of this new Myra. But Myra was ignoring him. 'It wasn't this man Pettifence,' she said decisively. 'It was Tim Goody. I saw him. Although of course I wasn't going to tell the police that.'

'Really, my dear.' The Bishop nodded vaguely. He had decided that whether this was a nightmare or not, the best way to survive it was simply to agree.

She fixed on him a martial eye. 'Hubert, this won't do at all. You must phone back the police and tell them they've got the wrong man.'

'Oh, dear,' said the Bishop. 'Must I?' He remembered his last conversation with the inspector and inwardly quailed. 'I don't think they'll believe me, my dear.'

'Why not?' demanded Myra.

'Because they say they've matched his clothes. They found the trousers he'd worn, all torn and covered with blood, and the other shoe.'

It was Myra's turn to look confused. 'But I could have sworn it was Tim Goody.'

The Bishop grimaced. 'Maybe in the dark,' he hazarded, 'it was difficult to see. Maybe you made a mistake.'

Myra looked at him uncertainly, and the Bishop rose falteringly to his feet. 'Myra,' he began, 'I think, just possibly, I might have made a mistake ... I appear to have misunderstood.' He swallowed, 'I'm very sorry, but I have to say I have very little idea of what's going on. Why should it have been Goody trying to break in here anyway?'

As he said this last, he looked at her pleadingly, half dreading that his earlier suspicions would after all turn out to be right. He was reassured by seeing a sour expression pass over Myra's face, almost as if she could not bear even to think of him. 'That man,' she pronounced angrily, 'is a complete and utter swine. He's a lecher, and for the past two months, ever since I told him how stupid he was being, he's been making my life a misery. He's completely mad. He ought to be defrocked.'

The Bishop could only blink in amazement but, now that Myra had at last managed to say this much, the floodgates suddenly opened and the whole unpleasant story poured out. 'He's been following me around everywhere,' she ended up. 'I've been really scared. I thought he might be going to attack me.'

The Bishop was appalled. 'My dear, I had no idea.'

'No,' said Myra ruefully, 'I was trying to keep it from you. I thought you had enough problems.'

The Bishop winced at the unvoiced criticism. Things had come to a sad pass he reflected, if his wife was too afraid to confide in him. A thought suddenly occurred to him. 'Perhaps all the anxiety you've been feeling,' he said, 'was why you automatically assumed that the intruder the other night was Goody.'

Myra looked doubtful. 'Maybe,' she agreed. 'But if that's so, why should Oswald Pettifence have been trying to get in?'

The Bishop shook his head. 'I have absolutely no idea, my dear. All I can say is I'm very glad we've at last managed to talk about all of this.' He looked at her hesitantly. 'Perhaps if you had told me about it in the first place, it could all have been avoided.'

His wife hung her head as if in remorse, but inwardly she felt the most enormous relief, as if some fearful monster had been routed. 'Yes, Hubert,' she said meekly. 'I'm so sorry. If it ever happens again, I promise I'll tell you straight away.'

The Bishop looked at her fondly. He could quite understand why other men might conceive such passion for this jewel of a wife. He determined that in the future he was going to listen more, and that he was going to take very good care of her. Very good care indeed.

24

Carl had at last gone away. Pepper could hardly believe it. He had been behaving so oddly of late, having people round at all hours collecting the little white packages he dispensed, and all the time seemingly obsessed with what was happening over at St Prosdocimus. Every time he opened his mouth, it was to complain about that 'fucking priest'. Pepper could not understand why he seemed to hate him so much, but in some mysterious way it was as if Dougal had become the symbol of all Carl loathed and feared. He had even begun to mutter in his sleep about destroying him and Pepper had started to feel really frightened, sensing that the violence throbbing away deep down in Carl was bubbling ever closer to the surface.

He had given no prior hint that he was going. He simply came into the tiny kitchen one morning and announced, 'I'll be away a few days.'

A wild bubble of disbelieving joy exploded in Pepper. 'When will you be back?' she asked breathlessly, with difficulty keeping the excitement out of her voice.

He looked at her narrowly. 'A few days. Why? What's it to you?'

She was alarmed. 'Nothing, Carl.' She rose hastily to her feet and twined her arms around his neck. 'I just miss you when you're away. That's all.'

'Hum!' He grunted, pleased, and then pushed her away. 'If anyone asks, ye don't know where I am.'

'But I don't anyway,' she pointed out.

He left then, taking a small holdall with him, and Pepper immediately began to rush round the flat, gathering together the last of her clothes and stuffing them untidily into a couple of carrier bags that she had saved from her last trip to the supermarket. That done, she peered out of the door to make sure the coast was clear, and then scuttled as fast as she could over to Maisie's.

'Tonight's the night,' she said excitedly, as soon as Maisie opened the door. 'Carl's gone away.'

Maisie, taking one look at her flushed face, felt a sudden stab of quite irrational fear. 'Are y' absolutely certain?' she asked apprehensively.

'Course!' said Pepper, pushing past her. 'He's taken a bag and some stuff. He won't be back for at least a couple of days now.'

She sounded so sure that Maisie pushed her unease to the back of her mind. 'Come on then,' she said briefly. 'Y'd better start to pack.'

They had agreed before that when the time finally came for Pepper's escape, she would pack the large suitcase they had bought from the market during the day, but not actually go until after dark. 'The less people know the better,' Maisie had pointed out reasonably and Pepper, though dying to make a start, had been forced to agree. She could not risk Carl coming after her.

Now Maisie dragged out the case from under her bed, and settled on her knees to help the other girl pack. It was certainly time to leave she thought, glancing up at Pepper covertly as the latter moved swiftly about the room, folding and then laying the clothes in neat piles for Maisie to place in the case. The bulge of her stomach had become increasingly difficult to hide of late, and there was a kind of bloom on her cheeks that Maisie thought had to do with incipient motherhood. She felt rather envious.

Across the street, Danny watched Pepper's arrival at Maisie's with interest. It was not the first of such comings and goings that he had observed over the last few days, and he felt mildly curious, wondering what could possibly be in the bulging bags. But he had other concerns on his mind and soon abandoned the puzzle of Pepper to consider his own predicament. The more he thought about it, the less he felt inclined to carry out Carl's commission. He was not sure whether he was afraid or not, but there was a peculiar feeling deep down in his gut whenever he thought about harming the priest. He could not make sense of it. He desperately wanted revenge, but whenever he considered how he might actually accomplish the deed, it was as if a restraining 'something or other' insinuated itself into his mind, paralysing his capacity to think. Danny was rather frightened. He began to wonder if it was God.

At that moment there was a loud beeping and a long black car slid to a stop in front of him. For once Carl had got his cassette player turned off, and Danny stared in surprise as the window wound silently down. 'Get in,' commanded Carl briefly. 'I want to talk.'

Danny felt a wave of unease but experience had taught him it was unwise to disagree with Carl. He skipped round the side of the car and clambered in and immediately Carl let out the clutch and they glided away. 'Where we goin', man?' demanded Danny.

His eyes fixed on the road, Carl inclined his head slightly. 'Nowhere particular. I just want a chat.' He was silent for a moment, negotiating a corner, then resumed, 'When ye goin' to do for this priest then?'

Danny swallowed. 'Soon,' he promised.

'If you can't do it, I'll get someone else.'

Danny felt a cold sweat break out across his brow. 'Course I can do it, man,' he protested. 'I've jus' bin waiting for the best time.'

This time Carl glanced across at him. 'I'm goin' away for a few days,' he said. 'I want it done by the time I get back.'

'Okay.' Danny's agreement was, he knew, a little too quick and he licked his lips nervously. 'Is that why Pepper was going round to stay at Maisie's?' he asked, hoping to divert the pimp's attention. ''Cause you're goin' away?'

Carl slammed on the brakes so hard they both lurched forward. 'What ye mean?' he asked, spinning round, his hand at the same time lunging out for Danny's throat.

Danny was so surprised he almost fainted. 'Nothing,' he gasped, his fingers scrabbling wildly at Carl's hand.

Carl gave him a shove and his fingers tightened. 'What are you talking about?' he said again.

He shoved his face up close to Danny's, and Danny felt his hot stale breath on his cheek. ''Onest, man,' he gasped. He felt as if his lungs were about to explode. 'I jus' saw 'er going round earlier, that's all. She 'ad a couple of carriers with 'er.'

Carl regarded him for a long moment, then gave a final vicious twist of his hand, crushing Danny's windpipe. Then abruptly he let him go. 'Why do you think she was staying there?' he asked.

Danny, now retching as he fought for breath, decided Carl was insane. 'I dunno, man,' he spluttered. 'It jus' looked like she was carryin' clothes, that was all ... I jus' thought.'

There was a loud angry beeping from behind, and Carl broke off to raise two fingers in the mirror. Then he drove on, a deep frown on his face. 'What's she up to?' he asked, more to himself than to Danny.

Danny thought it politic not to reply. He rubbed his bruised throat gingerly, and wondered how long it would be before Carl set him down. He didn't have long to wait. Carl pulled abruptly into the side of the road and, reaching across him, swung open the door. 'Get out,' he ordered. 'Remember what I said. I want it done now.' Danny clambered out as fast as he could. He was unlikely, he thought, to forget. As he stepped quickly away onto the pavement, Carl called behind him, 'Don't tell no one you've seen me. Is that clear? Especially, don't tell Pepper.'

He drove off with a screech of tyres, and Danny stared after him resentfully. 'Bleedin' nutter,' he said under his breath. He discovered he could not have managed a louder voice even if he had wanted, his throat hurt too much. A puzzled expression settled across his face. He felt even less inclined now to carry out Carl's instructions. If he were that desperate to have the priest topped, then let him do it himself! But Pepper ... ? That was an entirely different problem.

A sudden feeling of nausea overwhelmed him, and he sat down on the nearest step. Typical, Carl had dropped him miles from where he had picked him up. It would take him ages to walk back. He considered briefly whether or not to steal a set of wheels, but the street was empty for once and after a second he abandoned the idea. It might take him ages to find a car and there was no guarantee the police wouldn't become involved. Danny normally enjoyed a good chase but he suddenly felt the most terrible urgency to get back. He could not risk time being taken into custody. He had to find Pepper and warn her there was something wrong.

Back at Maisie's, Pepper finished stowing her clothes and then went out onto the street. She would, she thought, take one last opportunity to earn some extra cash. She positioned herself on the pavement, adjacent to the Wigspittle and Pole. A fine drizzle was beginning to fall, and she briefly considered abandoning the plan and going and taking refuge inside the pub, but after a moment she dismissed that idea. Time enough soon to cosset herself. She began to imagine her new life, somewhere quiet where nobody knew her and she could let her pregnancy show. She imagined herself with the baby once it had been born, and found herself wondering whether it would be a boy or a girl. She hoped desperately it would be a girl. Pepper's experience with males had not been very good. But whatever it was, she knew she would love it, and she was absolutely convinced that if this child *was* a boy, he at least would be different. More like that priest bloke maybe. He seemed okay really.

She was still thinking about the baby clothes she was going to buy, and the pushchair she would have, when there was a terrible screech of brakes, and Carl's car ground to a halt in front of her. She was so startled she jumped back, and in the same instant the sun came from behind the clouds and illumined her in a halo of light. Carl, flinging open the car door as he reached across, looked up and suddenly saw the swell of her stomach outlined against the light. At that moment an artist might have thought Pepper, unmistakably manifesting the growing signs of life, indescribably beautiful, but not Carl. His jaw dropped open. "You're pregnant!' he said incredulously. 'You stupid cow.'

Pepper could only stare at him, paralysed with terror. She tried to speak, and found her voice had dried up. In a trice he was out of the car. 'How long?' he demanded viciously.

She licked her lips and, thinking she was refusing to reply, he raised a hand to strike her. 'No!' she said, cringing back, the movement releasing her.

'How long then?' he barked again.

Along the street the other girls watched curiously. Carl ignored them. He lunged at Pepper and his hand caught her cheek. 'Sixteen weeks,' she said, sobbing. 'I've been meaning to tell you, 'onest.'

For answer, he hit her again and then, with one cruel movement, bundled her into the car. 'You stupid cow!' he shouted again, aiming a kick at the door. Then he ran round the other side, leapt in, and roared off. The girls all stared after them stunned, and then drew together in a frightened little knot. 'Wot d'ye think 'e'll do to 'er?' inquired one.

The others shrugged, and then another said, 'Do you think she's really pregnant?'

'Could be.'

They all looked mournful. Carl's jealousy was legendary and, while Pepper was too reserved to be universally popular, most of them thought she was alright.

'I'm going to go and tell Maisie,' announced one of the younger ones suddenly. 'Pepper's her friend. She might know what to do.'

Over at the rectory, Dougal forced himself to try and get ready for the Bishop's visit later that night. But he felt so depressed and fed up, it was all he could do to try and work out some sort of itinerary. The loss of the centre was a serious blow, because it meant he had nowhere to take the Bishop as a starting off place, and somehow just walking round the streets and chatting to the girls, although it was what he had been doing, seemed bland and inane in the light of all that had happened.

It would have been nice to have been able to take the Bishop to look at the restoration work but, since The Roxburgh had reclaimed the paint, despite Eliston and Regina's best efforts, the whole enterprise had ground to a halt. He supposed he would have to show it to the Bishop at some point, but somehow, in its state of half-finished abandonment, it looked more like a damning affirmation of guilt. Dougal discovered he felt intensely ashamed, as if all that had happened somehow revealed him as being inadequate and naive. He felt he wanted to hide away, but that was impossible.

Looking outside, where it was now raining in earnest, he decided that they would start with a visit to the Wigspittle and Pole, followed by two local clubs the girls frequented, and then move on to a tour of the streets later, when, hopefully, it might be drier.

He was interrupted in his plans by a wild and insistent ringing at the door, as if the person outside was too overwrought to remove their hand. Peeved, he got up and shuffled through to the hall. 'All right, all right,' he called waspishly. 'I'm coming. Stop it will you!'

He wrenched back the door and discovered Maisie standing there looking distraught. 'Y've got to 'elp us, Father!' she panted, eyes wild. She erupted past him into the hall. 'Carl's taken Pepper.'

Dougal, squashed up against the wall, decided there was some finer point here he was missing, but it struck him as not worth the effort of pursuing, because Maisie was clearly about to spill it all out anyway. Bowing to the inevitability of her onslaught, he tried vainly to shut the door, but Maisie was standing so close, and the hallway was so small, he found he could not move. 'Please, Maisie,' he said irritably, 'either go in or out, but whatever you do, let me shut the door.' Then he added, 'It's cold.'

Maisie blinked at him in surprise. She had never seen Dougal irritable before and was rather taken aback. 'Oh, I'm sorry,' she shrilled. 'But it's an emergency.'

Dougal sighed. In his present state of gloom, he could imagine very few things worse than what had already happened to him, and he felt in no mood to dispense sympathy to Maisie in an imagined crisis. It was probably of the order of a hole in her tights anyway, he reflected bitterly. 'Just go through into the sitting room, Maisie,' he said aloud, allowing just a hint of the sourness he was feeling to creep into his voice.

Maisie stared at him, perplexed, then whirled on her stilettos and walked through into the room. "'E's taken 'er,' she announced again in tones of utter devastation, flinging herself onto the sofa. Then to Dougal's complete astonishment, and not a little embarrassment, she suddenly burst into tears.

He could only stare at her, dumbfounded. Dougal was not very good at the best of times at expressing sympathy, and up until that moment he had not actually been feeling any. 'There, there, Maisie,' he said awkwardly, still standing by the door and staring at her, appalled. 'Don't cry. There's a good girl. It can't be that bad.'

For answer Maisie broke into a fresh paroxysm of noisy sobs and after a second, in the absence of anything better to do, he fished into his pocket for a handkerchief and thrust it towards her. Then he wondered if he ought to hug her or something, but decided against that. Diocesan guidelines recently had been very clear about that sort of thing, and besides ... he felt an idiot.

Maisie took the hankie and blew her nose loudly. It was not a very feminine sound and, when she looked up, there was mascara streaked down both cheeks. "'E grabbed her off the street,' she said dramatically.

'Did he?' Dougal frowned. Even immersed as he was in his own concerns, he was beginning to realise that there was something wrong here, and that he ought, out of Christian charity, to do something to help. But Dougal still did not feel very Christian. 'For heaven's sake, Maisie,' he said brusquely, 'pull yourself together. What's the problem? After all, he is her pimp, isn't he?'

Maisie stared at him in outrage. 'So?' she snapped. 'What y' saying? That gives 'im the right to do what 'e wants with 'er, does it?'

'No, of course not.' Dougal shook his head irritably and then sat down. Not for the first time when dealing with Maisie, he had the feeling of being caught in the backwash from an oil tanker. 'I'm just saying,' he said reasonably, 'that from what I've seen, this kind of thing isn't that exceptional.'

As if she could not quite believe what she was hearing, Maisie raised both hands to her face, pressing her fingers together across the bridge of her nose, and glared at him. Then she bit her lip and said furiously, 'I thought you were supposed to be our friend. To care about us! Pepper's pregnant. Don't y' understand? That's what the problem is, and Carl's found out!'

Her words took Dougal by complete surprise. They came as such a shock, he felt almost as if someone had delivered him a blow straight to the solar plexus. As if in pain, his face contorted. 'What's up?' demanded Maisie, in turn staring at him in amazement. She had wanted a reaction it was true, but this struck even her as a trifle excessive.

'Nothing,' mumbled Dougal, appalled at his own reaction. Maisie glared at him suspiciously. 'You ill, or what?'

'No.' Still clutching at his stomach, Dougal shook his head. A terrible feeling that he was slowly slipping down into a great vortex of mind-consuming chaos suddenly rose up all around him. 'If you must know,' he said miserably, 'it's Amanda.' Maisie waited. 'She's pregnant too, By someone else.'

At this pronouncement, even Maisie seemed floored. She sat there in complete silence and, suddenly incensed, Dougal exploded, 'I can bloody well understand how Carl feels. If it's not his kid!'

That at least appeared to touch her. She cast on him a look of such complete and utter disgust that he involuntarily recoiled, and then she said witheringly, 'Don't be so bleedin' daft. It's not at all the same.'

Dougal stared at her. He had been rather expecting sympathy, and maybe even an offer to make him a cup of tea. He felt his ego deserved a bit of remedial massage. 'Aren't you even going to tell me you're sorry?' he demanded, outraged.

Maisie pulled a face. 'No, I'm not,' she retorted. 'I'm glad. She's a cow. I'm just glad y've found out.'

This was too much. Dougal could not believe his ears. Shaking with rage, he sprang to his feet. 'Maisie!' he shouted, 'You really are the limit. My life's in complete ruins, and all you can say is you're glad!'

'At least you've still got a life!' shouted back Maisie, in turn springing to her feet. 'Pepper may not have. Not now.'

He went white. 'What do you mean?'

He was answered by a fresh storm of tears, and she flung herself back down again onto the sofa. Then she dragged his hankie once more across her face and, between hiccups, blurted out, 'Carl's goin' to kill 'er. I know it. 'E doesn't give a damn whether it's his kid or not. 'E just won't let her have one'

In spite of himself, Dougal found his gaze riveted by the grubby black streaks extending across his once pristine handkerchief. 'Oh come now,' he said, 'don't be silly.'

Maisie glared at him as if he was completely deranged. 'Silly?' she screamed. 'Is that all y' can say? I tell you 'e's going to kill her, and all you can say is 'Don't be silly'.' She imitated his voice mincingly and he winced.

'No, of course not, Maisie,' he began again, infinitely reasonable. She really was being most unfair attacking him like this. 'People don't kill someone just because they're having a baby.'

It was Maisie's turn to go white. She leapt to her feet. 'You might not,' she cried hysterically. 'But try telling that to Carl. 'E don't let any of 'is girls get pregnant. 'E always makes them get rid of it ... But it's worse for Pepper cos she's 'is woman!'

Not for the first time in their acquaintance, it struck Dougal that Maisie had a tendency to over-dramatise. That Carl would be annoyed he agreed. He was himself annoyed with Amanda. And he felt he could even understand if the pimp were to insist that the girl had an abortion. Not that Dougal personally had any sympathy with this point of view, of course, but he could quite see that Carl might feel the pregnancy of one of his girls was bad for business. But the suggestion that Carl might go beyond this and physically try to injure Pepper, Dougal found bizarre. People simply didn't do that kind of thing.

Maisie, however, clearly thought they did. She glared at him, anger mounting as he failed to respond, trying to work out what to do. And then she suddenly exploded, 'Y're just like all the rest aren't y'? Full of all these bleedin' platitudes about wot y're goin' to do, but deep down y' don't give a damn!'

As she said this, Maisie flung her hands in the air, and Dougal recoiled, completely taken aback by the violence of the movement. He was not used to being spoken to like this. Especially by parishioners. He opened and shut his mouth uselessly, and began to wonder if Maisie was perhaps unwell. For her part, Maisie danced around like an infuriated dryad, so blazing with indignation at what she felt to be Dougal's betrayal, that she was temporarily bereft of the power of speech.

It was perhaps a mercy she was. 'Would you like a cup of tea?' hazarded Dougal, remembering that this was good for shock, and feeling that he at least would benefit from it.

Maisie refound her voice. 'No I bleedin' wouldn't!' she screamed. 'I want ' elp to find Pepper!' And with that she flung from the room, a loud crash that made the walls of the house shake, testifying to her departure.

Dougal was so stunned that he just stood there, staring blankly at the space where she had been a minute before. He felt as if a tidal wave had swept over him, and he felt himself almost fall into a deep pit of remorse. But it was mixed with anger too. Everyone always wanted him to care about *them*, but who the hell ever bothered about him? He had just shared with Maisie his own anguish, and all she had done was round on him. Then he thought of Pepper, and the bitter antagonism that always seemed to churn away just below her surface, and he thought savagely, 'She knew the score.' In that one moment it seemed to him entirely unreasonable for Maisie to care so much for her, and so little for him. And then at last he allowed himself to think of Maisie herself. She was absolutely terrified, he thought stunned ... for someone else. She really cared. He had always assumed that she, along with all the other girls who inhabited the streets, was entirely self-regarding; a lesser form of life. He realised, with a sense of the most incredible shame, that he had actually thought she was incapable of caring. But she was right. It was not she who didn't care, it was he himself. When it really came to it, he was the one who was self-obsessed. And on top of all his loathing for the rest of humanity, in that moment Dougal felt a deep and terrible self-loathing.

*

By the time Danny got back, it was growing dark. The heavy clouds that had been rolling in all day hung low and heavy in the sky, blotting out any glimmer of light from above. Danny dashed along the streets, his feet almost unconsciously taking him in the direction of Maisie's. He had very little hope of finding either girl there at that hour, but still, he told himself, it was worth a try. As he ran, his eyes raked round, but the streets were deserted and his boots, ringing on the pavement, filled him with icy dread. He hurried past the Wigspittle and Pole, ignoring the cries of Biff and Darren who, as ever, were draped over the door, past the rectory and on to the row of run-down shops above which Maisie lived. Ahead he could see a light on in her flat and, obscurely encouraged, he ploughed on determinedly. As he pushed open the street door and ran past the smelling bins that filled the short alley, on his way to the stairs that led up to Maisie's flat, a dog howled and Danny shivered. His gran had always told him that when a dog howled like that, it was because it saw the angel of death. Danny was not overly superstitious, but in that moment he felt he could see it too.

He ran up the remaining stairs and hammered on Maisie's door. 'Maisie!' he shouted, reinforcing the summons, 'Let me in! It's Danny. I've got to talk to you!' He hammered again. 'Open the door!'

White-faced, Maisie pulled it back and stared at him. She could think of only one reason why Danny should hammer on her door like this. 'Wot is it?' she whispered, passing a dry tongue across her lips.

Danny shook his head. 'Where's Pepper?'

Maisie's eyes grew even larger, two pools of such unfathomable fear that Danny felt himself drowning in their depths. 'Wot's 'appened to 'er?' he said, suddenly terrified he was too late.

For answer Maisie stood back, motioning with her hand for him to come in. For a second she seemed to be too overcome to reply and then she said, her voice barely audible, 'Carl's grabbed 'er.'

Danny could not help himself. He sank into the nearest chair, his head falling forward on his hands, and gave a great tearing sob of despair. 'Oh God,' he blubbered, 'it's my fault.'

He raised an ashen face to Maisie and she stared at him appalled. 'I told 'im,' he said. 'I told Carl I saw Pepper comin' over here. I didn't know there was anything wrong. 'Onest.'

Maisie's tiny face, pinched suddenly and old with futility, gazed at him. 'It wasn't your fault,' she said. 'I always knew deep down 'e'd find out.'

A lot had happened to Maisie in the few hours since she had left Dougal. For a start she had trudged endlessly around the streets, scouring them for any sign of her friend; determined if at all possible to do something to help. But though she had gone to every place her imagination could suggest, and a few more, she had found no trace. Not of Pepper. Not of Carl. And finally she had come back in despair, like an animal returning hopelessly to its lair. She had tried to soothe herself at first by getting out the crystals she collected, and placing them around her in a circle. But they had seemed so cold and dead that she had, quite unreasonably, felt angry with them. What could a few lumps of dead rock do anyway?

After that she had tried to calm herself with some yogic breathing exercises she had read about once in a magazine, designed to promote peace, but it was no good. Whatever they did for the Tibetan monks, it didn't work for Maisie, and the thought of Pepper kept flooding back. And then she had thought of Dougal.

She felt indescribably angry with the priest. She felt he had let her down, betrayed her almost. But as she sat there glaring at the crystals winking back at her in the light, she had a stab of insight into the pain that he was feeling too, and she was so tired that her anger with him simply evaporated.

'Oh, God,' she said miserably, feeling indescribably weary. 'Why doesn't anything ever go right any more?' And in a great rush of anger, she suddenly lashed out at the crystals, scattering them across the floor. Even that, however, did not help, and after a second Maisie shouted, 'If y' really are there, God, why the hell don't you do something to 'elp for a change?'

The air around her seemed to shiver slightly, as if affronted by the noise, and Maisie collapsed crying onto her arms. In that moment she felt indescribably alone. Nothing seemed to help. Not her crystals, not the stupid spells and charms she had learnt, and certainly not the tarot. She was so incensed with this last that she abruptly jerked to her feet, almost ran to the drawer where she kept them, and flung them willy-nilly across the floor. Then she stood there shaking and crying. 'Oh, God,' she cried again. 'Please do something. Please let me find 'er before it's too late.'

It was at that moment that Danny had hammered on the door, and Maisie had been so startled that she had frozen, momentarily disorientated, while a terrible and quite irrational fear had gripped her that something awful had happened and that Danny was bringing news.

Now she stared down at him and said tremulously, 'She's pregnant, do you know that?'

Danny shook his head.

'I'm worried wot Carl'll do to 'er.'

She didn't need to say any more. ''E'll kill 'er,' breathed Danny.

Maisie swallowed, and then nodded. ''Elp me find 'er.'

Danny needed absolutely no urging at all. 'Course,' he said. 'Where you looked?'

25

As the Bishop clambered into his car in preparation for his foray to St Prosdocimus it dawned on him that, just as he had been so disastrously wrong in assessing the situation with his wife, so he might be similarly wrong in what he had assumed to be the truth about Dougal. He pondered this, staring at the steering wheel and trying to work out what it was that he actually knew as incontrovertible fact, and he arrived at the highly unsatisfactory conclusion that it was really very little. In fact the only thing he knew with any certainty was that Amanda was pregnant. Maybe by Nicholas, but equally, maybe not. Accordingly, it was with a far greater sense of humility, and a readiness to listen to whatever it was Dougal might have to say, that he eventually set off.

He found the young priest in what was quite clearly a state of barely controlled agitation. In the time since Maisie had left, Dougal had conducted his own search for Pepper but, like Maisie, he had drawn a blank. It was as if the girl had disappeared off the face of the earth. Everyone seemed very ready to tell him how she had gone (and he realised with a sense of shock that he had at last been accepted) but no one had seen hide nor hair of her since the abduction. With each abortive enquiry his misery deepened, but it was no good, and at half past eight he had been forced to acknowledge that simply wandering the streets like this was ridiculous and that he really must return in readiness to greet the Bishop, and learn his own fate.

'Dougal!' said Bishop Hubert warmly, as Dougal drew back the door. 'My boy.'

Dougal regarded him hollowly as he stood back to allow the Bishop to come in. He felt, after all that had happened, that his superior's greeting lacked sincerity.

For his part, the Bishop came to a halt in the poky little hall and scrutinised Dougal carefully. The pale overhead light cast a sickly glow and, looking at Dougal's ashen pallor, the Bishop felt a quite unexpected stab of remorse. He felt that somehow he had contributed to the state this young man was so clearly in. But even worse, he thought it suggested an unvoiced acknowledgement of guilt and fear of what was to come. 'Oh dear,' said the Bishop, and a great heaviness descended on him. He began to suspect that, after all, Dougal really had fallen from grace.

At that moment, however, Dougal roused himself and said, 'Sorry, Bishop, we've had a bit of a crisis here tonight, I'm afraid. One of the street girls has been snatched by her pimp and there are fears he's going to harm her.'

'Really?' The Bishop brightened at this and realised, not for the first time that evening, that he really wanted Dougal to be all that he had once seemed. 'Tell me about it,' he said eagerly. 'Perhaps I can help.'

In the absence of any better idea they set off, as Dougal had originally planned, on a tour of the pub and clubs. That was their best hope, Dougal said, of picking up any news. Accordingly, they went first to the Wigspittle and Pole, and the Bishop was amazed and pleased to see that overall people seemed to know their young priest and, even more importantly, to greet him with respect. The Bishop, who was used to his clergy complaining that they had no contact with their parishioners outside of those few who came to church, was stunned. He felt Dougal really was having an impact on the community. Then he found himself being introduced to a group of street girls relaxing in the pub before going out for their night's work, and he was utterly astounded to find them talking to Dougal as a friend. He found himself wedged at a battered table between a young girl in a quite obscenely short skirt and fishnet tights on the one side, and a rather older young woman in a pink plastic mac and very little else, on the other. 'My dear,' he asked, concerned, 'aren't you afraid of catching cold? It's very chilly out tonight, you know.'

It was while they were thus occupied that Bingo came in. He had learnt days before that there was no use coming to the area too early on in the evening because it was relatively dead, and it had been his intention now to grab a swift half in the warmth of the pub, before taking up position outside the rectory in readiness to stalk Dougal as he began his rounds later on. When he saw that the priest was already there, and who was with him, his eyes almost popped out of his head.

Bingo recognised the Bishop instantly. He had done a quite lengthy article on his investiture for one of the more upmarket tabloids but also, this evening, the Bishop was wearing his purple shirt, and Bingo knew full well that only the most senior of prelates were allowed to wear that particular shade. Then he registered that the Bishop was drinking what looked like a pint, and that his companions were quite obviously not the newest recruits to the Salvation Army, and his jaw dropped even further. He wondered briefly whether he should dash back to the car he had hired and grab his camera, but then he dismissed the idea. Wonderful though the picture would be (and even more startling the caption) he knew that to take it inside the Wigspittle and Pole would only serve to arouse attention of the worst kind. He decided therefore to bide his time, have a drink, and then follow them when they left.

Dougal was entirely oblivious of his presence. Indeed, he did not know who Bingo was, although he had long since registered the fact that someone must be following him. But now, in happy ignorance, he made a round of everyone in the pub, asking them whether they had seen Carl or Pepper. Darren and Biff, who were with their mates, asked him derisively and with hoots of laughter whether he wanted to score and then, when he turned away, muttered to each other that it wasn't going to be long now! Dougal, who was growing used to this kind of thing, ignored them, but the remaining customers were similarly unhelpful.

'Carl grabbed 'er!' he heard one of the girls confiding to the Bishop as he came back, her eyes round. 'It was 'orrible. 'E punched 'er an' then shoved 'er in the car. She was terrified.'

'Good heavens!' said the Bishop, clearly appalled at this testimony to violence. 'The poor girl.'

'I think we ought to move on and try The Inferno,' said Dougal. 'It's a club near here, and there's just a chance Carl may have gone there. Apparently he's due to meet someone there tonight.'

The Bishop downed his glass eagerly. He was, he discovered, feeling quite excited by all of this. It had been ages since he had had this kind of hands-on engagement with parish life. Across the bar Bingo, seeing his prey prepare to leave, tossed back his own whisky and soda and prepared to follow.

When the Bishop had heard the name 'The Inferno', he had imagined an exciting, rather exotic looking place with flaming red doors and beyond a row of bright, maybe flickering lights, leading into a darkened crypt pulsating with mysterious life. He was a bit of a romantic at heart. He discovered, however, that the reality was a good deal less exotic. They trotted quickly down a rather dingy and otherwise unremarkable side street, and arrived at a grubby looking doorway that seemed to plunge straight into the bowels of the earth. The Bishop gazed around, puzzled. It did not look like his idea of a club at all. In fact, apart from the yellowing pictures of near nude girls pinned around the doorframe under a thin covering of murky plastic, he would have had no idea it was there at all. Then, propped up against the wall in the shadows at the side, his eye fell on a large and rather garish board, with a painting of a voluptuous girl sprawled across it. It invited the passer-by to enter for naughty delight and, looking at it, the Bishop shuddered. Whatever it was that this particular establishment offered, it was not delight.

Dougal led the way in past the doorman. 'Evenin', Father,' called out that worthy, registering who it was. 'We're a bit quiet so far, apart from a gang of rowdies'

Dougal stopped to chat. 'Seen anything of Carl, Alec?' he asked.

The doorman shook his head. 'But it's still a bit early for 'im,' he advised. 'Wouldn't expect to see 'im before chuckin' out time. Unless 'e's got business, of course.'

They went on down the short flight of narrow stairs, the base of which disappeared into a well of inky (and, to the Bishop, menacing) black. At the bottom Dougal pushed open a door and they went in. Above them, at the same moment, Bingo slid in and past the doorman like a dark shadow, his coat collar turned up. Alec merely nodded. He was used to geezers like that.

If it had been seedy above, the Bishop found it was even seedier below. He had never actually been in a place like this before, and he stared round fascinated. It was not very large, he discovered. Stretching the length of one wall was a smoke-wreathed bar. In front of that were scattered a few tables, and then, set in the centre of the room, was a small stage with what looked like a large bird cage on it. But it was the occupant of the cage that caught the Bishop's eye, because inside a scantily clad girl writhed and gyrated, her pale moons of buttocks seeming very large and white. The Bishop averted his eyes hastily, feeling his face flame, but not before he had seen the expression of intense boredom on the girl's face. Dougal, he noted, seemed almost oblivious to her, although he waved a hand as he went past on his way to the bar, and the girl waved back. The Bishop felt himself gape.

As they settled themselves down on two rickety stools and Dougal began to chat to the barman, the Bishop noticed at a table over in the corner a group of about seven young men. They were clearly rather the worse for wear, and appeared to be engaged in a rather noisy drinking contest. The Bishop stared at them fascinated. From the tones that wafted every so often in his direction and the general look of them, he could tell that they were rather well-to-do. In fact they looked, to his eyes, like a group of young solicitors or city types.

'Stag night,' said the barman briefly, following the direction of his gaze. 'Bloody nuisance if you ask me, but they'll be out soon. They're doin' the rounds.'

At the same moment, one of the group in question looked up and his eyes fastened on the Bishop. 'It's the Strip-o-gram!' he shouted happily. 'He's here. He's even got a party shirt on!'

Six pairs of eyes swung towards the Bishop. 'I ordered a bird!' complained one bitterly. 'Not this old geezer.'

Bingo, who had been held up by an urgent call of nature, pushed open the door just as they were shouting out to the Bishop to come on over and get it off. His eyes bulged. He had retrieved his camera and had already taken a shot of Dougal and the Bishop talking to the doorman on their way in, but this promised to be even better. He walked a couple of paces forward and then checked, wondering if he could risk taking out the camera.

Ignoring him, and clearly incensed at the Bishop's failure to respond, the Hooray Henries staggered to their feet with loud whoops and cries of glee, and four of them began to push their way tipsily across to the bar. The Bishop, discovering them suddenly bearing down on him, looked askance and Dougal, realising that something untoward was going on, looked up and round. Bingo, watching gleefully, decided this was definitely worth the risk, and surreptitiously pulled out the camera from under his coat. At the same moment the four young rowdies lurched drunkenly up to the Bishop, and one of them flung his arms beerily around his neck. 'Come on,' he breathed beerily. 'Gerrit off!'

The Bishop was so startled he almost fell off his stool and the next instant he found his collar being tugged at in a vicious twisting motion that threatened to choke him. 'A ... Aagh!' he let out, giving a strangled cry as he fell off the stool and onto his knees. Two pairs of hands grabbed him and jerked him upwards, and to cries of 'Off! Off! Off!' he found his clothes being pecked at with sharp little tweaks that made him feel as if he was under attack from rampaging birds.

The young men were in no way hostile, but they were extremely persistent. Also, they were too drunk to have any very clear idea of what they were doing. Without more ado, Bingo pulled up his camera and a bright flash illuminated the scene.

The effect on the Hooray Henries was electric. They appeared to think the light was a part of the Bishop's act, and they took it as encouragement. Two more pairs of clammy hands wrenched drunkenly at the Bishop's trousers and they fell round his knees. At the same moment, one of the customers not involved with the group, and extremely irritated by what he saw as this interruption to his enjoyment, rose to his feet and planted a fist in the face of the nearest of the Bishop's assailants. 'Shove over!' he shouted. 'You're blocking the view!'

His victim let out a small 'Ugh!' and collapsed, and two of his friends, realising they were under attack, let go of the Bishop and turned on their assailant. The other three, still sitting at their table, now also rose to their feet and staggered across to give assistance. All hell broke loose.

'Blimey!' said the barman, struggling to be heard above the din, 'Get security down 'ere!'

The lights flickered, went off, and then came on again, and the girl on stage shrieked, flung open the door of her cage, and scuttled away. Bodies flailed back and forth across the floor, to the accompaniment of grunts and shouts, and Dougal tried vainly to reach the Bishop, who seemed once again to have fallen, and drag him to a place of safety over at the side.

The Hooray Henries were large lads. As the Bishop had correctly divined, they were newly qualified solicitors, but they also all played rugby for the local club, and enjoyed a good scrum. They took what was happening now to be a part of the evening's jollity and entered into the fight that suddenly erupted with gusto. As the Bishop panted and strove to pull his trousers back up, they tumbled backwards and forwards, punching blindly at anything that moved and giving noisy shouts. Dougal was hit on the jaw, and had to restrain himself from planting one back. But for all his efforts, he could not reach the Bishop.

The whole fiasco came to an end only some five minutes later, when the doorman and two security men summoned from above managed to push their way in. Unfortunately, however, they announced their arrival with a loud and extremely piercing whistle and, watching helplessly from the side, Dougal witnessed an amazing phenomenon. One moment the Hooray Henries were all scuffling and fighting and giving noisy cries of encouragement, and the next, as if by magic, the floor had suddenly cleared, and they had gone.

Dazed, and at a loss to know what had happened, Dougal looked round, but it was as if aliens had suddenly arrived and scooped the stag party up. There was not a trace left of their presence. 'Back door,' said the barman briefly, looking up from the debris behind the bar and catching his confusion. 'They didn't want to tangle with security. They've legged it.'

The tiniest breeze of cool air, wafting in just at that moment, seemed to give confirmation. 'I can't believe it,' said Dougal stunned.

''Appens all the time, mate,' said the barman.

Vainly, Dougal stared round for the Bishop. But of him too there was now no sign. 'Quick,' he said, turning back to the barman, a horrible suspicion beginning to form at the back of his mind. 'The Bishop. Where is he?'

In the act of retrieving a broken bottle of brandy from amidst the peanuts scattered across the floor, the barman looked up. 'Sorry, rev,' he said laconically. 'I thought you realised. One of 'em screamed as 'ow they 'adn't 'ad value for money yet ... so they took 'im with 'em.'

26

Danny and Maisie were also doing the round of the clubs, and with the same forlorn hope as that inspiring Dougal. As luck would have it, they arrived at the front entrance to The Inferno at precisely the same moment the Hooray Henries and the Bishop catapulted out of the back and into the tiny alleyway behind. That some sort of fracas was going on below was obvious, because the door was now firmly shut, and from the depths came a sound vaguely reminiscent of pigs being slaughtered. Danny and Maisie looked at each other and, as if by common consent, turned and walked briskly in the opposite direction. 'We've got to get away,' said Danny. 'It sounds bad. The cops'll be 'ere at this rate.'

'But wot we goin' to do?' wailed Maisie, on the brink of tears. 'If Carl is down there, we'll never get to 'im now.' Her voice broke. 'We're never goin' to find Pepper. An' maybe it's 'er all this is about!'

Danny hardly even bothered to look at her. His face was set. 'Come on,' he said. 'I know the back way out. If Carl was down there, 'e won't 'ave 'ung around.' He broke into a run and, after a second's startled surprise, Maisie took to her heels in pursuit.

Down in the darkened alley the young solicitors were trying bemusedly to get their bearings. Two of them held the Bishop firmly by either arm, and one of them had run on ahead to try and find the quickest way back to the main street. As the rest checked and tried to gather themselves together, Bingo, who had been watching developments like a hawk, emerged from behind them into the open air. Unfortunately, even after the murk of the club, it was extremely dark and, as his eyes strove to adjust, he bumped noisily up against one of the large bins standing round the door.

'Unhand me!' shouted the Bishop, taking advantage of the sudden quiet. The Hooray Henries, who were finding the effects of the open air beneficial, looked round in surprise. Having been out in the dark that much longer, their eyes had adjusted to the general gloom, and they made out Bingo perfectly. 'I say,' said one of them, who had discovered his brain was beginning to function again, 'that's the bounder that started all this. He took a photo!'

Bingo suddenly discovered how it must feel to be a fox cornered by hounds. Seven pairs of eyes fastened on him, only one pair of which might be termed even vaguely friendly. The Bishop was looking at him hopefully. The Hooray Henries, however, were still clearly in party mood. They were enjoying themselves immensely. 'What shall we do with him?' shouted one.

'Debag the louse!' shouted another.

'Teach the fart a lesson!'

Next second they had seized the terrified Bingo and upended him bodily into the nearest bin. Giving a strangled cry, he found his head wedged into a mass of decayed spaghetti. The smell was appalling. They gave him a shove and he managed temporarily to jerk his head clear. 'He..e..elp!' he shrieked. Then something reminiscent of rotting cabbage rammed itself into his mouth and he broke off, choking. But the stag party had not finished with him yet. As he struggled head downwards, legs waving in the air, hands wrenched at his trousers and tore them off. He had an impression, from the raucous shouts of encouragement that followed this, that they were flung away somewhere. The next second he heard footsteps pounding away into the distance and realised, with a forlorn sense of desolation, that he was alone.

Danny and Maisie arrived at the head of the alley just as the Hooray Henries, still keeping a tight hold of the loudly protesting Bishop, hurtled out and past. 'Fuck,"' said Danny, 'Wot was that?'

'Who cares?' said Maisie. 'It's not Carl.'

They peered around distractedly, and at the same moment a long black car turned into the top of the street and began to nose its way slowly down. 'No,' panted Danny, who saw it before Maisie. 'But I'll lay odds that is!' He grabbed Maisie's arm, pulling her back into the shadows, and together they watched as the car suddenly swerved drunkenly, narrowly missing a lamp post, and then spun in a wide sweep into the alley, scraping the near side bumper against the wall.

'Wot the 'ell's he doing?' breathed Maisie, petrified that the driver would at any moment turn his head and see them.

'Carl parks down 'ere,' said Danny briefly. 'When 'e's got a deal on. 'E says it's safer.'

The moon came out briefly as the car screeched past, and for a second the two occupants were illumined in its watery light. From inside the car came sounds of a noisy arguement, and the passenger was clearly visible pulling at the driver's arm, who responded by raising it and lashing out.

'Blimey,' said Maisie shaken. 'It's Pepper with 'im.' She turned, ashen-faced, to Danny. 'Come on,' she said urgently. 'She looks in a bad way.'

She had already started down the alley and Danny cried, 'No, Maisie, stop! Carl'll kill us!'

She paused and stared at him witheringly. 'If we don't, 'e might kill 'er.' Then she said urgently, 'Come on. 'E can't go anywhere now. It's a dead end.'

Inside the bin, Bingo finally managed to pull himself right side up, and cautiously raised his head to peer over the top. A long strand of spaghetti dangled over his ear, and a frayed looking lettuce leaf adorned the top of his hair, but Bingo ignored them. His most pressing need was to recover his trousers and, to that end, he peered round. The alley yawned emptily in front of him. Bingo felt reassured. He brushed the spaghetti away and prepared to heave himself out, but at that moment he became aware of the car inching its way slowly towards him.

It had its lights dimmed and, as he watched it curiously, a wave of terror flooded over him. Afterwards he was not entirely sure why, but in that split second he felt as if he could almost taste something cruel and menacing coming towards him. After all he had just endured, he felt he couldn't take any more. Hardly daring to breathe, and praying the driver hadn't noticed him, he relaxed his grip on sides of the bin, and allowed himself to slide gently down.

The car slid to a stop almost directly adjacent to where poor Bingo huddled terrified. He heard a car door open, and then a low moan and the sound of someone crying. A girl.

'Don't, Carl,' he heard her say pleadingly. 'Please.'

It struck him that she sounded ill. He heard a man's voice then, lower and harsh, the words unintelligible. But whatever it was he said, the girl began to cry in earnest now, sobs tearing at her, pleading with him to stop, not to do it, to leave her alone.

Another man might have leapt to her rescue, but Bingo, acutely aware of his trouserless state and not by nature overly brave, huddled down even lower. It sounded to him as if something extremely unpleasant was going on. And then, as he listened with bated breath, petrified in case he should be discovered, he heard footsteps pounding towards them down the alley, followed by a cry, and the man below cursed.

'Carl!' screamed a woman's voice. 'Let 'er go!'

'This ain't your business, Maisie!' shouted back the man. 'Just go away.'

'It is my business!' came back the woman's distraught voice. 'She's my friend. Leave 'er alone will ye!'

The footsteps drew close, and now Bingo distinguished another voice. 'Leave 'er, Carl!' shouted a man. 'You'll kill 'er.'

There was an unpleasant laugh and the man below shouted back, 'Yeah, Danny. Maybe I will.'

Bingo could restrain himself no longer. He was still frightened of course, but whatever it was that was going on below, he felt they would be too occupied now to notice him. Very cautiously he raised himself and peered once again over the rim of the bin. The sight that met his eyes made him goggle. He discovered the driver of the car was so close that, if he had wanted to, he could have reached out with his hand and touched the top of his head. In the fitful moonlight he could just make out the hard line of the man's jaw, and the cruel gleam of his eyes. Bingo gasped and, unable to help himself, craned further up. He saw the man had his hand twisted in the long hair of a young girl, and that he had forced her to her knees, so that she crouched awkwardly at his feet. She looked, thought Bingo, in agony and, as he stared down, she squirmed and raised her head so that, in the same moment, he saw her face. He felt it ought properly to have been a beautiful face, but it was battered now and bruised, so that the features ran together into a raw mass of bloodied flesh.

'Oh y' sod!' screamed out Maisie, pulling up short.

The man brought his free fist crashing down into the upturned face of the girl, and she gave a terrible squeal of pain. The next moment Bingo became aware of the last remaining participant to the drama. With a terrible cry Danny launched himself at Carl, who was forced to let go his hold on Pepper in an attempt to ward off the attack. He flung her roughly up against the wall, and she collapsed, inert. The movement, however, gave Danny his opportunity, and he fastened onto Carl like a bulldog, clenching his arms round his neck and refusing to let go, despite the other man's rough attempts to dislodge him. But he was younger and far smaller than the pimp and quite clearly not as strong because Carl, tiring of the struggle, now lifted him bodily and crashed him backwards onto the wall. Yet still Danny clung on, scrabbling and kicking at Carl for all he was worth, determined not to let go.

It was never an equal contest. In the moonlight there was the sudden flash of a knife, and Carl laughed cruelly. 'You out of your league, little brother,' he rasped.

Then there was a cry and Danny fell off him and back, clutching his arm. Maisie screamed, and tried to push her way over to Pepper, but Carl shoved her away violently. And then Danny, reeling, staggered to his feet and threw himself back onto Carl again.

In the moonlight, Bingo saw Carl once again raise his arm and bring it crashing down, and again Danny fell. Then Carl turned back to Pepper and again caught her up by the hair. But this time, in his other hand, he still held the knife. With absolute precision, and as if in slow motion, Bingo saw Carl aim a kick at the girl's stomach.

'NO ... O ... O!' cried Danny.

He strove desperately to pull himself to his feet as Carl, with a cruel laugh, prepared to bring down the knife. But suddenly there was another player in the scene being enacted below. With a roar like an enraged bull, Dougal erupted out of the club door. He charged straight at Carl like a bullet and the pimp, caught unawares, gave a small, 'Plgh!' of surprise and spun round, trying to defend himself. But he found this no easy task, because whereas Danny was still only a boy, in Dougal, Carl found an equal. The two men were of about the same height and weight, and in that moment Dougal was so full of rage that all he could think of was smashing his opponent. All his years as a fly half came flooding back, and Dougal caught the pimp in a flying tackle that detached him from Pepper and sent him crashing down the street.

Bingo almost fell out of the bin as he recognised who this latest participant was and then his fingers scrabbled for the camera, trying to locate it amongst all the rubbish. He missed what happened next because he was struggling with what felt like chicken entrails, but the next minute his fingers closed over the camera and he again crawled his way up. When he poked his head above the edge this time he saw Carl steadying himself against the far wall, as if just recovering from another scuffle, while Dougal seemed to be engaged in trying to pull Pepper away from the bins, at the same time feeling for her pulse. The black man looked angry now, his breath coming in rapid pants as he readied himself to attack, eyes narrowed, and Bingo saw him toss the knife almost lazily from hand to hand and then begin to advance slowly on his attacker. 'You!' he spat softly. 'I might have known it was you.'

'Father, be careful!' shrieked Maisie.

Dougal abandoned his attempts to revive Pepper and leapt back and away. Carl laughed. It was an evil sound and the two men began to circle each other warily. It was like watching an old gangster movie thought Bingo, and he began to think of the terrific story he was going to write. He was recalled to the present by Carl, immediately below him, suddenly lunging sideways and then pulling hard away. He was quite clearly intending to come up and catch Dougal on the back, and Bingo found himself crying out a warning. But the priest was ready for the pimp. In one swift and graceful curve that seemed to match Carl's every move like a dancer, he caught his opponent's upturned arm, twisted and then yanked him heavily onto the ground, sending the knife scuttering noisily into the shadows. Then, to Bingo's intense admiration, the priest followed up the advantage he had gained and brought his own fist smashing down onto Carl's face. The blow carried all the weight of his pent up rage and frustration, and of his utter desolation at all that had happened over the last few weeks. In that second Dougal was an avenging angel, and nothing could stand in his way. As Carl slumped to the floor Bingo almost cheered, but he had just enough presence of mind to click on the camera and aim it at Dougal, at that moment standing over his vanquished foe like some hero of old.

Flash! The sudden blaze of light made all the still-conscious participants of the drama freeze in astonishment. Maisie was caught, crouched down, with her hands raised before her face in horror. Danny was slumped on the ground still nursing his wounds and staring at Dougal as if he could not quite believe his eyes and Pepper, who seemed to be regaining consciousness, was moaning slightly, her body (despite Dougal's best efforts) still twisted awkwardly against the stinking bins.

Dougal was the first to recover. He turned round dazedly, as if not quite sure what had just happened, and his eyes fell on Bingo. 'Who are you?' he asked.

Feeling inordinately pleased with himself, and all thought of his missing trousers forgotten, Bingo heaved himself up and out of the bin and hurried forward. 'Bingo Drubbins,' he said, holding out his hand. 'Delighted to meet you.' He grabbed Dougal's nerveless hand and shook it energetically and then added, 'May I say that was absolutely splendid!'

Maisie, who had now scrambled to her feet and was attempting vainly to pull down her skirt, looked up at this point and said indignantly, ''Ere, I know you! You're the bloke wot wanted to know all about Father and the centre! Y're that journalist bloke.'

Bingo had the grace to blush. 'Ah,' he said. 'Yes ... well ...'

At that point he was thankfully spared by another and rather louder moan from Pepper, and they all of them turned to her in consternation. Dougal stooped and pulled her out gently, raising her head, and they saw, for the first time, the full extent of her injuries. She looked a mess.

'Oh, God,' blurted out Maisie, unable to help herself. 'Wot's 'e done to 'er?' She burst into tears.

'Get an ambulance, Danny,' said Dougal tersely. Danny, himself injured and clearly frightened, made to respond, but Bingo said, 'No, hang on a minute. I've got my mobile here.' He reached down for his pocket and then remembered he was still missing his trousers. 'Hang on,' he said again, embarrassed. 'It's in my trousers. They're round here somewhere.'

'Where?' demanded Maisie, staring at his knees.

'I don't know,' admitted Bingo. 'Some yobs tore them off me and then chucked them away. But they're round here somewhere.'

Maisie looked as if she was about to enquire why, and Dougal said hastily, 'Then just find the damn things will you. We need help.'

Ten seconds later, a triumphant cry from Danny revealed that they were hanging from the sooty windowsill of The Inferno. He passed them to Bingo, who groped in the pockets and then said, 'Yes, here it is. Won't be a mo.' He punched in the emergency number and then said, 'Where the hell are we, by the way?'

Maisie looked at him witheringly. 'Give us it 'ere,' she said. With a calm that amazed them all, she gave the exact location and a brief summary of Pepper's visible injuries. 'Ten minutes,' she said, giving back the phone to Bingo. 'That's 'ow long they said they'd be. The police are comin' too.'

They were startled at that moment by a sudden movement from the shadows. They had all been so concerned for Pepper that they had managed temporarily to wipe Carl from their minds. Now, however, he forced himself back into them.

'Don't think you've won,' he rasped, staggering to his feet, a hand clasped to his jaw, and glaring at Dougal. 'I'll be back, and when I am, you're finished. I'm going to sweep you away like the scum you are!'

Dougal, still cradling Pepper's head, stared at him coolly. 'I don't think so,' he said. 'You're evil, Carl, but you can't do anything. If I were you I'd go back to your rat hole before the police get here. It's you who are finished!'

Carl cast on him a look of hate. It was so fixed, and so full of loathing that Maisie, Danny and Bingo instinctively drew together, as if afraid of what he was going to do. But he only looked for a second longer at Dougal and then said softly, 'No, not me, priest. I'll get you in the end.'

The next second he was gone. In one quick movement, like a snake, he had slid into the front seat of the car, switched on the engine, and then rammed the car into reverse. It hurtled back down the alley, tyres screeching, just seconds before the ambulance turned in.

''E's gone,' said Maisie. She sounded stunned, but then she flung herself on her knees beside Pepper, all other thoughts gone. 'Is she going to be alright?' she asked.

Dougal shook his head. 'I don't know,' he said. 'She's not conscious.'

27

The police arrived just as the paramedics were finishing inserting a drip into Pepper's arm. Maisie, who had been clinging throughout the procedure in absolute terror to her friend's hand said loudly, 'I want to go with 'er in the ambulance.'

'We'd like you to answer a few questions first, love,' said one of the policemen, not unkindly, coming up just as the paramedic stood back.

Maisie sniffed and wiped away a tear. 'There's nothing to tell,' she announced. 'It was Carl.'

Since the ambulance had arrived and all her worst fears appeared to have been confirmed, she had been almost catatonic with dread, her face ashen. At one point it had seemed briefly as if Pepper was going to regain consciousness. Her eyelids had flickered open and she had turned her head, but the eyes that stared up at the world were glazed and unfocussed, and she did not respond as the paramedic called her name. She looked to Dougal, standing watching at the side, as if she had slipped into some terrible 'other' world from which she could not be recalled. And then Maisie had shrieked and said, 'God! She's bleeding.' It had been a cry to the Almighty dragged from the very depths of her soul, and she had pointed a trembling hand at the dark sticky stain appearing between Pepper's legs.

'Haemorrhage, Mike!' the paramedic had called briefly. 'She's losing it.'

Then there had been a terrible ten minutes, which had felt like hours to Dougal, as they had clustered round her, pushing, prodding, examining, doing things he hardly even registered, and then he had heard one of them say in a low voice, 'If we're not careful, we're going to lose her too.'

Maisie, so wrapped in grief, her gaze fixed on Pepper with an intensity that seemed to be willing the other girl to live, did not hear. She simply clung onto Pepper's hand fiercely, and Dougal heard her muttering, 'Y' goin' t' live ... Come on ... y've got to ...'

Dougal felt totally useless. He went over and laid an awkward hand on her shoulder, but she shook him off impatiently and then, glancing up and seeing who it was, said penitently, 'Sorry, Father, I thought it was one of them ambulance blokes. They keep tellin' me to move.' Her eyes were two luminous pools of horror. ''Ow could 'e do this?'

Dougal shrugged helplessly. Now that the excitement had passed he felt he had fallen into a void. He was numb. He looked round to where Danny was sitting on an upturned crate having his arm dressed. He too looked deeply shocked, and the chalky pallor of his skin made him look absurdly young. He glanced up at the same moment and their eyes locked. With a shock, Dougal recognised a strange kind of pleading in the boy's eyes. He glanced back down at Maisie to make sure she was all right, gave her shoulder a squeeze, and then, almost reluctantly, crossed over to Danny.

The boy's teeth were chattering. 'I'm s ... sorry,' he stuttered. 'I ... it's all my f ... fault.' He bit his lip and seemed to make a conscious effort to try and gather himself together.

'It's okay,' said the paramedic, who was tending him, soothingly. 'Don't worry.'

But Danny would have none of it. 'I told Carl Pepper was going round to Maisie's,' he said, his eyes fixed on Dougal. ''E cottoned on something was up.'

Dougal suddenly realised he was hearing a confession. He had always disliked Danny, unconsciously categorising him as a mindless yob, but in that moment he found himself looking beyond the rather unpleasant veneer to the frightened child beneath. 'It's not your fault, Danny,' he said gently, sitting down beside him on the crate. 'Carl would have found out soon anyway.' He grimaced. 'This was just a disaster waiting to happen.'

They sat for a while in silence, each trying to grapple with their own thoughts, and then suddenly Danny said, 'Thanks anyway.'

'What?' asked Dougal, looking up surprised. 'What for?'

Danny was looking at him awkwardly. 'You saved my life,' he said. 'When you went for Carl like that ... 'e was going to do for me ... So thanks.' And then, to Dougal's complete and utter astonishment, he wriggled away from the paramedic and held out his hand. For a second Dougal stared at it, and then in turn he raised his own hand and gripped the boy's hard. 'Mates then?' asked Danny, relieved. Dougal nodded.

The police wanted to know exactly what had happened. They wanted to know why Carl had been there in the first place, and why Maisie and Danny had happened along at precisely the same moment. When it came to Dougal's contribution, they looked perplexed, and one of them scratched his head and said, 'You mean, you just happened to come out while all this was going on and rushed in to the rescue, like Sir Galahad?'

Bingo intervened. 'Yes he did, constable,' he said enthusiastically, 'and he was marvellous. I saw it all.'

The policeman turned to him, 'And you are, sir?'

'Bingo Drubbins,' said Bingo, fishing in his pocket, 'I'm a journalist.' He produced his card and waggled it under the nose of the policeman, who looked even more bemused.

'And where did you witness the incident from, sir?' he asked.

'The bin,' said Bingo blithely.

'The bin?' echoed the policeman faintly. 'What were you doing in the bin?'

'A gang of rowdies thrust me in there.'

'A what?'

'A gang of rowdies who had been in the club.'

'A gang of pillocks more like,' muttered Danny.

Bingo ignored him. 'They resented my having taken a photograph of them. They did it in revenge.'

The policeman breathed heavily. Were it not for the severity of the injuries suffered by Pepper and the fact that Danny had been knifed, he would have thought this lot were taking the mick.

Bingo's words, however, had served to remind Dougal of something he had forgotten. 'The Bishop!' he exclaimed.

'Pardon, sir?' said the policeman, reeling.

'The Bishop,' repeated Dougal obligingly, at the same time smacking a hand to his head. 'Dear God, what an idiot I am! I'd completely forgotten him.' Then, seeing the look of total bewilderment on the policeman's face, he added, 'The rowdies ... they kidnapped the Bishop. That's why I came out here. I was in pursuit.'

After that things seemed to move quite rapidly. Pepper was bundled into the waiting ambulance, along with Danny, Maisie and a young constable. His colleague, left alone at the scene, then decided that this case was obviously far more serious than he had at first thought and he was clearly going to need the help of CID. He radioed back to the station and said, 'Kidnapping, Sarge. There's a group what's abducted the Bishop of Carbery.' He looked at Dougal for confirmation and Dougal nodded. 'One serious injury and a stabbing. They're dangerous.'

'Hang on ...,' began Dougal, rather taken aback by this construction the policeman had put on events.

But the policeman ignored him. 'One of the gang made a getaway in a black Mercedes, registration Juliet 581 ... Victor Foxtrot Delta (he had got this from Maisie). The others have escaped on foot. Approach with extreme caution. Armed and dangerous.' Then he turned back to Dougal and Bingo and gave a tight smile. 'Won't be long now. We'll soon round them all up.'

However, in this he was to be proved wrong, because the Bishop seemed to have disappeared off the face of the earth. Back at the station the policeman would have been suitably impressed if he could have seen the panic his information caused. Inspector Bateman, still trying to sort out the situation at Walsingham, was summoned back in and immediately went down to the cells, where Oswald was still being detained, pending bail.

'Okay,' he said angrily. 'Now we want the truth this time. What is this vendetta against the Bishop and his wife, and who's involved?'

Oswald looked astonished. 'I haven't the remotest idea what you're talking about,' he said. 'Vendetta? What vendetta? There's no vendetta against the Bishop.'

But the inspector was no longer prepared to play games. 'Look, sunshine,' he snarled, 'we know there's something big going on here, and we know for a fact you're a part of it. We only need confirmation from forensic and we'll nail you for the break-in. But we want to know what's really behind all this. Number one, why has the Bishop now been kidnapped?'

'Kidnapped?' repeated Oswald stupidly. 'You must be joking! I haven't the remotest idea why the Bishop's been kidnapped.'

And then he clamped his jaws tight shut and refused to say anything more till his solicitor should be present, at which point the inspector flung out angrily, more determined than ever to get to the bottom of this. The black Mercedes was traced, and two cars were dispatched round to Carl's. Unsurprisingly, however, they found he had gone and no one had a clue where. The police began to suspect that the Bishop's disappearance was somehow connected with drugs, and a car was sent to inform Myra of what had happened.

*

One of the worst things you can say to someone when imparting bad news is, 'I don't want you to worry, but ...' Unfortunately, the CID officer who had been sent to tell Myra of her husband's apparent abduction did not know this. Myra fainted. When she came round some three minutes later, it was to find the young WPC, who had come with the sergeant, holding a bottle of smelling salts under her nose and making soothing noises, while her superior seemed studiously bent on examining the nearest wall, the shade of which he appeared to find absolutely riveting.

'Hubert ...,' quavered Myra weakly, wondering what on earth was going on, and then memory came flooding back and she uttered a little cry.

'Ah, back with us then,' said the DS a shade too heartily, turning from his examination of the wallpaper. 'As I was saying, madam ...'

'It appears your husband *may* have been abducted,' broke in the WPC, glaring at him. She thought men were the absolute limit. She hated the heavy-handed way they steamrollered in.

Myra groaned and closed her eyes, trying desperately to fight against the swirling tides of black that threatened once again to engulf her. 'Where was he?' she managed. 'What happened?'

The DS flushed and shuffled his feet. He privately thought that the Bishop's wife was in it (whatever it was) up to her neck, and that they ought more properly to be questioning her, instead of concentrating all their efforts on Oswald. But even so, there were some things she ought surely not to know. Like her husband's little forays to sex clubs! He knew all about these churchmen and their naughty habits. He thought it was disgusting. But the WPC was again glaring at him. 'It was at the back entrance of a club on the St Prosdocimus estate,' she said firmly. 'He was with a priest, Dougal Sampratt. Apparently they were both just coming out.'

Myra nodded her head feebly. 'Oh yes, of course,' she muttered. 'He was going to go out on Dougal's rounds with him tonight.'

The sergeant was astonished. This was even more serious than he had thought. She not only appeared to know about the sex angle, but she seemed actively to condone it. He stared at her more closely, wondering if perhaps, after all, Myra were not at the centre of this plot.

Myra, in happy ignorance of the suspicions forming against her, staggered to her feet. 'What are you doing to find him?' she demanded.

'Our best, madam,' said the sergeant levelly. He decided he had had enough of all these church types. It was time to take off the kid gloves. 'We thought perhaps you might be able to help.'

But it was at this point that his hopes of a quick interrogation were blasted because Myra, good evangelical to the last, refused to talk to him any further and insisted instead on immediately calling a prayer meeting. 'Nonsense,' she said firmly, when he put to her the theory of a drugs-related conspiracy centering on St Prosdocimus, 'this is spiritual attack, that's all. The way to counter this is in the heavenlies.'

'The heavenlies?' he queried. 'And where might they be, madam? Is that an area somewhere round St Prosdocimus? Should we send a car?'

Myra looked at him witheringly. 'I mean the spiritual realm of course,' she said. 'I'm not sure your police cars have access there.'

However, before closeting herself away with the three friends who rushed round in answer to her agitated summons, she did consent to pass on all the information she knew to the WPC. It was not much, admittedly, but she said she rather thought that Dougal and her husband had been going to do the round of clubs where the street girls habitually went, prior to going out onto the streets to talk with them in situ. She further said that Dougal seemed to have been the object of a campaign of vilification over the past few weeks, and that it had been her husband's intention to try and get to the truth of the matter.

Her words, when they were reported back at the station, filled the investigative team with gloom. They began to think that the Bishop had perhaps been rather more successful in this endeavour than was good for his health and, in the absence of any other leads, suspicion now began to extend to Dougal. Two more police officers were dispatched to go and find him at the hospital, where he had gone to find out how Pepper was, and to bring him in for questioning.

Dougal, meanwhile, had found Pepper already wired up in intensive care, with Maisie sitting at her side. Danny had been wheeled, loudly protesting, to a bed up on the ward, and so Maisie was keeping vigil alone. She looked up as Dougal pushed his way in through the double doors, her face forlorn. 'They've taken away all her clothes,' she said miserably. 'They shouldn't ought to 'ave done that.'

Dougal came to a stop on the other side of the bed. Pepper did indeed look rather frightening. Under the bruising left by Carl's attack, her face was still almost totally unrecognisable and she lay motionless, naked under the thin sheet they had draped across her, wires and tubes protruding from all sides, while the monitors that stood all round beeped and whirred and cast a lurid light that made the whole thing look like a scene from a horror movie. 'They always do this, Maisie,' he said reassuringly. 'It's safer this way, easier to care for the patient.'

'It's not right,' repeated Maisie, distraught. 'An' they won't tell me what's goin' on. They just keep saying she'll be alright and not to worry … but I don't think I believe them.'

'Would you like me to go and try and find out?'

She nodded. 'Yes please. They'll talk to you, won't they?'

Dougal dutifully went and searched out a nurse. 'There's not really very much to say yet,' she said warily, taking in his collar. 'She's lost the baby, of course, and she's had quite bad internal bleeding, but we think she's stabilising. The major problem is that there might be some cranial damage. She must have struck her head when she fell.'

Dougal digested this. 'Or when someone hit her,' he said levelly.

The nurse shrugged, not dismissively but simply indicating that she didn't know. 'Could be,' she agreed.

Dougal discovered he felt sick. 'When are you likely to know?'

The nurse regarded him. 'It's still a bit early yet,' she said. 'The picture should be a bit clearer in the morning. We'll do a brain scan then. We suspect there's some internal swelling and something may have to be done to help that, but equally it might have started to reduce by morning. The really good thing,' she added, 'would be if she regained consciousness.

Feeling in full the weight of this bad news, Dougal went back to Maisie and reported what he had gleaned. Her face was a study. 'You know something?' she said abruptly, 'I've been praying. I knew there was something really bad 'ad 'appened to 'er. I asked Jesus to help.'

Dougal stared at her and then attempted a weak smile, 'I thought charms were more in your line.'

But Maisie shook her head vigorously. 'I'm finished with all that,' she said decisively. 'It's a load of crap. I went home before Danny came … I got out all me crystals because I was upset, and they were bleedin' useless. And I just suddenly thought how everything I've done has been wrong.'

He bit his lip, wanting to comfort her. 'Like what?'

'Like everything,' said Maisie savagely. The monitor beeped quietly as if in agreement and she glared at it. 'Bleedin' tarot for a start. The cards said it was all goin' to be okay.' She transferred her gaze back to Pepper, tears rolling unchecked down her cheeks. 'Look at 'er!'

Dougal could think of nothing to say. He came round the bed and put an arm round her shoulders. 'Don't give up,' he said softly. 'We've found her and she's alive. That's what matters. And now we've got to trust God to help.'

Maisie, still clinging onto Pepper's hand, whirled round and buried her face in his shirt. 'But will 'e?' she sniffed. 'Will 'e 'elp, or will it be just like everything else?'

The question somehow seemed to strike straight into Dougal's soul. He stared over Maisie's head into the middle distance and realised, with a start, that he had been asking himself the same question all night. Where on earth had God been over the last few months? He lowered his eyes and looked at her bent head, biting his lip, and a thought that was almost electrifying in its intensity, bubbled into his mind. If *he* were not here now, Maisie would be alone ... but *he* was here because God was. He gazed down at her and seemed to see himself as he had been just those few short months before. It was not a pleasant sensation. He saw how everything he had done had been a facade – an act. But it felt almost as if God had scoured it all away, as if He had sanded off the veneer to get at the wood underneath. And in that same moment, for the first time in his life, Dougal felt as if he actually caught a glimpse of God – of the immensity of the love that simply wouldn't put up with the second rate, not because of disapproval but because of the infinite potential that He had placed there, inside everyone. Almost, Dougal thought, he could feel God's pain and sadness at all the hurt and damage there was. 'Maisie,' he said awkwardly, groping for words. 'I don't know what's going to happen. None of us does, but I do know that God's here and that He cares.' His voice grew in strength. 'And I know that we can trust Him because of that, and that whatever happens, it will be all right.'

A fresh paroxysm of sobs greeted this reassurance. Maisie cried and cried as if her heart would break, and then at last she said brokenly, 'I wish I could believe. I really want to.'

It was while Dougal was still cradling her to his chest that the police arrived. 'Dougal Sampratt?' said one, regarding the scene. 'Vicar of St Prosdocimus?'

'Yes,' said Dougal, looking up surprised. 'Why?'

'We've got a few questions we'd like to ask, sir. In connection with the disappearance of the Bishop.'

Something in the strained politeness of their manner communicated itself, and Maisie raised a tear-stained face and stared at them. 'What's up?' she demanded, sniffing back the tears. She stared from one to the other of them and her face froze. 'Y' don't want him,' she broke out belligerently. 'He hasn't done nothing. He saved us.'

The policeman smiled, a tight little smile that left his eyes cold. 'Quite,' he said dryly, flicking a dismissive glance in her direction. 'We understand that.' He turned back to Dougal, 'As I was saying, sir, if you wouldn't mind coming down the station with us.'

This was too much for Maisie. After all that had happened that night, she suddenly had a focus for her rage. Years of not very happy relations with the local constabulary erupted in a blaze of downtrodden righteousness. 'Yes he bleedin' would mind,' she exploded. 'Why should he come with you? What d'y' think 'e's done?'

Dougal tried vainly to quiet her, but the policeman glared at her sourly. 'If you must know,' he said, 'we think he may have been involved in a conspiracy to abduct the Bishop.'

It was Dougal's turn to be amazed. His jaw dropped. 'But why?' he brought out.

Over by the door a little knot of nurses, drawn by the noise, came in and stood, open-mouthed. They looked as if they knew they ought to do something, but they all alike seemed riveted, incapable of doing anything that might interfere with the scene being played out before their eyes.

'Why?' repeated Dougal, shaking himself.

The policeman glared at him. He hated these sanctimonious vermin who made out they were so good, but inwardly were so corrupt. They were all such hypocrites. He was going to enjoy this. 'Because it appears that he was about to expose your sordid little goings-on,' he said blandly, 'and that he was going to ensure your removal from the church!'

Dougal was so shocked he could think of absolutely nothing to say. He opened and shut his mouth, but no noise came out. Maisie, however, did not appear hampered by any such constraint. 'Y' bleedin' mad,' she shouted, starting to her feet. 'There aren't any *sordid little goings-on* as y' put it. That Bingo Drubbins bloke made it all up. Ask 'im.'

'Bingo Drubbins?' repeated Dougal faintly. He had been so caught up in events over the last few hours that he had not actually made the connection between the journalist and the articles that had appeared before. There was no end, it seemed, to what he was learning tonight. 'How do you know that?'

'Because I told 'im. At least,' Maisie amended hastily, seeing Dougal's face, 'not what 'e wrote, that was 'is imagination. I told 'im all about the centre, and all the good you were doing.'

'Perhaps, madam,' said the policeman icily, growing bored, 'others told Mr Drubbins what he wanted to know.'

'No they bleedin' didn't!' Maisie rounded on him. 'I know exactly what the girls told 'im an' it wasn't any of that shit.'

At that moment a low moan from the bed caused them all to look down. Pepper had shifted slightly and her eyes were open. She stared round blearily and ran a tongue over her cracked lips, before her eyes came finally to rest on Maisie. 'Where am I?' she asked weakly. 'What's all the shouting about? What's going on?'

28

The object of all this concern had meanwhile found himself bundled roughly into a car with a blanket thrown over his head. This last was not from any desire to prevent him seeing the direction they were going in, but simply because Horatio, the young man whose stag party it was, had found it on the seat as he got in and tossed it aside. Spluttering, the Bishop wrenched it off and glared round in outrage, but he discovered that a car with eight bodies in it leaves very little room for manoeuvre and, although he now had a limited view out of a side window, he could not move.

The car swerved and then lurched wildly across the road, and the young men around him all shouted and cheered. The Bishop, closing his eyes in horror, began to think that if any of them survived this journey it would be a miracle. As the car mounted the pavement and than again bumped down onto the road he began to pray.

'Where are we going?' shouted Horatio.

'Coco's!' bellowed another.

'No, not there. Let's go and get Raphael, and then this Johnny can perform there too!'

From the response to this suggestion, the Bishop decided that the reference to Raphael was not, as he would have preferred, to the archangel, but probably to one of their cronies who had been unable to join them earlier. This was confirmed when, a quarter of an hour later, he found himself hauled unceremoniously out of the car, and discovered they were parked horizontally across the pavement before a tall Victorian building. 'Yoohoo! Raffie!' screamed the group. 'Open up, it's us!'

A window was opened above and a woman's voice called down crossly, 'For goodness sake, be quiet and go away!'

This, however, appeared only to amuse the group and they shouted even louder. Then, from the top floor of the house, another window was flung up and a voice, a man's this time, shouted back, 'For God's sake, shut up! I'll open the door.'

The Bishop now found himself bundled up the three shallow stone steps that led to the front door, and thrust into the hallway beyond. He hardly had time to take in his surroundings before, stumbling and sliding, he was frog marched up the three flights of stairs to the top.

This was not accomplished without difficulty, because Horatio now manifested a desire to sit down where he was and go to sleep. The first time he did this was directly in the path of those coming up behind, and there was a great deal of shoving and noisy encouragement before he could be persuaded to totter back to his feet and go on. The second time he simply collapsed across the stairs, and a loud snore emanated from between his lips. 'Come on, Horatio! You can't do this now,' shouted the others. 'This is for you!' And they all again stopped and tried to wake him up, urging him to go on.

The Bishop was mortified but he could do nothing to escape and then, at last, they were at the top and he found the door being held open by a dishevelled individual, who looked as if he had just got out of bed.

'Come on, lads,' said Raphael, complaining. 'I told you before I couldn't make it tonight. I'm on early tomorrow.'

This was greeted with whistles and derisory 'Ooohs', and the group tumbled past him and pushed their way into what was evidently the living room. 'Come on,' said one of them again, 'we've brought the night to you. We've brought the Strip-o-gram!'

He indicated the Bishop, and for the first time their host's eyes registered the presence of an unknown in their midst. 'Good Lord!' he said, growing pale. 'What the hell have you done?'

The Bishop, finding himself suddenly released, ruffled like an enraged hen and attempted vainly to smooth his clothes. Unfortunately his glasses were now lopsided across his nose, while his collar had detached from the shirt, so that his attempts were not entirely successful. Looking up, he discovered that the stag party had pulled across two chairs and the sofa, and were now ranged in a line, looking at him expectantly. All, that is, with the exception of Horatio who, finding himself seated, had finally succeeded in falling asleep. 'Come on then,' said one of them encouragingly. 'Hurry up.'

Raphael went even paler. 'Stop this,' he commanded. He pushed himself between the Bishop and his audience and then turned and said apologetically, 'I'm so very sorry, my lord ... Bishop ... I'm not sure what to call you. But I really must apologise for what seems to have happened here.'

'Get out of the way, Raffie!' screamed one of his affronted friends. 'You're interrupting the show.'

Raffie whirled on them furiously. 'Don't you idiots have any sense?' he snapped. 'This man isn't a Strip-o-gram, he's the Bishop of Carbery!'

Silence greeted this pronouncement. 'How do you know?' finally demanded one.

'Because I did some work last week for the consistory court and the Bishop was there.'

'Ah.' This statement had something of a dampening effect on proceedings. What the Bishop had been vainly protesting, ever since they carried him off, finally seemed to sink in and a sobering gloom came over the party.

'I'm so sorry,' said their friend again, turning back to him. 'I've no idea how this all happened but, let me assure you, they don't normally behave like this.' He ran a hand through his hair awkwardly. 'It's Horatio's stag do, you see. They're all drunk.'

A feeling of the most tremendous relief swept over the Bishop, leaving his knees weak. 'Quite,' he said feebly. 'That much at least would be obvious to the meanest intelligence.' Then he could manage no more. His knees suddenly buckled beneath him, and he sank weakly onto the nearest chair.

'Do you mean he really is a bishop?' enquired one of his now sobered abductors, in a small voice.

'Of course he's a bloody bishop!' snapped Raphael, whirling round. Then he suddenly recollected himself and went crimson. 'I'm sorry,' he said hastily, turning back. 'I didn't mean ...'

The Bishop waved a hand. 'It's alright,' he said, 'I understand ... I feel a little bit like swearing myself. I wonder, could I have a cup of tea?'

Minutes later, he found himself ensconced in the most comfortable chair the living room had to offer, with a cup of tea and a selection of chocolate biscuits placed in his hands. The Hooray Henries were trying to make amends. They themselves had very strong black coffee all round, which Raphael insisted on them drinking; with the exception of Horatio, who was still asleep.

'When is the young man's wedding to take place?' asked the Bishop, attempting to bridge the awkwardness that now descended.

'Three days' time,' replied one of them eagerly. 'In the cathedr ...' He trailed off, and an embarrassed silence fell, while his friends all turned and stared at the still inert Horatio in consternation.

'I see,' said the Bishop dryly, noting and rather enjoying their discomfort. 'And this is how you normally behave on a stag night is it?'

A couple of hours later, when they were all relatively sober and the Bishop had sufficiently recovered, a chastened little group escorted him downstairs. 'Of course we'll take you home,' one of them volunteered. 'Sebastian will be more than happy to drive you.'

The Bishop looked at them, looked at the car, and then back at the prospective groom, who had wakened half an hour ago and still didn't seem quite to know what was going on. 'I don't think so,' he said severely. 'You are all of you still over the limit.' Then a thought occurred. 'You say this young man is to be married in my cathedral?'

They nodded. A shade apprehensively the Bishop thought.

'May I ask if he and his fiancée have had adequate preparation for Christian marriage from Cathedral staff?'

Horatio, finding himself the sudden object of their concerted scrutiny, paled and then swallowed. He shook his head. 'No ... er ... I'm ... that is, I'm not sure. What do you mean?'

The Bishop regarded him, the thinnest of smiles curling his lips. 'It is diocesan practice,' he said evenly, 'that all engaged couples seeking Christian marriage should be prepared spiritually and emotionally for what a lifetime of commitment is going to entail.' He looked severely at the young man now staring at him with open dread. 'My impression, young man, from the behaviour of you and your friends tonight, is that none of you have the least understanding of adult behaviour.'

There was a chorus of protest. 'We were drunk,' offered one.

'I know that,' said the Bishop.

'It was just fun.'

'Not for me.'

Not for the first time that evening, silence again fell. 'I find myself asking,' continued the Bishop reflectively, 'whether any of you could possibly be considered as ready for marriage?'

'Oh yes, we are.'

'Really.'

'Honestly.'

'We're very mature really ... Normally.'

The Bishop fixed upon them a gimlet eye. 'I think I must be persuaded of that.'

The look of horror with which they now regarded him would, the Bishop reflected (had he been a vindictive man), have gone some way to assuage his wounded pride. As it was, of course, he reminded himself that he was not in the slightest bit vindictive; he simply had their best spiritual interests at heart. 'I think,' he said heavily, weighing every word, 'that you would all of you benefit from a course of spiritual instruction.'

Complete dread now fell upon them all. 'B ... but there isn't time,' stuttered Horatio. 'I'm getting married in three days.'

The Bishop stared at him, pursing his lips. 'What I have in mind, *for all of you*,' he emphasised, 'is something a little more long term. I would like to see you all enrolled on, and fully participating in, the twelve-week course we run on the basics of faith and Christian life. Otherwise,' he said loudly, checking their protest before it could be made, 'I might find I have to bring charges against you, which won't do any of your future careers much good. Indeed,' he added, having some time ago ascertained what they all were, 'I should imagine it would result in your all being struck off.'

They digested this. 'That's blackmail,' said one in a small voice.

The Bishop shrugged. 'What you did was kidnapping,' he reminded them.

When he left in the taxi they had called for him some ten minutes later, it was with a full list of their names and addresses in his breast pocket. He had assured them that someone would be in touch with all of them the following day and that full details of the course would be sent to them. As the taxi pulled away, leaving the group on the rain sodden pavement staring glumly after him, he felt rather pleased with himself. The evening might not have turned out quite as he had been anticipating, but he rather thought that the enrolment of seven young men, on a course usually dominated by women, was excellent. God, he reflected, moves in mysterious ways. He sat back and stretched slightly, feeling he had come to the end of a virtuous night, and then consternation struck. 'Good Lord!' he said loudly, sitting forwards and banging a hand to his head, 'I've forgotten poor Dougal.'

The taxi driver regarded him with interest in the mirror. 'Do you want me to go back and get 'im?' he enquired. 'They're all still out there.'

But the Bishop shook his head. 'You don't understand. The Reverend

Sampratt, I left him at The Inferno club earlier this evening. He must be out of his mind with worry.' He ignored the driver's look of surprise and said crisply, 'Driver, we will not go to the palace just yet after all. There's something I have to settle before I go home. St Prosdocimus vicarage, please!'

Muttering something unintelligible, the driver swung the taxi in a big arc and they set off in the opposite direction. When they arrived, however, they found it in darkness. 'Well what did you expect, mate?' advised the driver. 'It is the middle of the night.'

The Bishop cogitated. 'Wait here a moment,' he ordered. 'Perhaps he's asleep.'

'Lucky him,' he heard the driver mutter, as he clambered out. ''E's going to love being knocked up at this time.'

The Bishop ignored him. He walked briskly up the short path and rang a peremptory summons on the bell. The sound reverberated eerily into the emptiness beyond. The Bishop stood for perhaps three minutes, staring hopefully up at the faceless windows, but they all remained dark, and not a sound came from inside the house. He went back to the taxi. 'I fear I must trespass on your good offices a little longer,' he informed the now bored taxi driver. 'The Reverend Sampratt quite clearly is not here, and I believe there is every possibility he may be out still looking for me.'

The driver stared at him impassively. 'So what do you want to do?' he enquired.

The Bishop thought for a moment. He dearly wanted to go home to bed. He thought how nice it would be to curl up beside Myra, his arm protectively around her shoulders, the duvet pulled up to their chins. Then he thought guiltily about Dougal, out wandering the dark streets in search of him. 'We must search the parish,' he said crisply. 'I want you to drive down every road within the area until we find him.'

The driver clearly thought he was mad, but having established that his services were not going to come cheap, he seemed happy to comply. 'So why are you so keen to find this geezer?' he remarked chattily.

Finding nothing else to do as he stared out at the empty streets, the Bishop began to regale him with the story of the mission Dougal had set up, and the problems the young priest had been facing.

''Ere, I've 'eard about that,' broke in the driver excitedly. ''E's the bloke what's trying to do something about the tarts, isn't 'e?'

The Bishop winced. 'A trifle indelicately put,' he said, 'but yes.'

'Blimey,' said the driver. He sounded impressed.

Down at the station Dougal found himself in an interview room. Two doors down the rather dingy corridor, Oswald was similarly engaged, but neither at this point knew of the other's presence. 'It's my belief,' opined Bateman, 'that these two may be in it together. After all, they were both at Walsingham till Sampratt left to set up this mission. And why?' He tapped the side of his nose meaningfully. 'There's more to this than meets the eye. You mark my words. Why else would a bloke with everything in front of him leave a cushy number like that theological college, and go to a dump like St Prosdocimus? I'll lay odds there's some kind of scam going on, there must be if this bloke Carl's involved.' He thought for a moment. 'And the Bishop found out about it, and that's why he's been removed!'

He said this last triumphantly, and his subordinates gazed at him with respect. They wished they had the intelligence that could fit together clues like that. No wonder Bateman was an inspector. At his instigation, they decided to question the two men independently and then, when they had recorded both versions, confront them with each other. It would, said Bateman, be very interesting.

Dougal, having been made to wait for forty minutes, found himself being interrogated by two detectives, who let it clearly be known that they considered him to be guilty. 'But of what?' he kept asking.

'That's for *you* to tell us,' they replied.

One and a half hours later he had told them all about the drop-in centre and the problems they had within the community, the break-in, and the Bishop ... but still they kept needling him for more. 'Tell us about the drugs connection,' they kept prompting.

Along the corridor, Oswald's detectives were pursuing a different line. 'It's pornography, isn't it?' they said emphatically. One of the policemen had brought up the female clothing found in Brian's room. 'You've got some sort of sex ring going, haven't you ...? Do you like choir boys?'

Oswald was horrified and the solicitor he had retained said angrily, 'I really must object to this line of questioning. You have absolutely nothing to substantiate these allegations.' And turning to Oswald, he said, 'I advise you to say absolutely nothing. The onus is on them to provide evidence.'

Oswald more than happily complied with this advice, but inwardly he was feeling petrified. Could Tim Goody have been involved with a sex ring? he wondered. The possibility had never suggested itself to him before but, thinking about it, he would put nothing past Walsingham's principal. He shuddered violently, in the middle of a question about ritual abuse, and said suddenly, 'You've got to bring back Father Goody. He's the one who's involved in all of this, not me.'

For some reason he could not fathom, this seemed to be taken as some kind of admission and, shortly afterwards, Oswald found himself left alone with his solicitor and a grim-faced policeman, while his interrogators went out to share results with their colleagues. A little later they came back, accompanied this time by the inspector, who glowered at Oswald and then said heavily, 'We've had the results back from forensic.'

Oswald flinched, his mouth going dry. 'Yes?' he said breathlessly. He knew perfectly well that the results ought to exonerate him, but the whole situation had become such a nightmare that he felt prepared for anything.

'My client would like it to be known,' broke in the solicitor, leaning forwards belligerently, 'that ...'

'Save it,' said the inspector briefly. He turned back to Oswald, face blank. 'They appear to confirm the clothes are not yours.'

Oswald could not help himself. 'Oh, thank God,' he exploded, seeming to deflate in his seat. 'Now will you believe me?'

But even this, it appeared, was not enough to get him off the hook. The police accepted that he was not the perpetrator of the break-in at the palace, but they wanted to know how he had come by the clothes, and his anguished babblings about Father Goody's little problems only served to make them extremely interested in that individual too. 'So what you're saying,' finished Bateman, 'is that it's the principal of Walsingham who's actually at the centre of this ring. He's the mastermind behind the rest of you and once we've found him, then we'll have the key!'

Poor Oswald could have wept. He thought the whole world had gone mad. Whatever he said got twisted. Or else, he thought, he and the police were speaking different languages and they simply heard something entirely different to whatever it was he said. They appeared to think that he had committed some kind of crime in which drugs and perversion figured prominently, and nothing he could say would convince them otherwise. In desperation he wrote down for them the address of the Greek monastery Father Goody had gone to. But a little voice seemed to whisper to him that it would be no good.

29

If Oswald was having a frustrating night, so was the Bishop. From the safety of the taxi he scoured the streets, but of Dougal he saw no sign. He did, however, discover that the main road that ran parallel to St Prosdocimus was where the street girls plied their trade and, after having driven slowly up and down it a number of times, he instructed the driver to stop by a little knot of bored-looking girls. Then he wound down the window, leant out as far as he could, and beckoned to one of them to come across.

As luck would have it, she was one of the girls he had met earlier in the evening at the Wigspittle and Pole, and he brightened. 'Excuse me, my dear,' he said, 'sorry to bother you when you're working, but have you by any chance seen anything of the Reverend Sampratt?'

'Dougal?' said the girl obligingly. 'No, not since the pub. I think ...'

But what she thought the Bishop was destined never to find out, because at that moment a hand descended on the taxi door and a voice said menacingly, 'Excuse me, sir, may I enquire what you're doing?'

'I beg your pardon?' said the Bishop, startled.

A face appeared silhouetted in the grey square of window, blotting out what little light there was beyond. 'I said,' repeated the voice distinctly, 'what are you doing? Are you propositioning these girls.'

'Good heavens no!' said the Bishop, recoiling. 'Of course not. I was just ...'

'Please get out, sir.' The Bishop found the door suddenly wrenched open. 'We've had you under observation for the last half an hour. You've driven up and down this street five times. Ah!'

This last was as the police officer, which was what the Bishop discovered his interrogator to be, took in the Bishop's collar and purple shirt. He was only a patrol officer and had qualified a mere six months before, so he was still on probation. Together with his partner, still in the police car parked across the street, he had been out all night, and so knew nothing of the current crisis which had plunged his colleagues back at the station into such turmoil. They had watched the taxi going slowly up and down the street and he had said eagerly, 'That one's a punter, isn'the?'

His more expereinced partner had looked up lazily from his bag of chips and said, 'Yeah, looks like it. 'Spose we ought to do something.'

When the taxi had finally stopped Andy, the probationer, had been dispatched to issue a caution against kerb crawling. However, the last thing he expected to find when he flung open the door was an elderly priest. 'Just a minute, sir,' he said, swallowing and unsure now what to do. 'Just wait here a minute, please.'

He scuttled back to the police car and hissed to his partner, 'What should I do? It's a priest.'

The other patrol officer finished his last chip and said, 'It's not that Sampratt bloke is it? He's alright. We don't bother about him.'

Andy shook his head vigorously. 'No, I'd recognise him.'

'Humh.' His partner reflected and then slowly heaved himself out of the car. 'Okay, I'll come and have a look.'

It was while they were walking back across to the taxi that a message came over the radio, informing them that the Bishop of Carbery had been kidnapped by an armed and highly dangerous gang. In fact, control had been trying to reach them for some time, but the two policemen had switched off their radios when they had gone into the local chippie for something to eat. Andy's partner now looked the Bishop up and down speculatively and then withdrew a short way. 'That last message,' he enquired into his radio, 'the Bishop wouldn't be an elderly man, about five ten, receding grey hair, glasses, and a purple shirt?'

The radio almost fell out of his hand with the sudden explosion of noise. When he returned a minute later he looked thoughtful. 'Excuse me, sir,' he said, 'you wouldn't by any chance be the Bishop of Carbery?'

Back at the station, the team investigating the drugs and pornography ring was delighted to hear that the Bishop had been found. 'Bring him in,' said the inspector crisply, coming onto the radio and with difficulty suppressing the excitement in his voice. 'We'll get this sorted now!'

The Bishop was driven straight to the station and, rather to his surprise, was met at the door by Inspector Bateman, whom he recognised instantly as the same officer who had led the investigation into the break-in at the palace. 'Good to see you, my l ..., sir,' said the policeman heartily, remembering just in time the Bishop's dislike of being addressed as 'my lord'. 'Sorry to drag you over here after all you've been through tonight, but we've got a couple of suspects in and we'd like you to take a look at them.' He held open the door and ushered the Bishop through, 'We believe there may be some sort of sex and drugs ring going on, centering on the theological college. Although,' he looked at the Bishop more closely, 'we think you may know all about that, sir. That's why you were kidnapped, isn't it?'

The Bishop was aghast. 'What?' he said faintly. 'Me ...? Indeed not!' Then, discovering the inspector staring at him in complete and utter disbelief, he went, 'There's been a mistake. I was never kidnapped as such.'

A little group of policemen gathered round them curiously, and the DCI said ominously. 'Not kidnapped?'

The Bishop shook his head vigorously.

'Then would you mind telling us what did happen?'

'Certainly.' But the Bishop found this was no easy task. He had already promised the young men that he would not prefer charges if they attended the course, but as he tried to frame a reply that would be at once both innocuous and truthful, he found the whole incident sounded so improbable that he had not the slightest idea what to say. He took a deep breath. 'A group of young men,' he began nervously, 'were out on a stag night.' The inspector raised an eyebrow. 'They formed the mistaken impression I was a Strip-o-gram. They carried me off with them.' He swallowed, registering the looks of disbelief, but ploughed on bravely, 'Naturally they wished to let me go as soon as they realised the mistake they had made.'

'Naturally,' agreed the inspector dryly.

The Bishop ignored him. 'I was held up, however, because they wished to talk of spiritual matters and, once they realised the gravity of what they had done, they all expressed interest in joining a Christian commitment course.'

The Bishop suddenly discovered that Inspector Bateman's eyes had narrowed suspiciously, and he finished hastily. 'I came back to St Prosdocimus as soon as I could, of course, and then went in search of the Reverend Sampratt. Which was when,' he finished up, 'your two patrolmen stopped me.'

He dried up, aware of how lame his explanation sounded. There was a small pause, and then Bateman said evenly, 'I take it you can verify this, sir?'

He sounded annoyed, and in desperation the Bishop pulled the list out of his pocket and thrust it towards him. 'Yes,' he said, 'these are the names of the young men. Although I would really prefer for them not to be bothered. It was all just a bit of silliness.'

'Humph,' Bateman took it and stared at it grudgingly. In the same moment he seemed to become aware of the ring of interested faces peering over his shoulder and said waspishly, 'Haven't you lot got anything better to do?' Then he stopped and glared at the Bishop, before again looking down at the list in his hand, obviously trying to come to terms with this new development.

'Who are your two suspects?' broke in the Bishop nervously, wanting to fill the silence. 'Of what do you suspect them?'

That brought the inspector's head jerking back up. He glared at the Bishop and said frostily, 'Our two suspects are the Reverend Dougal Sampratt, whose version of events sounded, up till now, extremely unlikely, and,' he paused, drawing a deep breath, 'Reverend Oswald Pettifence.'

'Oswald Pettifence?' repeated the Bishop, stunned. 'The vice-principal of Walsingham?'

The inspector nodded grimly. 'We have evidence, by his own admission, sir, of his involvement with a vice ring centering on the theological college. The principal, Canon Timothy Goody, seems to be involved too. Although at present,' he added, 'we cannot trace that gentleman's whereabouts as he appears to have left the country.'

The Bishop opened and shut his mouth feebly. 'I'm sure there must be some mistake,' he brought out at last.

But Bateman was not about to allow that part of his case to collapse too. 'On the contrary, sir,' he said firmly, 'no mistake. We have forensic evidence now linking Canon Goody to the attempted break-in at the palace, and Reverend Pettifence further alleges that the principal has been stalking your wife for some time. Although,' he added grimly, 'we have yet to ascertain why. There seems, however, to be some sort of sex ring operating out of Walsingham, in which a number of the staff are involved, and we feel that all that's happened may be linked in some way to that.'

The Bishop was shocked. He thought at first it was all just another mistake, but then the police produced the forensic report of the clothing they had removed from Walsingham, along with records of items of women's clothing and photographs found in Brian's rooms. 'Are you trying to tell me Brian Mulligan has been consorting with women in Walsingham?' he asked in strangled tones.

The policeman looked at him. 'No, sir,' he said. 'We're not. We're trying to tell you that these articles of clothing were for his own use. Among other things, he's a transvestite.'

The Bishop found it hard to take it all in. 'But what about Pettifence?' he asked, bewildered. 'Where does he fit in?'

They were sitting now in Bateman's rather untidy office. Outside the door the Bishop could hear the normal sounds of a busy station: feet walking backwards and forwards down the long corridor, voices calling to each other, a steady hum of life. But he was beginning to feel as if he had gone to another planet, a place where the natural order was upended. He dreaded what he was going to hear next. In the event, it was even worse than he had anticipated. 'Ah yes, Father Pettifence,' said the inspector reflectively. 'He's interesting, he is. His story is that Canon Goody is an alcoholic and that he's been trying to help him.'

The Bishop brightened slightly at this testimony to Christian charity, but Bateman's next words dashed whatever slender hope had been forming. 'We find that there are certain discrepancies, however. It appears that he has on several occasions actually supplied Canon Goody with alcohol. In fact he claims that on the night of the break-in at the palace he met Canon Goody at the door and took him back to his room and then, at the Canon's request, went to get him further alcohol before he could persuade him to go to bed. He further says that the Canon then passed out, and it was then that he took the clothes we subsequently found in his possession.'

'But why?' asked the Bishop, even further lost in this labyrinth.

Bateman shrugged. 'That's precisely what we want to find out. We've been on to Interpol,' he added, 'to go and pick up Canon Goody, but we're running into some problems with access to the island. Apparently there are special rules attaching to the place that go back for centuries and the monks are proving a bit difficult.'

The Bishop nodded. 'A species of sanctuary I would imagine.' Then he roused himself. 'On the Reverend Sampratt at least I can allay your fears. He has had nothing to do with whatever has been going on at Walsingham, of that I'm absolutely certain. In fact, if what you say is true, that may well be why they wanted to get rid of him. Dougal at least is not involved. Also,' he added reflectively, 'I am not convinced of there being any drug element in all of this ... though honesty compels me to add that the sexual angle is not entirely a surprise.'

After that he asked to see first Dougal and then Oswald. Very reluctantly, the police then agreed to allow Dougal to go free, even Bateman being forced to acknowledge that there was now no crime with which he could be linked.

'Dougal, my boy,' said the Bishop, when Dougal was at last brought in. They looked at each other, and the Bishop said heavily, 'What a terrible night this has been.'

Dougal, who had by now been told of the charges being brought against Oswald and of the police's complete failure to find Carl, could only agree. He nodded miserably. 'Bit of a mess all round.' Then he told the Bishop about all the excitement after they had become separated and what had happened to Pepper. He did not, however, relate his part in the fracas and the Bishop merely nodded and sighed gloomily. It occurred to him that it seemed to be Carbery's destiny to stagger from scandal to scandal, each one worse than the one before. He wondered if any of them were going to be able to ride out the storm.

Pushing aside such thoughts, however, he went and asked if he and Dougal together might be permitted now to see Oswald. The custody sergeant looked as if he might demur, but Inspector Bateman, still at a complete loss as to what had actually happened, thought a confrontation betweeen Oswald and his superior might be beneficial, so he nodded and, after another interminable wait, the vice-principal of Walsingham was at last brought in, looking dishevelled and hollow eyed. When he saw the Bishop he swallowed awkwardly and said defensively, 'It wasn't my fault. Tim seems to have gone bananas this term.'

The Bishop looked at him gravely. 'As I understand it that process has not been helped by yourself.' Oswald hung his head and the Bishop said, 'Is it true that on a number of occasions you actually supplied him with further drink?'

Oswald nodded, too ashamed to speak.

'But why?' asked the Bishop.

Then at last Oswald looked up, his eyes fixed with loathing upon Dougal. 'Because I wanted to be principal myself,' he spat out. 'Only nothing I did seemed any use. When he was there,' he indicated Dougal with an angry jerk of his head, 'he seemed to get all the attention. It was all Dougal this and Dougal that. He organised all the conferences and student placements. The whole place seemed to revolve round him. And then once he'd gone Tim was absolutely useless, only no one would do anything because they didn't want to rock the boat. I could have done a far better job.'

The Bishop stared at him for a long moment. 'And so you thought you would help make his humiliation obvious, did you?' Oswald's silence was all the response he needed and, after a moment, the Bishop said heavily, 'What about the rest? The stories of pornography and sexual perversion ... are they true?'

Oswald made a sound like an express train coming out of a tunnel. 'No more so than usual,' he said contemptuously. 'Half the staff fancy each other, but then of course they always have been. And Brian likes dressing up, but he always has done ... I don't believe all this stuff about an organised vice ring.'

'Ah.' The Bishop looked as if a weight had been lifted from his shoulders. 'Even so,' he murmured, 'it's bad enough.' He raised his head and fixed Oswald in the eye. 'Father Pettifence,' he said severely, 'in the circumstances I can see no course for you other than to resign. I shall, of course, be happy to try and help you find a position elsewhere, but I feel you would benefit from a taste of normal parish life.' Oswald's head drooped. 'I shall also do my best,' continued the Bishop, 'to persuade the police that you are not quite the villain they seem to imagine, but I would advise you from this point on to be extremely careful.'

When Dougal and the Bishop emerged into the open air some half an hour later, they discovered that it was already light and traffic was beginning to move about on the streets. 'Good heavens,' said Dougal, looking at his watch, 'I hadn't realised it was so late. It's seven thirty.'

'Yes,' agreed the Bishop. 'It's tomorrow.' He stood on the pavement, scenting at the air as if trying to draw in something of its freshness. 'I'd better get home to my wife. I'm not even sure if anyone has told her yet that I'm alright.' Then he sighed heavily and said, 'There's going to be the most awful scandal when all this comes out.'

As if by common consent they turned and began to walk down the street. Dougal could think of nothing to say. He glanced sideways at the Bishop, who seemed deep in thought, an air of profound gloom about him. He was quite right, Dougal thought, there would be a scandal. It felt somehow as if a boil had been lanced but the question was, could the poison now be cleaned out and the area cauterized, or would it spread? A newspaper vendor on the street corner caught the Bishop's eye, and he stopped to buy a paper. 'Goodness gracious,' he said, staring at the front page, 'it's you!'

Jerked out of his reverie, Dougal stared across the Bishop's arm and saw a large picture of himself, standing over a vanquished Carl. The caption that ran alongside the photograph read, 'Battling priest goes to the rescue' and underneath the article began, 'Dougal Sampratt, the vicar of St Prosdocimus the Inferior spearheading the mission to clear up vice on the notorious St Prosdocimus estate in Carbery, and recently accused of immoral practices, has once again leapt to the defence of ...'

'Dougal!' said the Bishop, his jaw dropping as his eye ran down the article. 'You didn't tell me any of this. Is it true? That you actually rescued this girl ...?' He ran a finger along the page, 'And it says here that the accusations made against you have all been proved to be a tissue of lies.'

Dougal hung his head, crimson. 'Oh they always exaggerate,' he said. 'You know what the papers are like.'

The Bishop did know, but now he also knew what Dougal was like. He suddenly felt that in all the devastation and the gloom, God had put before him an assertion that there was still hope. 'My dear boy,' he said feelingly, 'I'm so very pleased.' And then suddenly a thought occurred to him. It was so simple that he could not understand how he had not thought of it before. It seemed obvious.

'Dougal,' he said abruptly. 'There are going to have to be a lot of changes in Carbery. For a start, Walsingham is either going to have to clean up its act, or it's got to be closed. But it can't continue as it is!' Dougal looked at him unhappily and swallowed but the Bishop was in full flight. 'My boy,' he said, 'Father Goody's gone, and now Oswald Pettifence and quite clearly Brian Mulligan will have to go too, and maybe others of the staff – though I hope not. But we have to root out the corruption wherever it's taken a hold.' His eyes glowed as he warmed to the theme, 'Many of the people there only need firm leadership in order to come back to the right discipline. They need an example of spirituality that will inspire and sustain them.' He looked Dougal firmly in the eye. 'Dougal, I now see clearly that the man for that job is you.' Dougal's eyes widened in astonishment, but the Bishop ploughed on. 'I want you to go back to Walsingham as principal. And I want you, with me, to clean that place up and make it once again a theological college worthy of the name.'

Dougal stared at him. He felt absolutely floored. For the past few weeks, and especially after Amanda had dropped her bombshell, all he had seemed able to think about was going back to Walsingham and sanctuary, but that had appeared impossible. It had felt as though he had been expelled from the Promised Land. And yet now here was the Bishop asking him – no, begging him – to go back! It was unbelievable. It was like a dream, like all he had ever imagined – only better. Promotion, and the mandate to guide the college as he felt led. Dougal reeled as he thought of the possibilities, and then, as he gazed with absolute joy into this cornucopia about to be realised ... he thought of St Prosdocimus.

'No,' he said, without thinking. 'I can't.'

The Bishop gaped, as if he had just been hit in the face by a wet fish. 'Why ever not?' he asked, astonished. He had been so carried away by the intensity of his conviction that it had simply never occurred to him that Dougal might refuse.

Dougal swallowed. 'I can't leave them,' he said. 'The people at St Prosdocimus. They need me.' The words cost him dear. Even to his own ears he sounded mad, and yet he knew it was right. He thought of Regina and Eliston. He thought of poor smashed Pepper and the violence that Carl had inflicted on her. And last of all he thought of Maisie, battling so valiantly and against all the odds to try and help her friend. He knew he couldn't simply abandon them all now, not just because he was being offered something better.

'I see.' The Bishop frowned. Then his brow cleared. 'Dougal,' he said, 'I completely understand and of course you're right. It's precisely this kind of thing that I'm talking about when I say that the staff and ordinands at Walsingham need an example of proper Christian service put before them.' He took a deep breath. 'But how would it be if the parish of St Prosdocimus was formally adopted by Walsingham? If you stayed as rector, but also took on the job of principal, and if the ordinands, as a part of their ministerial training, were then required, under your supervision, to work within the parish?'

'Good heavens,' said Dougal. He could think of nothing else to say.

The Bishop's hand closed over his arm. 'Think about it, my boy,' he advised paternally. 'Think about it ... and pray. And let me know your answer in the next couple of days.' He gave a quick, encouraging squeeze and then stood back, squaring his shoulders, a determined light in his eye. 'Now', he said firmly, I must go and see my wife. And after that, I have a phone call to put through to a certain monastery in Greece. Goodbye, my boy. Goodbye.' With that, before Dougal could reply, he strode away, his step considerably lighter. In the same moment, with a stab of almost prophetic insight, he had a sudden glimpse of the months ahead. They were, he felt, going to be enormously difficult, and there were going to be all sorts of attacks launched against him, some of which would be very hard to withstand. But he would withstand them, he knew now, and he felt absolutely certain that Dougal would help.

Overhead, the sun suddenly broke out from behind the dull covering of cloud, a quite unexpected brilliance poured onto the streets. In the Bishop's heart the little flame of hope, ignited by his new-found clarity, blazed up ... and he went on his way, very strangely at peace.

30

In her flat in Hampstead Amanda also saw the papers that morning and was overjoyed. She felt they proved her innocence quite incontrovertibly. She abandoned any idea of breakfast (which she had not wanted anyway, because she was as usual feeling sick) and rushed down to Carbery to see Nicholas.

She found him in his flat, morosely trying to compose a letter to the Bishop, telling him exactly what he thought of him and where he could stick his rotten job. Nicholas was feeling low. He had absolutely no intention of sending the letter, of course, but it relieved his feelings somewhat to write down all he would actually like to say. It was into this quagmire of self-pity that Amanda erupted like an effervescent dose of salts.

'Have you seen this?' she shrieked, waving the by now rather tatty paper in Nicholas's face as he opened the door. 'This just proves I was telling the truth all along!'

Nicholas frowned and peered at it distastefully. 'It doesn't say anything about your not sleeping with him,' he said at last.

'Oh, don't be so stupid,' said Amanda witheringly. 'It says the whole thing was a tissue of lies, put out to try and destroy Dougal's reputation.'

'Huh!' said Nicholas. He rather wished the attempt had succeeded. He turned round and pushed his way back into the flat and after a moment Amanda followed, wrinkling her nose in distaste at the rather foetid smell. Once in the sitting room, he turned back to her and said heavily, 'This doesn't actually prove a thing. After all, there's still that photograph of you coming out of his house in the morning, and you did admit you spent the night there. So how on earth can I believe you didn't sleep with him?'

Amanda looked at him angrily, her face flushing. Really, the man was impossible. She had been absolutely convinced as she drove down through the early rush hour traffic that this altered everything, and that Nicholas would read the article and simply wrap her in his arms, begging forgiveness. How wrong, she thought, could she be? With difficulty she bit back a waspish retort and said plaintively, 'But Nicholas, it's your baby. Just what do I need to do to prove that to you?' And then her patience finally snapped. 'Why do you always judge everyone by your own standards? Dougal isn't a bit like you!'

It was Nicholas's turn to feel enraged. He glared at her. 'Oh I see, your plaster saint is above all that kind of thing is he? I suppose he believes in immaculate conception for everyone.'

Amanda was stung. 'He's honourable, if that's what you mean.'

'Implying I'm not?'

Nicholas went white with fury and Amanda bit her lip. She did not want to quarrel, there was too much at stake. She dreaded having to recall the wedding invitations now. 'Oh Nicholas,' she said beseechingly. 'Don't be so stupid. Don't let's quarrel like this.' His face looked mulish, and she went on hastily, 'I'm simply saying that Dougal is a *very* moral person. He doesn't believe in that kind of thing. I'm not sure if he's slept with anybody yet, but he certainly wouldn't with me and I was his fiancée.'

Nicholas looked as if he was about to argue, and Amanda decided to go for broke. 'I love you,' she wailed. 'Of course it's your baby. I wouldn't lie about something like this.'

Somehow that seemed to get through to him. He stared at her glassily. He was still not convinced, but he thought suddenly of the little parish in Knightsbridge her father had mentioned, and of how he hated the subservience of his present job. He thought of how he could actually send the letter he had been writing, instead of just thinking about it and throwing it away. And he thought of what a frightful prig that Sampratt bloke was, and of how he detested him. Yes, he thought bitterly, that sanctimonious, holier than thou carrying-on was just the sort of thing Sampratt might do. God, how he hated him! Always making everyone else feel so grubby. 'Well, are you sure it's my baby?' he asked unthinkingly.

It was the wrong thing to say. Amanda looked as if she could strangle him, and then she said violently, 'You know it's your baby! Who else do you think I've been sleeping with?'

He weighed the situation. 'And you promise you and Dougal never actually ... you know... at all?'

Amanda glared. 'Yes,' she said, through gritted teeth.

'Humph.' As if he were making the most enormous concession, Nicholas finally reached across and took the paper from her hand. He looked at it, a rather nasty expression on his face. 'Quite a saint, isn't he?' he said, after a moment.

Amanda swallowed but said nothing, watching him apprehensively. She felt instinctively that there was a sea change going on, but which way things were going to fall out she still had no idea. She held her breath.

'Well, I suppose we could still get married then,' he said grudgingly.

'Oh yes!' Amanda was so excited, she gave a little explosive whoop of joy. She wouldn't have to contact the abortion clinic after all, she thought, relieved. And, more importantly, she wouldn't have to cancel the wedding. The humiliation of that would have been insupportable after booking the Abbey and the reception at Claridges. She spun round in a joyful circle and then looked at him, hands clasped before her, eyes glowing. He stared back at her owlishly, and for the first time she registered the two-day stubble on his chin and rather greasy hair. He was an unattractive sight and she pulled up short, rather startled. This was a Nicholas she had never seen before. But there was worse to come. As she stared at him she had a sudden blinding flash of all she had lost and, in that moment of would-be triumph, she suddenly saw Nicholas for exactly what he was. It was not a pleasant revelation and, with a dull sense of anguish, she suddenly realised that she did not want to marry him at all. After all he had done and the way he had acted, she felt she didn't even like him very much any more.

'What's wrong?' he asked, catching the expression on her face.

She swallowed, almost rooted to the spot, and then shook her head dazedly. 'Nothing ... I just felt the baby move, that's all.'

He nodded, and she could almost feel the rearrangement of perspective that was going on inside his head. Everything would be wonderful now, she realised, at least on the surface. He would tell everyone how lucky he was and how the baby was the most tremendous blessing to them both, but deep down ... deep down there would be nothing there. And she looked into the deadened pit of Nicholas's soul with horror.

'I was thinking,' he was saying. 'We could go to St Lucia for the honeymoon and then we could come back to a fresh start at St

Cuthbert's. It would make a natural break.'

She did not answer, instead staring at him stupidly, and after a moment he said, 'Amanda?'

She saw two paths before her, maybe three, none of them very attractive. She took a deep breath and made her decison. 'Yes,' she said wearily, 'I suppose we could.'

*

Dougal made his way slowly back to St Prosdocimus, his emotions in turmoil. His fortunes had taken such an unexpected turn in the last few hours that he hardly knew whether to laugh or cry. The idea of Walsingham felt to him like a restoration to Gilead, while the joining of it to St Prosdocimus was the icing on the cake. But then, hot on the heels of the euphoria that suddenly erupted like fire inside him, he had an unexpected vision of Amanda, and a deep stab of loss shot through him. What on earth was the point of it all, he wondered, if from now on he was going to be alone. In an almost physically painful glare of insight he saw his future stretching endlessly before him, a lonely celibate, married to his barren office and the Church.

He was still battling with his enraged feelings of loss when he turned into the square fronting St Prosdocimus. It was just as forlorn and grubby as ever. The same air of unsurprised abandonment. The same quota of battered tin cans and empty cigarette packets littering the scrawny grass. He sighed wearily and looked across at the rectory, trying mentally to resign himself to the thought that God might actually want to him to stay unmarried and that this might be his calling. In the same moment he felt a stab of surprise.

Maisie was sitting idly on the rectory wall, a cigarette dangling from her fingers, obviously waiting for him. She looked up as he approached and he quickened his pace, wondering if anything further had happened to Pepper. But her expression was radiant. 'Dougal,' she said, rising to her feet. Dougal noticed that the 'Father' had gone and he felt absurdly pleased. 'Dougal, I came to tell y' ... Pepper's goin' to be alright. They did one of them there brain scans at six o'clock, and they said everything's okay.'

His face broke into an answering smile. 'Oh Maisie, I'm so pleased.'

'Yeah.' She nodded. 'She's pretty cut up about the baby of course, but at least she's alive.'

She looked as if she wanted to say something more but didn't quite know how and he said quickly, 'Come on in, and I'll tell you all about what happened to me. You can have breakfast if you like.'

She stepped forward eagerly, her face splitting in a huge grin. 'Yeah, I was wantin' to ask y' what 'appened with the police. Is everything alright?'

His key was in the lock, and he fumbled slightly as he unlocked the door. 'It's fine, Maisie,' he said over his shoulder. 'Amazing really. The Bishop wants me to go back to Walsingham.'

The sound of her sharp intake of breath as he stepped into the hall made him spin round in surprise. He discovered she was standing almost directly behind him, hands clasped across her chest, a stricken expression on her face. 'Does that mean you're leavin' us?' she demanded. With a shock, he realised she was close to tears.

'Oh no, Maisie,' he said quickly, 'of course not.'

Then suddenly the sunlight that had trailed him despondently home seemed to push its way into the tiny little hall and her face was abruptly framed with light, transforming it with a wholly unexpected beauty. Dougal realised that, in the short time he had known her, she had changed almost beyond recognition and he stared at her, almost feeling that he was seeing her for the first time. In that moment he saw her brittle cockiness and veneer of untouchability, but he saw a lot more too. He saw her essential honesty and courage, totally undimmed by all the squalor amongst which she had been forced to live. He saw her longing after something better. And he saw her truth. Then he thought of Amanda and into his mind floated the words 'A wife does what she does for love, but a whore does it for reward and position.' He had absolutely no idea where the words came from but they struck him with such force that for a second he thought someone had actually spoken them aloud and he gasped.

Maisie, however, was still looking at him with terror in her eyes and he shook himself. 'No, Maisie,' he said again. 'I'm not going at all. I'm going to do both. I'll stay here as rector of St Prosdocimus, but from now on I'll combine it with Walsingham, so the two will be linked.'

Maisie's eyes grew round. 'Carl's goin' to love that!' she breathed.

Dougal could not help himself. He gave a great shout of laughter. 'Yes, Maisie,' he wheezed as soon as he was able to speak, 'he is, isn't he!'

An uncertain, rather baffled smile came to Maisie's lips but she said nothing and seeing her confusion, Dougal took a grip of himself. 'It's going to be fine now, Maisie,' he said firmly. 'You'll see.' And he looked across the tiny hallway, still smelling slightly from its newly applied coat of paint, and he smiled.